CW01497519

The Agon
of Modernism

The Agon of Modernism

Wyndham Lewis's Allegories, Aesthetics, and Politics

Anne Quéma

Lewisburg
Bucknell University Press
London: Associated University Presses

Associated University Presses
440 Forsgate Drive
Cranbury, NJ 08512

Associated University Presses
16 Barter Street
London WC1A 2AH, England

Associated University Presses
P.O. Box 338, Port Credit
Mississauga, Ontario
Canada L5G 4L8

The paper used in this publication meets the requirements
of the American National Standard for Permanence of Paper
for Printed Library Materials Z39.48-1984.

Library of Congress Cataloging-in-Publication Data

Quéma, Anne, 1960–
    The agon of modernism : Wyndham Lewis's allegories, aesthetics, and politics / Anne Quéma.
        p.   cm.
    Includes bibliographical references (p.   ) and index.
    ISBN 0-8387-5392-2 (alk paper)
    1. Lewis, Wyndham, 1882–1957—Criticism and interpretation.
2. Political and literature—Great Britain—History—20th century.
3. Modernism (Aesthetics)—England.   4. Modernism (Literature)—
England.   5. Aesthetics, British.   6. Allegory.   I. Title.
PR6023.E97Z85   1999
828'.91209—dc21   98-44002
                                                            CIP

Contents

Preface

My encounter with modernist literature occurred twenty years ago and had the metropolis of London and the mountains of Savoy for background. Since then a number of persons have encouraged me to pursue my passion for books and art. I would like to thank them here for their direct or indirect contribution: the late Bernard Lafourcade as well as Judith Bates of the Université de Savoie; John Healy, Ian Cameron, Ray Morrison, Roger Mesley, and Francisco Loriggio of Carleton University; Paul O'Keeffe as editor of *Enemy News;* Paul Edwards of the *Wyndham Lewis Annual;* Bernard Bergonzi; David Trotter of University College London; and the perceptive reader for Bucknell University Press.

I also wish to thank the British Library for its assistance, as well as the staff members of the Libraries at Royal Holloway College and at Carleton University for their warmth and support.

On the technical side, Norma Rankin was of enormous help at previous stages of manuscript preparation.

Finally, the writing of this book would have been impossible, had Paule Quéma and Danièle Gréverie not stepped in at crucial babysitting times. I dedicate this book to my husband James M. Thompson whose love, knowledge, and unflagging support saw me through all these years.

Acknowledgments

THE FOLLOWING PERMISSIONS ARE GRATEFULLY ACKNOWLEDGED: For the photographic reproduction: Wyndham Percy Lewis, *A Battery Shelled*, 1919. Oil on canvas, 182.7 × 317.7 cm (Michel P25). Reproduced with the permission of *The Imperial War Museum*, London.

For quotations from *The Art of Being Ruled, The Childermass*, and *Malign Fiesta:* The reproduction of copyright material was made possible thanks to Wyndham Lewis and the Estate of the late Mrs. G.A. Wyndham Lewis, and by kind permission of the Wyndham Lewis Memorial Trust (a registered charity).

I am also grateful to the Johns Hopkins University Press for permission to reproduce part of my article, "A Genealogy of Impersonality," published in *Philosophy and Literature*. Finally, I thank Paul O'Keeffe and Paul Edwards for permission to use parts of my article *"Mrs. Dukes' Million:* A Mystery" originally published in *Enemy News*.

Introduction: Modernism Reclaimed

METAPHORS OF GIGANTIC, TOTEMIC STATUES BURIED IN DUST, preserved in their primitive state, and awaiting to be discovered by the curious archeologist of earlier twentieth-century art haunt the critical imagination of those who have taken the time to read Wyndham Lewis's texts and examine his visual works. Invariably, a monograph on Lewis's artistic activities begins with the almost ritualistic statement that in him we have an ignored or simply unknown genius who should be recognized as a major contributor to the earlier development of modern art.

Although few in number, most of the successful critical studies of Lewis's works retain the visible marks of the shock of the new always produced by the first encounter with his paintings and writings. These affect us today the way they affected his contemporaries. When Fredric Jameson responds to Lewis's sentence production as "an explosive and window-breaking *praxis*,"[1] he echoes T. S. Eliot's enthusiasm for the writer who wrote with "the thought of the modern and the energy of the cave-man."[2] For Lewis is first and foremost an impressive transformer of energy, be it in the diagonal lines of his vorticist plates or in the exhilarating pyrotechnics of some of his prose. Beyond gender, beyond ideology, even beyond culture, the energy of Lewis's art will remain the surest means of beckoning to any fresh reader or viewer.

Born off the coast of Nova Scotia on his parents' yacht in 1882, brought up from the age of six as an English boy, brilliant student at the Slade School of Art, at the spearhead of the vorticist avant-garde in London, soldier in the First World War, incisive satirist and skillful portraitist, political pamphleteer, and artist in exile on the North American continent during the Second World War, Wyndham Lewis was practically saved from total critical anonymity by Hugh Kenner's monograph, *Wyndham Lewis* (1954), published three years before Lewis's death. Yet today Lewis remains among the least studied of the European modernists.

The posthumous assessment of Lewis's works has been plagued by a reputation that has fallen like a pall on his artistic achievement. This reputation is built on the notions that Lewis was a strange bird, combining mordant satire with inveterate paranoia; that he was a "lonely old volcano of the Right" (as Auden and MacNeice put it);[3] that he had the terrible habit of sowing his seeds here and there without due regard to the mother of his children; that he had "the eyes of an unsuccessful rapist" (or so wrote Hemingway);[4] and that he socked it to Roger Fry and Bloomsbury in *The Apes of God* and earlier in rebelliously seceding from the Omega workshops to establish his own vorticist group and magazine, *Blast*.

In addition, it is quite evident that the character of both his satirical writings and his ideological statements impaired what is crucial to the artistic survival of any writer—the transmission of texts to future generations of readers and critics. The negative effects were already recorded by Lewis who was convinced that there was an orchestrated boycotting of his texts by reviewers and editors. Hugh Kenner points out that without the reedition by James Laughlin's New Directions of modernist texts, writers such as Pound and Williams would never have enjoyed the renown and critical attention that have been granted them.[5] This type of reediting has functioned as a conveyor belt between texts and readers in academic spheres. In Lewis's case, the reediting of his major texts was not inaugurated until 1978 when Bradford Morrow's and Bernard Lafourcade's bibliography was published under the aegis of Black Sparrow Press.[6]

The lack of print transmission across generations of readers has also had another pernicious effect, on which it is necessary to dwell. On account of a general critical discourse that functions at the different levels of genre ("satirist"), ideology ("fascist," "right-wing"), psychology ("cantankerous," "egotist"), studies focusing on Lewis have in one way or another introduced, and indeed, analyzed him as the odd man out, the singular personality, the outsider, the true genius who cannot be categorized. This approach, which stems from the still-lingering notion of romantic genius, runs the risk of isolating Lewis's achievement from its ideological, cultural, and social contexts.

In contrast, the present study springs from the fundamental notion that, far from constituting an isolated case, Lewis's artistic achievement manifests major aspects of "modernism" and that these identify him as a central figure of the movement. The rough edges of Lewis's works allow the critic to sharpen our apprehension of modernism, which during decades of commentary and under the effect of temporal erosion has developed rounded, PreCambrian shapes. This is not to deny the singularity of the writer; but this singularity can no longer be regarded as oppositional and should be redefined from within modernism.

The decision to identify Lewis's writings as a manifestation of modernism is far from uncontroversial. Critics such as Reed Way Dasenbrock, Vincent Sherry, and Julian Symons see in Lewis a cornerstone of modernism. But how does one reconcile his modernism with the avant-gardist streak highlighted by Peter Bürger in his study of *Tarr*, the 1918 version of which was hailed as as a radical piece of literature? And how does one square his modernism with the postmodernist features noticed by Bernard Lafourcade in his reedition of *Snooty Baronet*, and by Sue-Ellen Campbell in her analysis of Lewis's critical writings? Suppose then that Lewis is a precursor of postmodernism. How does this hypothetical postmodernism fit his right-wing, elitist politics? Nor do contradictory interpretations occur only among critics. They actually occur within one and the same critical analysis: Fredric Jameson hails Lewis as a postmodernist alternative to the likes of Woolf, Eliot, and Lawrence, yet also sees in him a particularly exacerbated case of totalitarian and "therefore" modernist politics.[7]

My own approach to Lewis's works is based on a distinction between "modernism" and "avant-garde." In historical terms, the advent of what is conventionally referred to as postmodernism had the initial effect of either evicting modernism from the stage or of reducing it to disreputable "high modernism." At the same time, "avant-garde" was increasingly used to the point of either replacing the term "modernism" or of functioning as a synonym of it with positive connotations. Today the return to the usage of "modernism" coincides with an attempt to redefine the term as a descriptive tool, as Astradur Eysteinsson's *The Concept of Modernism* attests.[8]

Recent analyses have had the effect of honing the edges of modernism. At its most extreme this criticism attributes characteristics to modernism that used to be recognized as those of the avant-garde. For instance, Carol Hamilton claims that a direct link exists between the modernist aesthetic of order and chaos and the anarchist dialectic of creation and destruction as postulated by Mikhail Bakunin in 1848. H. Porter Abbott redraws the map of modernism by locating the imperative to innovate and make it new right at the core of Beckett's *modernist* texts. These two examples alone show to what extent the periodization of modernism depends on the radicalization of its defining characteristics.[9]

A distinction between modernism and avant-garde presupposes the definition of each term. After thirty years of poststructuralist deconstruction, the concept of definition might be considered as an accute case of naïveté or of crass logocentrism. In this respect James Kinneavy brings out the fact that the function of definition is to immobilize the meaning of words.[10] So it could be argued that, given this function, we are bound to end up with a dangerously petrifying definition of either modernism or avant-garde. One possible way of avoiding the problem is to pluralize either term. The pluralizing of avant-garde is taken for granted nowadays, while that of modernism is relatively recent and chiefly results from studies that reintroduce the writings of women and blacks into the mainstream of modernism. However, this strategy does not eliminate the problem that pluralization amounts to variations upon a single entity. So the task of defining the singular of these plurals has only been postponed.

While discussing the term "postmodernism," Jameson argues that without a definition stating the dominant features of this concept, we are left with a "view of the present as sheer heterogeneity, random difference, a coexistence of a host of distinct forces whose effectivity is undecidable."[11] Similar difficulties attend any other term of our critical vocabulary. The sense of loose heterogeneity translates into a loose use of terminology. For instance, Peter Nicholls describes the "Men of 1914" as a specific brand of modernism; yet, in connection with the question of artistic form, Nicholls refers to the "agonistics of this particular avant-garde."[12]

Let us make the hypothesis that while T. S. Eliot should be categorized as a modernist, Tristan Tzara the dadaist should be regarded as an avant-gardist. The traditional definitions of modernism tend to preclude this distinction. For example, when Lyn Pykett plausibly lists criteria such as self-reflexiveness, formal simultaneity, juxtaposition, paradox and indeterminacy, dehumanization, disintegration of the subject, and urbanization as defining criteria of modernism, one senses that all of these criteria apply equally to Eliot's and Tzara's writings.[13]

The list of criteria proposed by Pykett, commonly assented to by most critics, implicitly includes two types of criterion. One is formal and deals with the experimental potentialities of media (from language and music to painting, choreography, and cinematography); the other is "thematic" and includes the self, the city, time, and so on. Neither formal nor thematic criteria are useful in drawing a distinction between avant-garde and modernism because both types are relevant to both concepts. This implies that the hypothetical distinction between Eliot and Tzara should be located outside formalist and thematic criteria.

I propose to start looking at the problem from a different angle; that is, from the angle of sociocultural contexts for the production of modern art in the earlier half of the twentieth century. My intention is not to provide an exhaustive, let alone extensive, list of contextual parameters, but an examination of the question leads into a minimum of nine areas: 1) theoretical forays into language as semiotic system (Peirce, Saussure, Wittgenstein, Cassirer); 2) the perspectivist

(Nietzsche) as well as the psychoanalytical (Freud) gutting of the traditional "humanist" self and, simultaneously, the massive ideological reconstruction of the self (Marxism, communism, fascism); 3) the destabilization of gender identities and boundaries; 4) the bureaucratic and industrial organization of life, time, and space; 5) the social urban typology displacing rural typology; 6) the rise of economic nationalisms; 7) the progressive dismantlement of empires; 8) the waning of the social and political role of the author and, simultaneously, the development of mass literacy and entertainment; 9) consumerism and the commodification of the object.

The distinction between avant-garde and modernism lies in the positioning of the artists and their works in connection with these general parameters that make up the context for art production. In other words, the distinction is not governed by formal and thematic criteria but by the position shaping the use of form and themes and determining itself against these contextual parameters. Thus what distinguishes Eliot from Tzara is the position they took on the use of montage, juxtaposition, the disintegration of the self, and the role of the author. The next two steps then are to distinguish between the positions of the avant-garde and modernism, and then to establish their interaction. For the critical notion of distinction is useful inasmuch as it allows one to describe phenomena of dialectical exchange and interrelation.

The avant-garde's position towards the context I have sketched is one of radical transformation if not annihilation. It is a position overwhelmingly determined to turn its back on whatever represents and functions as the status quo. This revolutionary stance leads the avant-garde to identify itself with the most forward-looking elements of society. Hence avant-garde art identifies itself with discourses on the machine and the city, urban rhythm, the modern newsprint, investigation into and experiments with language, the unconscious, anarchic social undercurrents in order to transgress the status quo.

From this fundamental position derives a series of strategies that help us today define the avant-garde. The first set of criteria includes the well-known rejection of institutionalization, the codes of extremism and nihilism, the offensive practices of artistic and sociopolitical iconoclasm. Thierry de Duve makes an insightful distinction between two types of avant-garde. One develops by rejecting tradition because it is initially rejected by academies and institutions; the academicism against which the other type of avant-garde rebels is not the facile target of museum art, but "that which remains of previous avant-gardes when they have run out of their scissional energy."[14] The first type can be referred to as rejection or tabula rasa avant-gardism and is typical of the prewar Parisian avant-garde. The other can be referred to as secession avant-gardism and was practised in prewar Munich. Interestingly enough, and perhaps as a result of the influence of de Duve's theory, originally published in France in 1984, Parisian avant-gardism is also in the process of being reinterpreted. For instance, Philippe Dagen and Michel Décaudin argue that Apollinaire was open to the art of the past and of the present; and that like Duchamp he was suspicious of ideological closure, especially among avant-gardists.[15] This makes Apollinaire an avant-gardist of the secessionist type.

A second group of defining criteria refer to the collective characteristic of the avant-garde. As a group, the avant-garde addresses another group: we are dealing with a rhetoric of the public arena, hence manifestos and journalistic typography and technique are used to communicate with a targeted public. The avant-garde also adopts the discourse and practices of the specific social group: youth. Finally, a third group of criteria defines the avant-garde as a combination of anti-traditional radicalism and a temporality of the present. This is the reason why it is primarily a philosophy of action, be it in the form of the gratuitous act, gesture, gesticulation, or political agitation. This is what leads Peter Bürger to associate the avant-garde with social "praxis."[16]

While the avant-gardes develop transgressive strategies of self-identification with the practices and discourses of their times, modernism is saddled with an awareness of tradition. I use the term in a broad way as means of referring to values associated with past institutions as well as social systems, practices, and discourses. Modernism is partly defined by a backward gaze towards the past, and this gaze is not innocent as it has ideological associations variously identified as *nostos,* nostalgia, ideological repression of the transgressive unconscious, regressive protofascism, or any other position that indicates an allegiance to the past.[17]

However, *nostos* as a position of resistance towards the modern world does not yet constitute modernism. Modernism is constituted by the paradoxical relationship between *nostos* and avant-gardist radicalism. Modernists writers are modernists because they use avant-gardist practices and idioms to split apart systems of totality they have inherited from the past *and* by which they remain fascinated. As Wladimir Krysinski notes, the avant-gardes have a "mobilizing" function within the works of modernism.[18] The traditional values on which modernists were mobilized include social and political roles of authority, gender identity and patriarchy, social hierarchy, language and meaning, art and the social role of the artist. In other words, for modernism to become, the avant-garde has to be. The last twenty years of the nineteenth century and the first twenty years of the twentieth century are key to the creation and development of a succession of artistic avant-gardes engaged in an ever-increasing series of experimental challenges and counter-challenges. Most of the pre-modernist and modernist works were written in response to these avant-gardist breakthroughs.

The interrelation between avant-garde as mobilizing force and *nostos* as form of resistance accounts for the dual presence of the two positionings within the career of one and the same artist. Ezra Pound is a supreme example of such duality. Richard Sieburth has shown to what extent Pound's theories on monetarism cut short his contribution to *The Dial* of Scofield Thayer, whose aesthetic philosophy was based on the autonomy of the art object.[19] Sieburth's argument is crucial for it brings out the radicalism (which goes as far as the social scheme of handing the means of artistic production over to writers and consumers) of an author often categorized as "high modernist." The modernism of Pound consists in the explosive combination of radicalism and *nostos,* revolution and tradition.

From a cultural viewpoint, the modernists were the inheritors of two equally powerful traditions: a literary tradition and a philosophical one. As opposed to Victorians such as Dickens who "just" wrote, an impressive number of modernists were both artists and thinkers. It is no coincidence that three major male figures of international modernism should have had truck with philosophy *and* creative writing: Eliot wrote a doctoral dissertation on Bradley;[20] T. E. Hulme tried his hand at poetry; and Lewis studied time as a philosophical concept. What is equally striking is that although conceptual thinking is obviously an object of attraction and interest, it is also under suspicion. In his thesis Eliot wrote of metaphysical systems that they are "condemned to go up like a rocket and come down like a stick."[21] Hulme entitled his unfinished philosophical work *Cinders.* As for Lewis's philosophical work, *Time and Western Man,* the reason why it has only recently been taken seriously by academics is not that its ideas were considered dubious, but that it breaks the rules of conventional philosophical argumentation. The fascination with systematic discourse and the simultaneous itch to submit this discourse to avant-gardist strategies of questioning is typically modernist.

The modernism I am describing here represents a hinge between the nineteenth-century philosophical mega-systems and the second half of the twentieth century with its philosophies of suspicion and deconstruction. It seems that the modernist relationship to philosophy took the form of a dilemma: roughly speaking, either to subscribe to a system of thought that projects a humanist conception of the self expressed in a discourse governed by specific conventions; or to develop an iconoclastic philosophical vision and discourse spurred by the insights provided by the avant-gardist experimental practices of art. Derridean writing stems from the second alternative, while modernism is astride the two visions. In fact the modernist approach to discursive writing is best pictured as a spectrum that has T. S. Eliot's literary essays at one end, and Gertrude Stein's experimental criticism at the other end. Modernist contradictions coincide with abrupt swings of the pendulum from one end of the spectrum to the other.

It is no coincidence that parody should be a major characteristic of modernist texts. Michael McKeon's Bakhtinian definition of parody as "a single dialectical gesture of recapitulation and repudiation, imitation and disillusion, continuity and rupture"[22] is a particularly apt description of modernist incorporation and rejection of authoritative traditions. Generally speaking, Lewis's non-fictional views can be considered as a parody of the romantic tradition. This parody can also aim at modernism whenever the latter more or less surreptitiously borrows from romanticism. Lewis's parody of romanticism is seen most clearly in connection with the concept of time and its role in self-definition. For instance, Coleridge described in striking terms the romantic conception of time as a destabilizing and chaotic factor. In his correspondence he wrote that he felt "'whirled about without a center as in a nightmare—no gravity—a vortex without a center.'"[23] In his writing, Lewis borrowed the romantic vortex only to parody it. In *Time and Western Man* the vortex is frozen by a powerful dualism that divides time from space, body from intellect. Salvation does not lie in temporal excursions into the past, but in the capacity of spatial consciousness to arrest time. Hence the painted ship upon the painted ocean is not an image of hell but an image to be desired.

In his fiction Lewis's practice of spatialization does not consecrate the self as intellect; rather, it freezes the bodies—vessels of time—into ludicrous postures. His grotesque representations of the body are in part based on a parodic process of romantic epiphany. Robert Langbaum suggests that an epiphany is based on an empirical, sensorial perception that leads to an experience of surprise on a sudden glimpse of the extraordinary. This definition of epiphany fits the process experienced by the reader or the beholder of Lewis's representations of the body. However, the end result is not transcendental uplift but a scorching yet exultant encounter with dehumanization. The linearity of Lewis's narratives confirms the intention to parody what Langbaum refers to as the "static lyrical novel," the plot of which, as in *Ulysses,* is apparently pointless so that it may become epiphanic.[24]

The same demonstration can be developed in connection with Lewis's Berkeleyism. Bishop Berkeley's *esse est percipi* became extremely attractive to the romantics, who saw in the self an imaginative and creative agent in the act of perception. Thus in *Defence of Poetry* (1821), Shelley declares: "All things exist as they are perceived; at least in relation to the percipient."[25] In *The Revenge for Love* the description of Margot's perception of the National Guard's road-accident reads like a parody of the romantic reading of Berkeley: through her perception the world is created anew, but the creation is a case of abortion because organic vitality is mechanized and missing from the perceptual experience, which manifests itself as an uncontrolled series of disconnected percepts.

The literary relationship between modernism and tradition can also be observed in its approach to realism. Contrary to a common assumption, modernism did not constitute a clean break from realism. For instance, the role of an interpreting observer was already problematic in realism, and the transition from realism to modernism in part consists in foregrounding this latent problem. This is exemplified in earlier short stories such as "Tonka" written by Robert Musil before the World War I. Nor is it an accident that another German modernist, Thomas Mann, should have begun his career with the realistic *Buddenbrooks*.

Therefore it is crucial to maintain a dialectical relation between modernism and what preceded it. Marshall Brown argues the following: "we need to develop a more dialectical account than has hitherto been customary. . . . The new turns against the old, but it does so from a historical logic already inscribed in the old, and still preserved in the new."[26] Not only is there a need for a logic of diachronic interaction between historical trends, but there is also a need for synchronic interaction among currents and countercurrents of a same period so that they are not analyzed in isolation but as different manifestations of a common cultural quest. In a perceptive essay, George Dekker shows how the relation between Robert Louis Stevenson and Henry James can be read as an example of the dialectic between the claims of romance and those of realism.[27] This combination, which verges on paradox, between fiction as means of access to the object and fiction as construct constitutes a "mixed current" that, in my view, characterizes the whole movement of modernism.

Timothy Materer has interpreted the influence of Augustus John, Yeats, and T. S. Moore on Lewis in psychological terms.[28] However, Moore's influence also has literary connotations. Although not studied today as a major figure, Moore wrote an important study on Flaubert and realism.[29] It is difficult to imagine that, in his relation to Moore, Lewis was unaware of this critical study. Of course, this does not make Lewis Flaubert's parrot, but realism is certainly the backcloth for his earlier sketches of *The Wild Body,* in which innkeepers and Polish emigrants are socially analyzed. Artistic impersonality, discussed by Moore in *Art and Life* (1910) and by Lewis in *Men without Art* (1934), is the hinge between Moore's analysis and Lewis's modernism.

From a sociopolitical viewpoint, the twentieth century has been hailed as the era that saw the amplification of the feminist movement. The son of a divorced mother who had to make ends meet, Lewis was also a vorticist avant-gardist at a time when suffragettes rebelled against the patriarchal status quo. At the same time and despite recent critical efforts,[30] today modernism tends to be associated with male authors. This male dimension is involuntarily brought out by the type of criticism on modernism produced in the last thirty years. Perhaps the best way of summing up this type of criticism is to quote from Jeffrey Perl, who refers to Harold Bloom and Hillis Miller as the "most talented of Eliot's disaffected progeny."[31] Has one ever heard of the most talented of Gertrude Stein's, or Marianne Moore's, or H.D.'s, or Jean Rhys's disaffected progeny?

Although Lewis is often perceived as a "masculine author," and although he made a point of defending masculine values, I will try to show that his treatment of the gender question indicates a typically modernist ambiguity concerning the traditional roles associated with gender. His fictional and nonfictional approaches to the question show to what extent he belonged to the modernists who, from Oscar Wilde through D. H. Lawrence and Virginia Woolf to Thomas Mann, reflected on the relation between creativity and gender identity. In this respect, the modernist practice of dandyism can be interpreted as a strategy to reinvent a self beyond gender restrictions.

There is a political significance to Lewis's treatment of gender. Indeed, in what I see as a process of self-identification, Lewis tended to associate the male gender with sociopolitical values and figures of authority. But there is more to it. I will show that his texts display what looks like unconscious, if not repressed homosexual strategies as a means of repudiating sociopolitical authority traditionally associated with male roles. Therefore, Lewis's treatment of the gender question duplicates the double movement of incorporation and rejection that characterizes modernism in its relation to tradition.

Some of Lewis's major fiction supports Michael Levenson's recent argument that the novel is a means of expression that allows a transposition of the private into the public and the social.[32] Lewis achieves this transfer by means of the political and cultural allegories of his final narratives, in which the exegetical aspect of allegory and his veiled psycho-political reflexion converge. But before I can bring out the convergence of the private story and the public form, I need to elaborate on what I think is the private story. My study is therefore partly based on a speculative psychoanalytical interpretation of Lewis's writings. Today psychoanalytical criticism remains controversial. Forty years of Saussurean theory have had the effect of flattening the self that is hiding between the lines of a text. While engaged in a comparative analysis of modernism and postmodernism, Terry Eagleton observes the following: "Postmodernism . . . commits the apocalyptic error of believing that the discrediting of . . . representational epistemology is the death of truth itself, just as it sometimes mistakes the disintegration of certain traditional ideologies of the subject for the subject's final disappearance."[33] My interpretation of psychological inscriptions of the biographical self in literary texts derives from the conviction that the postmodernist emphasis on textuality has not dealt with psychological subjectivity satisfactorily: it has simply pushed the issue under the carpet.

As my study amply demonstrates, the idea is not to step back to the simplistic view of a direct transcription of the author's "life" into the text; rather, it is to acknowledge the creative and textual aspects of works while establishing psychological links between these aspects and the empirical and biographical information available to the critic. In other words, while postmodern theory felt the necessity to fight old critical demons by *opposing* textual analysis to biographical criticism, today contemporary criticism can take another look at psychocritcism because it has assimilated the lessons of textual analysis.

In spite of the controversy surrounding the psychoanalytical approach to homosexuality, and in spite of the argument that Freudian theory is but a theory—modernist at that—and that its scientific claim should be relativized, my theoretical point of departure is Freudian. Indeed, my research into the psychology of homosexuality has led me to believe that the Freudian model of interpretation provides the best approach to mechanisms of repression. In my study I do not assume that homosexuality is a disease, malformation, sin, or abnormality. Instead, I look at what happens when homosexual desire is thwarted.

The ultimate purpose of this speculation is to show that gender identity is one of the keys to Lewis's erratic excursion into the minefields of Hitlerism. The hegemonic tendency of psychoanalytical explanation is well known, and I do not intend to use psychocriticism either as a master narrative or as a genetic means of explaining Lewis's entire writing: today more than ever it is obvious that a text is an incredibly complex entity where the skeins of culture, history, politics, ideology, language, and psychology are entangled. However, I do think that a psychoanalytical interpretation has a role to play in the account for Lewis's political texts.

The tension between revolution and tradition is quite exacerbated in Lewis's texts, and the powerful irreducibility of both positions probably contributes to the reader's sense of Lewis's singularity. In terms of his early visual output, his editorship of *Blast*, and his publication of the 1918 *Tarr*, Lewis's artistic project was predominantly avant-gardist. After his return from the front of World War I, Lewis undertook a striking enterprise of rewriting that generally had the effect of toning down the linguistic avant-gardist experiments of the original versions. More than a process of maturation, this imperative to rewrite texts such as the previously published *Tarr* or the short stories of *The Wild Body* attests to the agon between avant-gardist tabula rasa and traditional *nostos*.

As an avant-gardist visual artist, Lewis certainly practiced secession when he convinced a group of painters working for Roger Fry's Omega workshops to leave and create a new avant-gardist movement baptized vorticism. His schismatic avant-gardism may be in part the product of his stay in Munich in 1906 before his vorticist years in London. The spirit and practice of secession avant-gardism are also manifest in the first number of *Blast* (1914), which raves against other avant-gardes such as cubism and futurism. Michèle Poli describes Lewis's avant-gardism as a dialectic of yes and no colliding in vorticist gyration. Thus in the second number of *Blast* (1915) Lewis exclaimed: "you must catch the clearness and logic in the midst of contradictions: *not* settle down and snooze on an acquired, easily possessed and mastered, satisfying shape."[34] There is also little doubt that vorticist abstractionism, its overtures to industrial mechanization, and its belief in the conceptual function of the artist all constituted an attempt to supersede the tradition of the artist as craftsman to which Fry still adhered. At the same time, Lewis's practice of secessional avant-gardism means that his salvos were directed at other avant-gardes such as Italian anti-traditionalist futurism. Significantly, the past and its painterly tradition is rarely if ever the target of Lewis's scoffing manifestos, which display admiration for painters such as Cézanne, Velasquez, or Ucello.

Ever since the publication of Peter Bürger's *Theory of the Avant-Garde*, the critical practice has been to assume that a divide between art and life, or high art and popular culture is maintained by modernists because their vision of society is fundamentally elitist if not anti-democratic. On the whole, I do not have any major quarrel with the notion that the modernist divide is politically motivated. However, I also believe that there is more to it. In particular, one has to question the supposed necessity that the divide between art and life is always politically conservative in nature: this necessity is not borne out by history.

A brief survey of the history of the relationship between author and mass culture reveals that the sense of a divide appears at both ends of the political spectrum. Within the British context, it looks as though the notion or experience of a divide was born with the establishing of the Commonwealth. This is the period when censorship was abolished and when a spate of pamphlets of diverse ideological persuasions poured out of the printing shops. Strikingly enough, it is immediately after this period that Milton, who as pamphleteer and poet denounced monarchical tyranny, also had the Son in *Paradise Regained* declare the following: "For what is glory but the blaze of fame / . . . And what the people but a herd confus'd, / A miscellaneous rabble, who extoll / Things vulgar, and well weighd, scarce worth the praise? / They praise and they admire they know not what; / And know not whom, but as one leads the other."[35]

If we now jump to 1800, we read the following taken from Wordsworth's preface to the *Lyrical Ballads:*

> a multitude of causes, unknown to former times, are now acting with a combined force to blunt the discriminating powers of the mind . . . to reduce it to a state of almost savage torpor. The most effective of these causes are the great national events which are daily taking place, and the increasing accumulation of men in cities, where the uniformity of their occupations produces a craving for extraordinary incident, which the rapid communication of intelligence hourly gratifies. To this tendency of life and manners the literature and theatrical exhibitions of the country have conformed themselves.[36]

Although the degree of Wordsworth's political engagement is subject to debate, one cannot suspect him of having sided against the underdog. At the generic level, his description of the St. Bartholomew Fair in *The Prelude* amounts to a transgression of heroic decorum since low, vulgar, popular culture is incorporated into high art.[37] Between Milton and Wordsworth one finds Pope, whose satire of Grub Street and simultaneous support of Bolingbroke's Jacobite patriotism constitute the two sides of the same coin. Although the political affiliations of the three authors are quite different, in all three cases one observes the notion of a cultural and political divide between the artist and the modern phenomenon of mass culture.

In addition, it is possible to argue that the development of phenomenology since Hegel also led the modernists to create a Maginot line between art and life as a safeguard against an invasion of phenomenal experiences. All too often modernist works are considered in the vacuum of autotelism in which they are supposed to feed off the tendrils of their own textuality. Occasionally studies such as Sanford Schwartz's *The Matrix of Modernism* or Judith Ryan's *The Vanishing Subject* remind us of the fundamentally phenomenological preoccupation of modernism with the world of things as they appear to consciousness.[38] In connection with this issue, I will establish a genealogy of the concept of impersonality, which shows that modernism evolved the concept as a means of signifying the presence of the object, while postmodernism took hold of the same concept with a view to erasing the object for the sake of an hegemonic "signifier."

The strategic reason for Peter Bürger's argument concerning the elitist divide between art and life, and high art and popular art is that avant-gardes can then be presented as the oppositional, left-wing alternative. My study questions this categorization. I suggest that avant-gardist strategies can easily coexist with right-wing ideology. Or to put it another way, avant-gardist vehicle and ideological tenor do not have to coincide. Incidently, such a situation has two implications: avant-gardist strategies do not automatically absolve one from blockheadedness; extreme-right ideology does not annihilate the capacity for creative innovation. Hence one ends up with French paradoxes such as Céline, ignored by critics until recently and finally recognized as one of the major innovators of novelistic writing in French twentieth-century literature.

As far as Lewis is concerned, the avant-gardist project reappears after the First World War in his self-reference as the Enemy. The term is not historically innocent, while at the same time it captures the military etymology of the French term "avant-garde." What is important to grasp is that the term "enemy" in Lewis covers not only an aesthetic project but also a political, sociocultural project. So, rather than discard Bürger's definition of the avant-garde as social praxis from the basis of art, I will apply it to Lewis's political texts even though they do not present typically left-wing features. Indeed his political views are not expressed in objective terms and, like the avant-gardist project of Peter Bürger's description, Lewis's political texts present themselves as artistic entities with, however, a socially pragmatic function.

In particular, I will show that, although his political writings are chiefly written as pamphlets, they in fact should be conceived of along allegorical lines. The pragmatic function of his allegorical politics is twofold: to organize social praxis from the standpoint of avant-gardist vorticism; and to convince the reader of the necessity of an authoritarian political regime. Therefore, if today Lewis's politics is perceived as regressive, reactionary, and repellent, its vehicle is paradoxically revolutionary and avant-gardist. Again, this agonistic combination of regressive dogmatism and progressive radicalism is typically modernist.

What emerges from my dicussion of the dialectical relation between modernism and tradition is a curious pattern of agonic self-contradiction. Thus against authority, modernism crosses gender boundaries, but in a movement of return, creates mythological figures of patriarchism. Against authority, modernism sides with avant-gardist experimentalism, but in a movement of return, also draws on the tradition of the past. Against authority, modernism endlessly satirizes the claptrap of bourgeoisie, but in a movement of return, secures stability and order in politically regressive systems. This striking pattern of contradiction is symptomatic of a movement that, in spite of itself, balks at ideological coherence and creative cohesiveness.

It is only recently that contradiction in modernist texts has caught the eye of critics. Helmut Lethen argues that modernism is located somewhere in the gap between hierarchy and anarchy, narrative and anti-narrative, ontological certainty and uncertainty, construction and destruction.[39] While Eysteinsson sees in modernism a poetics of "interruption," Richard Pearce refers to "the unbridgeable gaps, the intransigent obscurities, the intolerable contradictions, the dizzying leaps in perspective" of modernism.[40] Marianne DeKoven analyses textual ambiguities from the ideological standpoint of class, gender, and race. For her, modernist texts are characterized by contradiction generated by the juxtaposition of incompatible statements or representations. In an article presenting a concentrated version of her groundbreaking thesis, DeKoven argues that "modernist writing offers, constructs, in fact defines itself as radically inconsistent—literally, self-contradictory—though not incoherent."[41] More than any other corpus, the Lewisian corpus keeps its reader on the *qui–vive* by frequent interruptions in the process of making sense of the different texts. I use the term "agon," which I borrow from Lewis's *Enemy of the Stars* (1932), in order to express the particular tension of his discursive contradictions.

However, I question DeKoven's use of *sous-rature* and its post-structuralist connotations. The connotations imply that modernists always consciously created self-contradiction in the process of deconstructing traditional systems of meaning. I am skeptical as to the systematic aspect of this strategic consciousness, and I suggest that modernism also derives its singular dynamism from its *fascination* for contradictory yet irreducible systems of thought and representation. In other words, procedures of parody and self-irony can also be indicative of ideological allegiance that need exorcising because they cannot be easily erased. This ideological tug-of-war is best expressed by Terry Eagleton when he writes that modernism stubbornly refuses to give up the "struggle for meaning. It is still agonizingly caught up in metaphysical depth and wretchedness, still able to experience psychic fragmentation and social alienation as spiritually wounding, and so embarrassingly enmortgaged to the very bourgeois humanism it otherwise seeks to subvert."[42]

I would attribute programmatic self-contradiction to the avant-garde and its systematic, overweening nihilism. For instance, the magazine *Dada* exalts the "interlacing of opposites and all contradictions, utter absurdities, inconsistencies." Strikingly enough, Conrad uses the same tropes in the following excerpt: "The only legitimate basis of creative work lies in the scrupulous recognition of all the irreconcilable antagonisms that make our life so enigmatic, so burdensome, so fascinating, so dangerous, so full of hope."[43] What makes these tropes "modernist" is the Conradian metaphysics of life to which the hyperbolic string of adjectives alludes. This hyperbole is absent from the avant-garde tropes (or the hyperbole is derisory), but is the object of exorcism in modernism that is caught between hyperbole and anticlimax.

This character of modernism will remain invisible if we persist in ignoring the instability of meaning at the core of modernist texts. For instance, T. E. Hulme is known for chameleon-like changes of philosophical positions. Should we let this semantic dislocation speak for itself, or should we, like Levenson in *A Genealogy of Modernism,* rationalize Hulme's contradictions by incorporating them into a chronological, cumulative pattern?[44] Should we, as Quinones did in *Mapping Literary Modernism,* trace modernism on the basis of a four-stage development from radicalism to integration? My own inkling is that rather than smoothing modernist inconsistencies by fitting them into teleological moulds, one should let them jut out so that the tensions between ideology and nihilism, truth and counterfeit, belief and suspicion can be revealed. In part the perception of these modernist tensions derives from the reader's attempt to remain faithful to the frustrated process of finding coherence and continuity in a given text. Modernist contradiction occurs whenever the reader is unable to fill up the gaps and blanks referred to in Iser's analysis of the act of reading.

The principle of contradiction also implies that one cannot keep on studying the work of individual modernists in a piecemeal fashion. To study Eliot's "The Waste Land" without comparing the poem to "Tradition and the Individual Talent" misses the contradictory nature of modernist discourse. Louis Menand points out that the fragmentary aspect of the poem stands in total contradiction to the ideal of completeness advocated in the essay.[45] The poem itself breaks into two discourses: one is poetic, the other scholarly. The poem is nihilistic and dystopic, while the footnotes try to contain the poetic movement of dispersal and disunity. As Michael Kaufmann argues,[46] the footnotes aid and abet Eliot's critical desire to create wholes. In his "Reflections on the Death of a Porcupine" (1925), to take another example, Lawrence reaches a typically modernist aporia. Concerning his famous hierarchization of the dandelion and the hart's tongue fern, which contradicts his belief in the value of the individual, he concludes: "Even apparently contradictory truths do not displace one another."[47] The ideological argument becomes locked in contradiction because the author refuses or is unable to let go of either side of the argument. The "non-organic" character of these modernist works derives not so much from machine imagery or mechanistic metonymy as from contradiction that fragments meaning. What is important here is not the fragment itself, which, as Herbert Schneidau has argued,[48] can be epiphanic, but the lack of cohesion among fragments.

The notion that fragmentation is a defining characteristic of modernism has certainly gained wide recognition. Typically critics locate it at the different levels of time, self, and style.[49] Lewis's dualism of mind and body is a perfect illustration of the modernist discourse on the fragmented self. However, and this is the main thrust of my study, modernist fragmentation also affects the notion of an oeuvre as a semantically and ideologically cohesive whole. Thus what defines Lewis's vision is neither his fiction, nor his nonfiction: it is the contradictory, schismatic views spanning his fiction and nonfiction. One cannot study Lewis the novelist without inquiring into the essay-writing, be it concerned with philosophy, aesthetics, or politics. And the task of categorization is made all the more arduous as the Lewis of *The Art of Being Ruled* does not necessarily correspond to the Lewis of *Tarr*. A fracture exists between the fictional writing and the nonfictional that prevents his oeuvre from reaching creative cohesiveness.

Thus, while within a nonfictional context his belief in the intellect leads to the quasi-mythological creation of "Western Man," within the fictional context his pessimistic belief in the material factor in the self leads him to consider the concept of "Humanity" as an "ideologic phantom."[50] The two messages, one humanist the other Foucault-like, simply do not cohere: they create an agon at the level of meaning. Therefore Lewis's fiction cannot be interpreted as a systematic application of his philosophical positions. The same applies to the relation between his nonfiction and his pictorial art. Tom Normand's recent interpretation of Lewis's pictorial art is weakened by his decision to analyze the pictures chiefly in the light of the nonfiction without always pointing at the disjunction between the discursive ideology and the creative practice.[51] For instance, Lewis's lyrical vision of the Wild Body in "Inferior Religions" is in total contradiction with his pictorial, ruthless satire of the human body starting with "Two Nudes" (1903, Michel, pl. 1) in which, as a student at the Slade, he provided an already grotesque and acerbic representation of the body.

The modernist mechanism of textual self-contradiction is best analyzed at the generic level of texts. Lewis's corpus is generally characterized by the use of several genres. Here I will focus on four of them: the pamphlet and the essay with regard to his nonfiction, and allegory and satirical realism with regard to his fiction.

Of the four, the pamphlet and allegory are least examined and most neglected. On account of its powerful dogmatism yet fundamental elusiveness, the pamphlet has been referred to by Marc Angenot as a "vacillating and impossible site."[52] Lewis's extended use of the pamphlet is symptomatic of a culture unable to transcribe beliefs and credos in an authoritative language. As far as allegory is concerned, little has been written on this generic character of Lewis's writing, perhaps because he himself laid so much emphasis on satire in connection with his writing. And yet allegory in Lewis is chiefly responsible for creativity and fabulation. It is the generic signal that his imagination is taking off. It is also the means of throwing bridges between his art of fiction and his painting, which, more often than not, develops an allegorical narrative of some sort. While establishing the generic features of the fiction and the nonfiction, I will also try to show how the contradictions between the different parts of the corpus occur by focusing on the role of prosopopoeia, which functions as an invariable from one genre to the next.

My reading across the genres of Lewis's corpus faces the criticism that in doing so I ignore the difference in value of the works compared. For instance, *Mrs. Dukes' Million* is a potboiler and cannot be compared to *Tarr; Count Your Dead, They Are Alive!* cannot be compared to *The Art of Being Ruled*. I suggest that the pursuit of meaning often ignores categorization and value. Orwell read a great deal in detective stories and boys' weeklies; in *Mythologies*, Roland Barthes decoded the trivial and the insignificant; Michel Foucault saw significance in historical, anonymous documents; and Lewis himself ana-lyzed Donald Duck very seriously.

The three main parts of my analysis are organized according to Lewis's three main areas of writing: part one focuses on his discourse on the self and identity; part two on his statements on art and culture; and part three on his politics. I deal with the modernist textual and ideological contradictions of Lewis's writings first from a thematic viewpoint in chapter 1, then from a generic viewpoint in chapters 2 and 3. The conclusions from this generic analysis are used throughout my study to provide insight into other aspects of the author's writ-ings. I treat Lewis's ambivalent relation with tradition from the point of view of art in chapter 5 and 6, and from the point of view of gender identity in chapters 4 and 10. Finally I concentrate on Lewis's modernist dialectic relation with the avant-garde first in aesthetic terms in chapter 7, then in political terms in chapter 9. The reader will find an introduction to his political writings in chapter 8.

The Agon
of Modernism

Part One
Allegories

1
The Agon

IN 1927 WYNDHAM LEWIS PUBLISHED A VOLUMINOUS REFLECTION on the role of time in Western culture. The importance of the work, *Time and Western Man,* is threefold: first, it addresses a crucial issue in a timely manner; second, it contributes to a twentieth-century tradition of anthropological studies concerned with the role of time in culture; third, in its overt opposition to the modern valorization of time, it creates a problem for the periodization and definition of Lewis's entire corpus. In particular, the work was written by an author who was also the former avant-gardist editor of *Blast,* in which the past and the future are shelved to make room for the present equated with art. One could always argue that the author, having sown his wild avant-gardist oats, went on to become a modernist pipe-smoking sage. But such an explanation would leave Lewis's fictional output out of the picture. The crucial point I will argue in this chapter is that, although both *Time and Western Man* and Lewis's fiction tackle modern conceptions of time, the respective outcomes are antithetical. Roughly, the philosophical work is concerned with creating an ideal conception of the present in terms opposite to Bergsonian *durée,* with the aim of mastering time. The fiction reflects the same programmatic anti-Bergsonian stance, but cannot be read as an exemplification of the ideal temporality defended in the nonfiction. Instead, I will show that it is dominated by a temporality of eschatology and repetition. What makes Lewis's corpus so specifically modernist is the agon between these two contradictory accounts of temporality, which, with its still point and rushing velocity, the aporetic vortex captures so superbly.

Although the purpose of this chapter is not to investigate the general philosophical background for the development of Lewis's philosophical ideas, I find it relevant to refer to at least two events in the history of ideas that have a demonstrable relevance to what in my introduction I described as the modernist ambivalent relation with tradition.

In general Lewis's philosophical approach belongs to the movement of thought that emphasized the function of experience in our explanation of existence. However, his approach to experience does not consist in an unconditional surrender to materialism. Matter is not embraced but held at arm's length. To this extent, Lewis is a dualist whose aim is to maintain a gap between intellect and body, mind and matter, subject and object.[1] I suggest that Lewis's dualism of mind and body derives from the Darwinian debate. Gillian Beer has assessed the Victorian debate on the theory of evolution as a symptom of anxiety in the collective psyche.[2] There was a deep-seated fear that, at the level of biological processes, man and animal might merge. Yet writers such as T. H. Huxley argued that the gap between man and animal could no longer be maintained. Only twenty-three years separate Lewis's birth from the the publication of Darwin's work, which means that his intellectual development took place in a society still recovering from the Darwinian earthquake.

The Darwinian impact on twentieth-century thought is recorded by John Dewey in "The Influence of Darwinism on Philosophy," a lecture given at Columbia University in 1909 and published the same year. The paper should actually be read as an introduction to the questions raised by Lewis in *Time and Western Man*. For Dewey, Darwinism has dislodged the "conceptions that had become the familiar furniture of the mind . . . [which] rested upon treating change and origin as signs of defect and unreality." Before Darwin, "change as change is mere flux and lapse; it insults intelligence. . . . Completely to know is to relate all special forms to their one single end and good: pure contemplative intelligence." After Darwin, flux, process and change have become recognized modes of explanation: "The influence of Darwin upon philosophy resides in his having conquered the phenomena of life for the principle of transition, and thereby freed the new logic for application to mind and morals and life."[3]

Dewey's account of the impact of Darwinism on the philosophical concept of time is invaluable because it helps bring out the crucial connection in Lewis between his dualism of mind and body and his conception of temporality. Indeed, his decision to keep space and time separate overlaps his philosophical dualistic antinomy of intellect and body. In fact Lewis's antithesis of space and time is an indirect statement of what he believed was the dual nature of the self. It is indeed characteristic of Lewis's thought to associate space with the intellect and time with the body.

The Darwinian background also accounts for Samuel Butler's extremely important influence on Lewis. A child of his age, Butler rebelled against his forebears, particularly Darwin.[4] There is a certain evolutionary pattern from Darwin through Butler to Lewis. Explicit references to Butler are found in his "Essay on the Objective of Plastic Art in Our Time" (1922), "The Foxes' Case" (1925), "Creatures of Habit and Creatures of Change" (1926), and *Snooty Baronet* (1932).[5] In *Tarr* (1928) the eponymous hero begins his anti-female complaint with a parody of Butler's poem, "A Psalm of Montreal" (1884): "Oh Sex! oh Montreal! How full and wrong this haunting of women is! . . . It is like a slop and spawn of children and the bawling machinery of the inside of life, always and all over our palaces."[6] In 1926 Lewis quoted a passage from Butler's *Notebooks* that describes the encroachment of origins on the self:

> "No sooner do we think we have got a *bona fide* barrier than it breaks down. The divisions between varieties, species, genus, all gone; between instinct and reason, gone; between animals and plants, gone; between man and the lower animals, gone; so, ere long, the division between organic and inorganic will go and will take with it the division between mind and matter."[7]

This breaking down of barriers between mind and matter precisely constitutes the apocalyptic threat against which Lewis tried to build a bulwark.

The endeavour to erect a dualistic system is not unique to Lewis. Other modernists resorted to the same type of argument even though their dualism was not as thoroughgoing as his. T. S. Eliot argued that one "must be either a naturalist or a supernaturalist. . . . if this 'supernatural' is suppressed the dualism of man and nature collapses at once."[8] One also recalls T. E. Hulme's concern with the "reestablishment of the temper or disposition of mind which can look at a gap or chasm without shuddering."[9]

Modernist manifestations of dualism such as Lewis's, Eliot's, and Hulme's should therefore be regarded as attempts to maintain a philosophical sense of traditional stability that Darwinism had overturned. However, confining modernism to Butlerism and dualisms of all stripes would be a mistake. Along with the desire to cling to the aura of authority that pre-Darwinian stasis and Platonic idealism provided, one finds the equally powerful will to question and reject a conceptual tradition that no longer cohered with the phenomenological experience of an ever-changing world.

Thus the second event in the history of ideas to be mentioned is what Judith Ryan refers to as the movement of "new psychology." The so-called new psychologists included Franz Brentano, Ernst Mach, and William James who, as a European traveller and student, was deeply influenced by the first two. James is also at the centre of Lewis's discussion of time in *Time and Western Man*.

The new psychologists' reflection on the role of perception in our experience of the world led to a redefinition of self, reality, and their interrelationship. Brentano's theory was that subject and object do not exist independently of each other, which implied a loss of clear boundaries between the two. Mach presented the self as a bundle of impressions or atoms in constant change. James modified these positions by establishing a relation of functionalism between subject and object. So, the "flux" and the loss of "clear outlines" of Lewis's critique in *Time and Western Man* are in fact elements deriving from a type of discursive analysis initiated towards the end of the nineteenth century, and affecting the fields of philosophy and the arts in the first half of the twentieth century.

The new psychologists' analysis reads like a philosophical systematization of what the romantics and, along with them, German Idealists such as Fichte had grasped. New psychologism is concerned with what, in "Tintern Abbey," Wordsworth referred to as the "mighty world / Of eye, and ear,—both what they half create, / And what perceive."[10] However, the difference between the romantics and the new psychologists is one of context. The new psychologists' reflection contributed to the demise of a traditional explanation concerning the relation between self and phenomena in the context of developed industrialization and of urbanized, fragmented communities no longer significantly held together by religious belief.

Ryan's studies of individual authors such as Joyce, Kafka, or Musil clearly show that the modernists were the inheritors of this important debate. One could argue then, as Ryan implies, that these writers were the receivers of philosophical ideas with which they experimented in their fictions. I suggest there is another way in which new psychology and modernism converge, and that is in the definition of "modernity." Matei Calinescu has established that the earlier stages of modernity in art were characterized by a sharp consciousness of time and especially of the present and transitory, as in the case of Stendhal's and Baudelaire's art.[11] There is then a definite parallel between this sense of modernity based on a new awareness of time on the one hand and, on the other, the transitory nature of the self as argued for by the new psychologists. This seems to indicate less of a causal relation between art and philosophy, and more of an "episteme" of temporality à la Foucault.

With its satirical critique of the flux and of the loss of clear outlines concerning the self and the external object, *Time and Western Man* is a clear attempt to break away from modernity as defined by Stendhal,

Darwin, the impressionists, the new psychologists, and Bergson. Granted their disparity, all these figures contributed to a movement of thought that defined our experience of the world in monistic terms. From a philosophical viewpoint, Lewis's dualism is a response to this ubiquitous monism. His positions are never presented explicitly; instead, they show through his critique of what he calls the Bergsonian, or time-space, or abstract school. While a critical spotlight is directed on this school of thought, the positions from which the critique is conducted are left in the dim areas outside the flow of light. Thus Lewis's position on object is defined in opposition to the Bergsonian subject, and his position on subject is defined in opposition to the Bergsonian object.

The contrast between Bergson's mental world and a Lewisian objective world of concrete matter is similar to the contrast between the Great Within and the Great Without established in *Satire and Fiction* (1930). The Great Within is characterized by temporal subjectivity, while the Great Without is characterized by spatial objectivity. Bergson and Einstein are both rejected as the high priests of the creed that aims at coalescing time and space. In fact, for Lewis time and space in Bergson do not coalesce; space is taken over by time. Lewis's dualistic division between mind and matter is implicit in passages such as the following: "*The world* [of birds] *is not a world of distinct objects. It is an interpenetrating world of direct sensation*. It is, in short, Mr. Bergson's world. . . . It is a *mental,* as it were an *interior* world, of palpitating movement, visually indistinct, electrical."[12] However, in taking a stand against temporal subjectivity, Lewis does not argue in favor of matter in general. His materialism has been carefully sifted and what is foregrounded is special matter, both spatialized and visualized, for matter can also be temporal and auditive. Lewis deals with temporal and auditive matter insofar as it is synonymous with Poundian or Bergsonian matter—that is to say, insofar as it is an object of satire.

In his analysis of the Bergsonian school, Lewis spells out all the major points of criticism that the tenets of new psychology had raised. For instance, the Bergsonian process of perceptual experience results in the dissolution of identity, while the world of objects no longer presents a point of mooring for drifting consciousness. Thus "you lose not only the clearness of outline, the static beauty of the things you commonly apprehend; you lose also the clearness of outline of your individuality which apprehends them" (*TWM,* 175). The critique of the time-school leads to the creation of tropes that are important because they will reappear in the context of non-philosophical, political discourse. Thus temporal succession and the

Jamesian stream of consciousness transform the self into a "crowd of
Me's" (*TWM*, 362), or a "crowd of hurrying shapes, a temporal
collectivity. . . . a *history*" (*TWM*, 181), or again, into a "phalanstery
of selves" (*TWM*, 175).

Lewis's account of the clear outline of individuality is provided
through the critique of the Bergsonian representation of the objective
world. He first establishes a contrast between the Bergsonian world of
sensation and what he describes as spatial consciousness. Bergsonian
subjectivity is rejected for being characterized by a fundamental lack
of stability: things have lost their contours in a flux of sensation.
"Time for the bergsonian or relativist," Lewis argues, "is fundamentally sensation; that is what Bergson's *durée* always conceals beneath
its pretentious metaphysic. It is the glorification of the life-of-the-
moment, with no reference beyond itself and no absolute or universal
value" (*TWM*, 27). Lewis's aim is to nip vitalism in the bud by
mechanizing the temporal flux. While discussing Whitehead's theory
of organic mechanism, he asks: "locomotion and movement, 'organism' in the making, or *becoming*, not *become*, what is that but a machine?" (*TWM*, 178–79).

Lewis's response to the Bergsonian school faces a dilemma. How
does one provide stability of identity and clearness of outlines while
still working within a perceptual and phenomenological framework?
His solution is to privilege one aspect of perceptual experience at the
expense of others. A relation of intentionality is established between
subject and object, which are defined in isomorphic terms because
both are spatialized. Thus, on the one hand, "our consciousness is
quite static and still, as serene and unmoving as our position upon
the earth in the midst of Space appears to be" (*TWM*, 233); on the
other, the world of perceived objects is defined in these terms: "there
is such and such a thing, or person, one moment, then it ceases to
be: that is the 'spatializing' truth" (*TWM*, 233). Lewis has therefore
obtained an equation of some sort that allows him to provide not
only a definition of subject and object that is modern insofar as it
rests on the notion of the present and the contingent, but also one
that is equally antimodern insofar as it tries to evacuate the subjective
effect of time: "the world of Space—as opposed to the mental world
of memory—is the world of a 'pure Present.' For the past of that
space-world is dead and gone" (*TWM*, 232).

"Spatializing truth" is supposed to provide a sense of continuity in
contrast to the world of the abstract school defined as "one of succes-
sive, flat, images or impressions" that "are, as far as possible, naked
and simple, direct sensations" (*TWM*, 409). However, the weakness
of the Lewisian spatializing process lies in its creating a world breath-

lessly reborn every second, yet constantly stillborn: "there is such and such a thing, or person, one moment, then it ceases to be." In effect, spatializing truth would destroy the traditional sense of continuous matter while confining the self to a phantasmagoria of disconnected percepts. To some extent, Lewis's definition exacerbates the sense of contingency created by the new psychologists without the benefit of a sensuous continuum. This is the reason why, by the end of his argument and haunted by a Berkeleyism bereft of a divine act of perception, Lewis suddenly reintroduces memory with this time a cognitive function: "every time we open our eyes we envelop the world before us, and give it *body,* or its quality consisting of *objects,* with our memory" (*TWM,* 408). Memory thus defined allows the object to be complete by providing the front of a house with a hidden yet memorized back; by the same token the sum of all the perceiving acts results in a sense of continuous identity.

Lewis is not so much concerned with explaining reality as with dealing with it. In other words, his analysis is not descriptive but programmatic. He presents the different time philosophies as ideologies of the body that incarnates time. In his interpretation of Spengler's organicism, he argues that "the reference is directly to the organic mechanism of your body, with systole and diastole, periodic changes, and its budding, flowering and decaying. The 'mind' has ceased to exist. The universe is an animal resembling your body, with a mind composed of *time*" (*TWM,* 283). Ultimately, the thought of *Time and Western Man* is transcendental in the sense that it aims at creating a self that rises above the commonplace or the anonymous body. The following passage provides a clear expression of Lewis's dualistic transcendentalism: it "is in non-personal modes of feeling—that is in *thought,* or in feeling that is so dissociated from the hot, immediate egoism of sensational life that it becomes automatically intellectual— that the non-religious Western Man has always expressed himself, at his most profoundest, at his purest" (*TWM,* 271). The reason why Bergson is his bête noire is not anti-Semitism. Rather, in Lewis, Bergsonian thought functions as a means of externalizing as well as evacuating the body and its flux. The triumph of spatializing truth demands the sacrifice of the body: hence Bergsonism will be pilloried.

As the Enemy, Lewis's intention was to present *Time and Western Man* as the alternative to modernity as represented by the abstract school and the modernist writers. However, such binarism ignores the ambiguity of modernism with which Lewis's campaign was not concerned. For instance, Bergsonian duration functions as a paradoxical means of providing a sense of permanence in the midst of contingency. Ryan points out that Pater's position on the flux was far from single-minded: "at the same time as he maintained that life was a perceptual flux in which the boundaries between self and world were merely labels given by the reflective mind, Pater also held that this mind was essentially isolated." It has also been the convention to regard Stephen Dedalus's definition of beauty in *A Portrait of the Artist as a Young Man* (1916) as an ironical statement. By contrast, Ryan proposes to replace this definition in the context of the debate on new psychology: "Stephen's phases of apprehension all move in the same direction: to identify, to analyze, and consolidate the individual particularity of the object."[13] If such is the case, then the definition can be said to participate in the search for a point of stability or for the clear outlines in the midst of the flux. Rather than seeing an ironic contradiction between this aesthetic statement and the subsequent apparent fluidity of *Ulysses,* one can suggest the presence of a tension between an awareness of the perceptual flux and the desire to still the flux to let the object stand out.

Again, Ryan points to the sense of ambiguity characterizing Virginia Woolf's thinking on the question. In her diary Woolf asks herself: "Now is life very solid or very shifting? I am haunted by the two contradictions. This has gone on for ever; will last for ever; goes down to the bottom of the world—this moment I stand on. Also it is transitory, flying, diaphanous."[14] The key word here is "contradictions," which is symptomatic of the whole debate and reflects a sense of transition if not crisis. It seems as though meaning in modernism underwent a redefinition not only because a new world superseded an old, but also because meaning could no longer be equated with unequivocal statements on clearly defined problems. The time question is important because symptomatic of such modernist ambivalence and contradiction.

While the arguments of *Time and Western Man* contribute to the construction of binary meaning opposing spatial consciousness and spatial matter to temporal flux, Lewis's creative writing works directly against this binarism. The dualism of mind and body is still implicit in the fiction but the dominant, determining factors are time and the body. The shift from the nonfiction to the fiction corresponds to a reversal of meaning: in the nonfiction the perceptual process governed by a spatial bias leads to the potentiality of a meaningful world characterized by a traditional sense of stability; in the fiction the same perceptual process destroys any possibility of meaningfulness. In effect, Lewis's vision displays the same modernist contradictions as those expressed in Pater, Joyce, and Woolf. What is specific to Lewis is that the contradictions of meaning chiefly occur between the nonfiction and the fiction.

In particular the fictional representation of the act of perception fails to establish the self as an intellectual consciousness and the object as a static object. Instead, the representation is divided into a solipsistic eye and a moving, and therefore, temporal body. Nor does the act of perception correspond to the language of the intellect. In *The Childermass* (1928) an apparently digressive anecdote reveals the rift between seeing and saying. Pullman tells his companion Satters an anecdote concerning the Victorian physicist Tyndall, who once suffered from an electrical shock during a public experiment: *"while he was reassuring* the audience, his body appeared to him cut up into fragments. For instance, his arms were separated from his trunk, and seemed suspended in the air. . . . his optic nerve was quite irrational. It reported everything in a fantastic manner. . . . Had it been the optic nerve speaking it would have said, 'As you see, I am all in pieces!' As it was, he said, 'You see! I am uninjured and quite as usual.'"[15] A disjunction between rational discourse and subjective perception has occurred, which destroys the unity of the self. The description of Tyndall's fragmented body could actually be used as an ekphrastic description of Picasso's *Man with a Pipe* (1912). Here Berkeley's *esse est percipi* is not suported by cognitive memory, and is tinged with cubistic and surrealistic hues.

With the resurgence of the body in the fiction, the nonfictional emphasis on the intellect is superseded by the fictional emphasis on the will or energy. The critique of vitalism is continued in the fiction without, however, the inclusion of a counter-representation of the intellect. In a purple passage from *Tarr* (1928), Soltyk is described at his duel, while taunted by Kreisler's verbal provocations. The narrative describes the self suddenly beleaguered by destructive energy:

> Soltyk became white and red by turns: the will was released in a muffled explosion, it tore within at its obstructions, he writhed upright, a statue's bronze softening, suddenly, with blood. His blood, one heavy mass, hurtled about in him, up and down, like a sturgeon in a narrow tank. . . . His hands were electrified: will was at last dashed all over him, an arctic douche and the hands become claws flew at Kreisler's throat. (*Tarr*, 280)

The description is governed by a dissociation between Soltyk's passive consciousness and the energy of the body. This taking-over of the Wild Body is typical of Lewis's characterization: it appears in "Dean Swift with a Brush. The Tyroist Explains His Art" (1921) where vitality is said to be "immense, but purposeless, and hence sometimes malignant";[16] and it rules the actions of characters such as Victor

Stamp in *The Revenge for Love* (1937) or Augustine Card in *The Red Priest* (1955).

Should one see in these violent manifestations of the will an aftermath of Lewis's experience at the front during the First World War? The earlier *Wild Body* short stories testify to the fact that violence of the body was a Lewisian concern from the start. "Le Père François," published in 1910, is a case in point. A French tramp, François is suddenly under the sway of irrational and uncontrollable motion: "He grew more and more violent, often getting up and whirling round without reason, like a dervish, with his ruined umbrellas shaken at arm's length" (*CWB*, 283). Far from being the sole expression of a postwar trauma, the violence of Lewis's characters stems from early modernist primitivism that, at the turn of the century, characterized visual artists and painters alike.

Throughout Lewis's fictional writings, the prevailing devices of characterization are reification and mechanization, which coerce the will into rigidity and help spatialize the flux of the body. The outcome, however, is not the beauty of spatializing truth as praised in *Time and Western Man,* but grotesque representations of a ludicrously specialized self. For instance, Kreisler "compared himself to one of those little nursery locomotives that go straight ahead without stopping; that anyone can take up and send puffing away in the opposite direction. . . . He was a thing, scarcely any longer a *Mensch*" (*Tarr,* 117). In *Blasting and Bombardiering* (1937), the autobiographical self is represented as a soldier-puppet that has just been wound up: "I instantly wheeled with the precision of a well-constructed top; and with the tread of an irresistible automaton I bore down swiftly and steadily upon the adjutant; I brought my heels together with a resounding spank, gave my rifle a well-deserved slap, and stood looking over the adjutant's head."[17] The mechanization of the body constitutes a halfway victory by shaping the flux, but it never leads to the representation of intellectual, spatial consciousness whose character is incompatible with the temporal nature of narration and art in general. Spatial intellect is condemned to utopia, and that is the reason why Lewisian characters such as Macrob or Arghol, who are more intellectually than physically defined, do not survive by the end of the plot.

Nor does Lewis's description of the body stay at the surface of things as is prescribed in *Satire and Fiction*. The novelistic narratives teem with Swiftian blow-ups of individual parts of the body, providing telling insights. The primitivism of *The Wild Body* short stories creates a nightmarish vision totally apart from the ideal of Western Man. For instance in "The Cornac and His Wife" the Breton community and the narrator gather for a show presented by circus acrobats:

"We had to visualize a colony of much-twisted, sorely-tried intestines, screwed this way and that, as they had never been screwed before. It was an anatomical piece" (*CWB,* 99). In *The Childermass,* the mouth of a youth, "which is a coarse hole, promises as well the complete absence of mind, nothing but matter and its gaping traps" (165). Or biological processes of the body are used as tropes to describe the soul's posthumous voyage. The Bailiff informs his audience that the

> souls forced peristaltically into this metropolis from the earth, as though almost by muscular propulsion, forget by a divine ordering of the mirrors of their consciousness the phases of their journey. . . . They arrive completely transformed, cooked in this posthumous odyssey. . . . they reach the anus symbolized by the circular gate over there more cloacal even than at the moment of their engulfing on their earthly deathbeds. They will be found to have assumed a more ultimate form as well (though equally cloacal) than was possible in terrestrial life. (*CM,* 134)

The description parodies the Parousia or "Second Coming" of Christ, according to which posthumous life will be enjoyed in heaven in the form of a renewed physical envelope. With its references to digestion and defecation, the parody reads as if Ubu's scatological pataphysics had been applied to Dante's *Inferno*.

Because the body cannot be annihilated without annihilation of the total self, time is endured and never abolished. The plots and structures of Lewis's novels and plays can be said to be determined by the temporality of the body. On the whole and in a spirit of antimodern temporality and subjectivity, his plots are chronological, but this chronology should not be taken for a straightforward treatment of time. Instead, the chronology is often destabilized by scenes laden with a sense of crisis, which more often than not have the body for chief concern. The "pure Present" of Lewis's philosophy is replaced by an eschatological type of temporality.

It is no accident that *Tarr,* Lewis's first major novel, should capture the modernist agon between a sense of stasis and continuity and one of chaos and disruption. A hiatus exists between the title of the work and the conception of its characterization. Tarr is both the name of a major protagonist and an acronym for art, presumably of the static type as he is a painter. And yet the bulk of the narrative concentrates on the failed artist Kreisler who, like a cork tossed by the turgid element of a vortex, is unable to control time. The central part of *Tarr* is a case in point. "Bourgeois-Bohemians" constitutes the third part of the novel and consists of two chapters. The second chapter, which describes Kreisler's mad dance with a Victorian partner, symbolizes the modern conception of a vitalistic, irrational self. The central vortex of the novel is described in the following terms:

> He took her twice, with ever-increasing velocity, round the large hall, and at the third round, at breakneck speed, spun with her in the direction of the front door. . . . Another moment and they would have been in the street, amongst the traffic, a disturbing meteor, whizzing out of sight, had they not met the alarmed resistance of a considerable british family entering the front door as Kreisler bore upon it. . . . They received this violent couple in their midst. The rush took Kreisler and his partner half-way through, and there they stood embedded and unconscious for many seconds. (*Tarr*, 149–50)

Oscillating between the comic and the erotic, such a description temporarily lifts the plot out of its chronological frame and imparts an exhilarating sense of apocalyptic ending. Numerous descriptions concerning Kreisler's acts are based on tropes alluding or referring directly to the vortex. This symbol appears whenever the vitality of the Wild Body or even the will conceived of at a cosmological level reach a paroxysmal point.

The vorticist dance as expression of apocalyptic energy recurs throughout Lewis's writings, from the earlier Breton stories and *Mrs. Dukes' Million* (1908–10) through *Snooty Baronet* (1932) to *Malign Fiesta* (1955). The same motif reappears in his pictorial art, especially in the early stages of his career. In *The Dancers* (1912; Michel, pl. 13), three figures are enclosed within sweeping arcs, as if they were caught in the blue amber-like maelstrom of their frantic dance. In an earlier sketch, *Dancing Figures* (1910), five dithyrambic figures, three females and two males, are arrested in the midst of action, their bodies convulsed and contorted by the implied rhythm of an absent tune. They have been plucked out of the stream of life. The female figure on the lower right is spinning like a top, and in the upper area of the picture, a man and a woman revolve around each other. Angular, jagged strokes as well as curves are used to depict the dancers. While the angular outlines translate a sense of syncopation, the curves provide a sense of gyration. One can even see the five figures as belonging to an ellipse starting with the fat Breton on the left, curving with the broken back of the bending female figure, and ending with the gyrating girl. The whole effect is enhanced by the slanted surface of the dancing-floor, flat and merged with surrounding walls, as if the fast spin of the dance-vortex had flattened out the shapes and outlines of the objective world. This sketch recalls the "Breton Journal": "the dancers at every minute turning riotously between the narrow walls [of the inn]" (*CWB*, 195).

The Lewisian sense of an ending is also manifested by the myth of metamorphosis, which is concerned with a beginning and an end forever enacted and forever postponed. Brunel puts it this way: "metamorphosis is at one and the same time the phantasy that the body is discarded and the expression of the body's irreducible character."[18] In this respect the posthumous publication of *Mrs. Dukes' Million* is invaluable because it gives access to a formative piece of writing in which Lewis creates the "phalanstery of selves," which were to become the butt of his satire in *Time and Western Man.* The temporality of the novel is in part based on the myth of metamorphosis that allows a cathartic multiplication of selves to occur within the plot of a thriller.

The plot reflects a modern conception of identity that breaks down the barriers among temporal versions of the same self. This is exemplified by the protagonist's various impersonating metamorphoses. Besides impersonating Mrs. Dukes, Royal also appears as a bohemian artist, a chauffeur, a German band player, and an aviator. All these impersonations are avatars of Royal whose identity in the novel is never singular but always the sum of two images. Also, at a time when D. H. Lawrence was getting ready to write *Sons and Lovers,* Lewis's text played with onomastics to signify a self that lived beyond the appearances of rationality. As an artist, Royal's name is Ernest Nichols whose painting Mrs. Dukes finds apalling and horrible. Mrs. Dukes has a son whose name is Cole. Although he is an adult, Cole is the infant smoking the pipe, at which he sucks as if it were "an indiarubber tit."[19] He is the regressed creature, living under the surface of social life, in the warm dirty entrails of the Dukes' house. He belongs to the Great Within and, like Faulkner's Benjy, he is inarticulate, if not mute: "He had been queer, morose and delicate as a boy, and had grown into a man for whom all intercourse with his fellows was impossible, and who, besides, seemed in no way desirous to have any. He had always lived with his mother" (*MDM,* 20). What is remarkable is that Cole's name is inscribed in the painter's name: Nichols/Ni-Cole-s. Thus, by means of an allograph, Lewis creates a very convincingly modern unconscious, which he later took pains to repudiate.

A narrative device close to metamorphosis is the double that appears in *Mrs. Dukes' Million* and later on in the postwar novels. The role of the double in Lewis is to chop up the sequence of self-representations, to spatialize the temporal phalanstery of selves. The making of Snooty Baronet rests on such a strategy. The duality of the character is indicated by what Kenner refers to as the metaphysics of names in Lewis. Indeed, Snooty is also known by the double-barreled name of Kell-Imrie. It is reported that whenever he pays a visit to his mistress Lily, the Baronet assumes a Butler-like personality, "tucked up in the lion's skin of the famous author of 'The Way of All Flesh.'"[20] The Baronet's impersonation is an uncanny means of playing hide-and-seek with the self: he impersonates Butler in order to become anonymous and hide his true identity from his mistress. This play on identity is based on the biographical fact that, as Peter Raby reports,[21] Butler used to visit a prostitute without revealing his name. Thus the self who enjoys sex with Lily and who breaks the bona fide barriers between intellect and body remains unnamed or unnamable.

In a chapter located right in the middle of the novel, the Baronet is confronted with his physical double, but this time in a context of visual perception. Peering at a hatter's shop-window, Snooty discovers an automaton in action, staring back at him: "There was something abstruse and unfathomable in this automaton. Beside me a new arrival smiled back at the bowing Hatter's doll. I turned towards him in alarm. Was not perhaps this fellow who had come up beside me a puppet too? . . . Of course he was, but dogging that was the brother-thought, *but equally so am I!*" (*SB*, 135–36). The automaton acquires an allegorical meaning and constitutes an archetype for the characters of the novel who are all governed by the actions of the mechanical Wild Body. While metamorphosis fosters a sense of transition and succession, the double creates a sense of crisis and dual confrontation. This is particularly conspicuous in the encounter between Snooty and his literary agent, Humph. As body, Humph is reduced to a chin and an onomatopoeia. Officially the Baronet has a purely scientific interest in the agent who represents a "specimen" of behaviorism. In point of fact, his report on their meeting betrays a curious sense of anxiety. What is supposed to be a banal scene of polite greeting turns into an expressionistic nightmare:

> My hand gripped in his granite paw, he pushed me back against the wall. . . . we stood, or rather danced or shuffled, up against the wall, he gradually edging and thrusting me back into the corner, which was also the jamb of the door, my hand imprisoned all the while in his fist of stone—wooden and dour and blank, his at once full and hollow face staring up in mine, with never a muscle moving upon its meat-flushed, tanned-hide, surface, with never the shadow of a smile. . . . I was paralyzed with repulsion, as I now shrank stiffly back. (*SB*, 118)

The description rests on the dissociation between Humph-the-Wild-Body and Snooty-as-consciousness. An agon develops between the loathed body and consciousness paralyzed by disgust. The ghostly, outlandish characteristics of the double, catalogued by Karl Miller,[22] feature in the description: "—wooden and dour and blank, his at once full and hollow face staring up into mine . . . with never the shadow of a smile." The apocalyptism of the relation to the double is expressed in oneiric scenes such as the Baronet's dream of falling into wells: Humph "was down here and as soon as I reached the bottom he would attack me. He was armed and I was not" (*SB*, 227). Snooty falls into the well of the unconscious, which is at the nether end of Lewis's vertical symbolism. What awaits him there is both his double and most intimate enemy.

By killing Humph, Snooty gets rid of his double or Wild Body. This murder represents the possibility of interrupting the succession of doubles and Wild Bodies. Although Snooty does not actually plan Humph's murder, a sense of finality subsists. While planning his trip to North Africa with Humph and Val, Snooty declares: "As to me, in the charge of these machines, they should—up to the last moment—have their way with me. *Up to the last* grain of sand, when the sand *at last* ran out" (*SB*, 131). If the psychological logic of the double is pushed to its conclusion, then Humph's murder, which occurs in the midst of a "fantasia," corresponds to a veiled suicide. Yet Kell-Imrie survives, not just as detached observer but as agent, since his murder confirms him as an embodiment of the will. The cathartic elimination of the body is postponed yet again, leaving the prospect of an endless chain of impersonations.

This is the reason why the other major manifestation of Lewis's fictional temporality is repetition. The conclusion to *Tarr* presents a comic temporality of repetition with a sustained pattern of alternate love partners. But the last great pieces of Lewis's career emphasize a more sinister type of repetition that heralds Beckettian temporality.[23] In *Self Condemned* (1954), René's and Hester's experience of time is one of unrelieved, frozen eternity: "In the Rip van Winkle existence of René and Hester . . . a thousand years is the same as one tick of the clock. It was a dense, interminable, painful vibration, this great whirring, agelong, thunderous *Tick*."[24] The "one dully aching throb of time" of the novel is a far cry from the "eternal Present" of *Time and Western Man* and a grotesque twin of Bergsonian duration. In *Monstre Gai* (1955) Mannock describes to Pullman the temporal properties of Third City: "The central fact is that time does not exist here. Or it exists in a kind of unprogressive way, it halts one at one's earthly self, at some specific date."[25] The "Heaven of the Young" actually conceals an eternal physical hell from which one can escape only by means of an act of apocalyptic magnitude. Hence John Rigate announces with eagerness the imminent attack of Lucifer's forces on

Third City: he is waiting for Godot. Apocalyptic destruction occurs, but near the beginning of the plot, which looks rather ominous.

A mysterious process of destruction or "storm" develops with shift from light to darkness, followed by seismic movements as well as the deafening sound of an overpowering, Miltonic "Hiss." The description of the storm draws on the biblical topos of the apocalypse with its rain of flies, locusts, splintered glass, stones, blistering heat, and deafening noise. A supernatural battle develops opposing the forces of Lucifer to God's:

> The apparent slamming of monstrous doors would correspond for those attuned to terrestrial battle, with the detonation of shells and bombs. But the doors which seemed to be slamming must have been shutting out areas as large as the city itself. . . . What would not be familiar to the human soldier would be three or four mammoth voices on high, crashing out the alphabets of Heaven and of the Pit. The nasal tongues of giant viragos at one time conducted a screaming argument among the clouds, which, if translated, was totally absurd. This terrific contest degenerated into something like a zoological madness. The giant sounds shrank to a hubbub of monkeys, and a psittacine screaming. As abruptly as it had begun this chaotic orgasm ended—like a vast squib it hissed and spluttered, it chattered and squawked to an end, an end at which no one was present. (*MG,* 59)

The description combines extra- and intratextual references. The historical and biographical background is not the Second World War but the First World War of which Lewis had firsthand experience. The metaphor of door-slamming to describe detonations was actually used by Lewis in a letter to Ezra Pound, which he wrote on June 19, 1917: "The perpetual opening and shutting, slamming and slapping of doors that goes on here, the ceaseless rush of outgoing shells, and fatigued complaint, or surprised whistle, of incoming ones."[26] The other reference is of course Milton's epic of *Paradise Lost* with its titanic confrontations between good and evil. However, the bathos of the intertextual reference is evident as the contest is described in terms of a "zoological madness" or a "chaotic orgasm" involving fighters of dubious origins (as they are referred to as "viragos"). The occurence of the contest is also something of a paradox because all the inhabitants of Third City are left unconscious and unable to witness the event. This is the typically Beckettian quest for the end that remains frustrated because it cannot occur outside time and yet, as long as there is time, there is no end in sight. The self is therefore condemned to endurance. The first object of awareness on Pullman's awakening from his temporary coma is the body described in reifying terms: "it was an impossibly ramshackle mechanism which forced the eel-like limbs into the tubes of cloth, and forced the feet into two shoes of iron" (*MG*, 73). The apocalypse of *Monstre Gai* is meaningless because it leads to a painful rebirth into the world of matter.

While *Monstre Gai* treats temporality from the standpoint of an impossible ending, *Malign Fiesta* tackles the same problem from the standpoint of a new beginning. This last volume of Lewis's trilogy is characterized by a two-stage plot: the first part is concerned with describing an inferno of tortured flesh and reaches its nadir with the visit to the Punishment Cells. The second part is concerned with the creation of a new world or the genesis of the Human Age. Pullman organizes a huge "fiesta" to celebrate the Devil's betrothal, symbolizing the new order among the giant-angels so far maintained in a state of physical purity. The Creation of *Malign Fiesta* is as meaningless as the apocalypse of *Monstre Gai*. Indeed, what is celebrated is the birth of the Wild Body with its terrible energy. Elements of the carnival are therefore used to turn genesis into a parodic act. Creation coincides with the Fall, sexual licence and the murder of an angel who "lay, toes upwards, the handle of a long knife sticking up expressively, above the region of the heart; a nail had been hammered into each of his eyes."[27]

Ultimately this creation is parodic because it is a vast empty stammer: the "interminable animal survival" (*MF*, 480) dreaded by Pullman continues. It is within this temporality or misfired apocalypse that creativity is alluded to in the evocation of Lewis's personal artistic genesis on the Breton coast while observing the life of alien rustics. This return to origins is hinted at in the description of vorticist dances organized for the fiesta and performed by Spanish, French, Irish, and Scottish dancers. Even the first act of creation is represented as Pullman notices "an angel busily writing, as well as drawing, in a little book" (*MF*, 503). Thus creativity is temporalized and materialized.

The comparison between Lewis's nonfiction and his fiction brings out an important paradox that we will see recur in other contexts of analysis: his fiction tends to be cognitive to the extent that it reveals something about the world of experience. This revelation always takes place within a fundamentally dystopian universe. By contrast, the nonfiction is the locus of Lewisian utopia, where the creative illusions, whether they go by the name of spatializing truth, not-self, or the Great Without, are given full expression. To say therefore that *Time and Western Man* is more representative of Lewis than, say, *Snooty Baronet,* or vice versa, is to ignore the tense and chiasmic relation between the fiction and the nonfiction. While the argument of *Time and Western Man* characterizes art as the product of spatializing truth and as a means of transcending the material conditions of life, Lewis's novels such as *Tarr* and *Snooty Baronet* as well as the two sequels of his major trilogy annihilate this transcendental aspiration. Now, this dislocation of meaning between the nonfiction and the fiction I have interpreted from a philosophical and thematic viewpoint, but such an analysis does not cover all the aspects of the problem. Indeed, Lewis's contradiction between fiction and nonfiction coincides with a shift of genres. In the next two chapters I will try to bring precision to the terms "fiction" and "nonfiction," and assess genre as a factor of meaning in Lewis's corpus.

2

Genre and Meaning: The Nonfiction

IN *TIME AND WESTERN MAN* LEWIS GIVES US A GLIMPSE OF WHAT the language of spatial consciousness would be like: his ideal logos is on a par with his ideal of spatial intellect to the extent that they share objectivity and purity. Lewis's definition of good language is based on the criteria of clarity, logic, and simplicity. "There," he says, "you get the minimum of fuss or mannerism. When the mind is most active it is least personal, least mannered" (*TWM*, 134). In *Satire and Fiction* Lewis conceives of the language of satire as an extension of the visual, spatial intellect. In short, Lewis's visual logos is supposed to beget a realism providing the clear outlines of the Great Without. Such a theoretical view of language seems to support Margot Norris's generalization that "the cultural ideological agenda of the high modernist's deployment of a highly controlled and disciplined style betrayed its protofascist intentions."[1] So when the reader prepares to read a Lewisian creative piece, s/he should expect either one of two things: an objective realism with a scientific, detached omniscient voice, or an allegory of the self as visual intellect.

In fact, the creative pieces tell quite a different story. Lewis's isomorphism between perceiving subject as spatial intellect and the perceived object as spatial matter never constitutes the ideological basis for contructing a narrative. Lewis's fictional narrative is characterized by a discontinuity between the said and the seen, the narrator and the focalizer, the act of telling and the act of perceiving. This means that the logos as a means of communicating the clear outlines of the external world does not govern the narration of his fiction. In *Enemy of the Stars* (1932), the logos gets split between Arghol's two voices: one is "raucous and disfigured with a catarrh of lies, contracted in the fetid bankrupt atmosphere of life's swamp"; the other is "clear and splendid among Truth's balsamic hills" (*CPP*, 147). In *The Vulgar Streak* (1941), Vincent's lower-class background provides the frame for language determined by Halvorsen's voice compared to "a can-opener . . . an instrument of the will" or by Vincent's "old evil-smelling, aitchless and g-less" father.[2]

At first sight, the presence of what is variously referred to as the omniscient, third-person, or extra-diegetic narrator in Lewis seems to indicate an authoritarian, monological type of narration. But this is to assess the fictional corpus without taking account of the nonfictional corpus. The fictional narrative strategies acquire their full meaning only when they are analyzed within the context of transition from nonfiction to fiction, or vice versa. Thus the split between the seen and the said, the focalizer and the narrator in such novels as *The Revenge for Love* and *Self Condemned* manifests the failure of the Western Man project. Theoretically Western Man should be able to tie intellect, logos, and spatialization all in one. In the fictional corpus the reader is faced with a shell-shocked narrative where the three components have split off.

Of all the Lewisian narratives, *Snooty Baronet* is perhaps the most revealing. With his analytical "behavioristic" analysis of the human species, intellectual self-detachment, and cool narrative voice, the Baronet seems to be a promising narrator à la Western Man. However, the novel is characterized by a narrative false bottom. Behind the Baronet's voice there is another voice. Thus the narration oscillates between Snooty as first-person narrator and a third-person narrator reporting on events and characters including the Baronet-narrator. Significantly, the "objective" narrator steps in whenever Snooty as a narrator loses control over the report on events. For instance, the sexual scene between Snooty and Val is first narrated by Snooty:

> as I spoke I went to meet her—as I started my mechanical leg gave out an ominous creak (I had omitted to oil it, like watches and clocks these things require lubrication). I seized her stiffly round the body. . . . Her waist broke off and vanished into me as I took her over in waspish segments, an upper and a nether. The bosoms and head settled like a trio of hefty birds upon the upper slopes of my militant trunk. . . . Squatted upon the extremity of the supper-table, with my live leg (still laden with hearty muscles) I attacked the nether half of my aggressive adversary, and wound it cleverly round her reintegrated fork. (We were now both suspended upon my mechanical limb). (*SB*, 48)

The offhand, analytical description, which Snooty dubs the "picturesque method," is supposed to indicate a sense of control and detachment. Yet the Baronet's sexual experience proves emetic, at which point the impersonal narrator intervenes: "Eventually, [Snooty] sank into an arm-chair, whose big square hollow shelf fronted the fireplace. Repeatedly he carried his hand to that part of his skull where there was a silver plate" (*SB*, 49). Never do the two origins of the

narration merge. In fact, by the end of the novel the objective voice
has been taken over by the voice of Snooty as unreliable narrator.

Lewis's dualism of mind and body is partly responsible for the
fundamentally ambivalent aspect of his narratives. Rather than endowing the organization of the narrative with the exclusive authority
of the intellect, this dualism forces the narration into uncomfortable
splits. As early as 1915 the fractured logos was promoted in *Blast:*
"You must talk with two tongues, if you do not wish to cause confusion" (*Blast* 2, 91). The act of narration in *The Wild Body* is ambiguous because the narrator introduces himself as a dual being: a blond-
skinned gut-bag and a detached observer. From what source does the
narrative draw its authority: from the gut-bag or from the detached
observer? There is no straightforward answer. Recognition of the fact
that Lewis's creative writing is dialogical should help dismiss the critical myth according to which his characters are mere puppets coerced
into a hierarchy of the intellect, and ruled either by a privileged protagonist or the narrative consciousness of the text.[3]

Now, if one takes another look at *Time and Western Man,* one
discovers a striking paradox: the work is characterized not only by
the presence of a powerful narrative persona but also by an elusive
philosophical position. In fact the book has often been criticized for
confining itself to destructive analysis and for failing to provide any
positive alternative. The criticism is not entirely fair, but it certainly
points at something peculiar about the work. There is indeed something peculiar about a book that is shaped by a dualistic conception
yet that manages to elude any direct statement concerning such a
conception.

It seems to me that the modernity of the work precisely lies in this
paradoxical combination of assertiveness and elusiveness. To emphasize the assertive aspect only is to bypass the flitting aspect of Lewis's
thought. Equally, to emphasize the elusive aspect only is to ignore
the fact that Lewis did hold identifiable if not always explicit views.
It is important to recognize this fundamental ambivalence because
such recognition helps explain how the contradiction of meaning between Lewis's nonfiction and his fiction occurs. My claim is that this
contradiction already lies in nonfictional texts such as *Time and Western Man*. In particular this phenomenon becomes apparent as soon
as one tries to determine the genre of the work.

My general assumption is that genre is not an exclusively literary
category and that it can be fruitfully used when dealing with nonliterary texts. Tzvetan Todorov sees genre as a means of codification of
the different discourses of a given society.[4] Literary genres are nothing but a choice of codes among other discursive codifications estab-

lished as social conventions. He points out that both the sonnet and scientific discourse follow specific rules of presentation: for instance, one may have prosodic constraints, the other is expected to confine itself to the use of impersonal narrative and the present tense. To regard genre as a general feature of discourse opens new vistas concerning the relationship between the fiction and nonfiction of one and the same author.

Generally speaking, Lewis's nonfictional writing falls into two genres: the essay and the pamphlet. In *Time and Western Man* these two genres share a concern with the expression and analysis of ideas and concepts. In this respect, they have some sort of truck with philosophical genres. At the same time, by virtue of their rhetorical strategies, they also overlap with literary genres. It is precisely this overlapping with literary genres that produces friction at the level of meaning, and that makes the work unreadable for certain practitioners of philosophy.

In *La parole pamphlétaire,* a brilliant and thorough analysis, Marc Angenot has established a functional generic model of the pamphlet. His model chiefly draws on the 1868–1968 period of French nonfiction concerned with pamphleteering. Here I do not intend to apply systematically Angenot's model to Lewis's nonfiction for, in point of fact, the application would turn out to be unsuccessful. Indeed, although Lewis's nonfiction presents notable traits that suggest the category of the pamphlet, any effort to force the writing into the pamphlet mould is thwarted by its essayistic characteristics.

As a typical pamphleteer, Lewis makes the point that his nonfiction is not the most important part of his activities, but the product of a duty or necessity to defend his artistic activities and choices. Angenot also notes that any self-respecting pamphleteer will introduce himself as a solitary scribe whose positions endanger his career and reputation. Lewis's statements on Bloomsbury's nefarious influence on his publications, and Auden's depiction of the author as "that lonely old volcano of the Right" both confirm this typology.[5]

Although subversive, the pamphleteer's discourse is fundamentally "doxological," which means that it does not transgress the dominant ideology but works within it. Hence, Angenot underlines, its accessibility that is also a characteristic of Lewis's writing. It is striking that the notion of "spatializing truth" issues from the terms of the debate initiated by the new psychologists, Bergson and others. Clearly Lewis works within familiar conceptual territory. The relation of the pamphleteer to "truth" is not one of transgression but of revelation. Angenot shows convincingly that pamphleteering rests on the paradox that both pamphleteer and the target of the pamphlet are defending the same values, but that only the pamphleteer has access to truth: "the pamphleteer is the vehicle of dazzling truth such that it should obviously pervade the whole field where he aims to take action—and yet he finds himself alone to defend truth and marginalized by an inexplicable scandal. . . . he aims at confronting imposture, that is to say falsehood which, by superseding truth, excluded him and his truth from the empirical world."[6] We have here an almost perfect description of the rhetorical strategies of Lewis's nonfiction. His targets are either the writers who share with him the value of the intellect yet betray it, or the bohemian artists who share with him the value of art yet betray it. In both cases, Lewis the Enemy or outsider tries to reestablish the true intellectual and the true artist. From a rhetorical standpoint, the themes of conspiracy and betrayal are not the product of a fantasy but topoi of the pamphlet.

Similarly, the depiction of the opponents as impostors or make-believers—Angenot cites tropes based on circus-life and clowns—converges exactly with the Lewisian theme of illusionism identified by Hugh Kenner,[7] and more generally with the recurring trope of false bottom that was the original title of *The Revenge for Love* (1937). Another major topos of the pamphlet identified by Angenot is that of the world upside down: "The world of scandal is not only blind to truth and apt to worship false idols: a perversely rigorous processus has *systematically inverted* . . . the 'natural' order of phenomena."[8] One has in Lewis's ideological critique of homosexuality as inversion an extraordinary use of the topos.

Besides tropes, topoi, and typology, the pamphlet is distinguished by what Angenot refers to as its "parole", or by what I will call "voice." The pamphletic voice is profoundly ambivalent as it is torn between self-assertion and self-questioning. The philosophical authority of *Time and Western Man* is proclaimed in the preface where Lewis presents his credentials as a painter's "bias" for the spatial and the visual. In other words, the philosophical basis, from which the conceptual critique of *Time and Western Man* is conducted, is not developed argumentatively: it is asserted, as it were, at the top of the narrative voice. Like satire and polemics, the pamphlet is therefore marked by the strong presence of the enunciator who does not have any doubt as to where truth lies.

Inevitably the agonistic, strong presence of the pamphleteer's voice coincides with a dogmatic approach to ideas that tolerates little argumentation. The first sentence of "The Meaning of the Wild Body" offers an example of this dogmatic proclivity: "First, to assume the dichotomy of mind and body is necessary here, without arguing it" (*CWB*, 157). As opposed to rationalistic argumentation, the writing of *Time and Western Man* often veers towards satirical attacks on thinkers and writers which, within the frame of rational philosophy, amounts to *ad hominem* argumentation.

At the same time, within the general philosophical context of *Time and Western Man,* the pamphletic voice functions as authorial intrusion, or parabasis, typical of modernist narrative experiments. The iconoclastic character of the work derives from the clash between the context of philosophical genre and a pamphletic voice that refuses to conform to the rules of logocentric discourse. Although the work displays the persuasive authority of the pamphletic voice, it does not leave the reader with the sense of argumentative objectivity. But there is the rub: indeed, *Time and Western Man* presents itself as the defense of spatial objectivity by means of a pamphletic voice whose chief characteristic is to lack and even reject objectivity.

The pamphletic voice in Lewis is therefore highly ambiguous: on the one hand, on account of its self-declared subjectivity it pecks at theoretical and systematic constructions of objectivity; on the other, it condemns itself to sclerotic dogmatism. It is within this context that Lewis's nonfictional use of the essay is best grasped. In fact one can already say that the sense of paradox between generic experimentalism and ideological dogmatism is reinforced by the rhetorical features of the essay as genre.

In "The Essay as Form" Theodor Adorno defines the essay as a genre based on a critique of systematic, methodical discourse. By discarding the scientific and logocentric model of argumentation, the essay offers the best possibility of escaping from the dogmatism of ideology. For Adorno the essay "constructs the immanent criticism of cultural artifacts, and it confronts that which such artifacts are with their concept; it is the critique of ideology."[9] His view of the essay as the heretical means of transgressing philosophical orthodoxy signals a milestone in the genealogy of one kind of philosophical discourse culminating in Derridean grammatology. As a critique of time ideologies, *Time and Western Man* is an important if highly ambiguous stage in this historical process.

The unsystematic, anti-methodological character of the essay can be detected in *The Caliph's Design* (1919), which some critics have diagnosed as a poorly written text or a bag for stuffing ideas without discrimination. In fact, the essay reads like the blueprint for the massive study of time in *Time and Western Man.* Time remains the object of analysis of the items of discussion, which present themselves as digressions but actually converge towards the concept of time as spokes towards the hub.

Lewis's use of the essay also produces the effect of tension between art and theory, experience and objectification that Adorno ascribes to the genre. By virtue of its conceptual concern, the essay tends toward theory or philosophy; by virtue of its experimental character, the essay tends toward art. In fact Richard Chadbourne refers to the *poesis* of the essay that does not develop side by side with the conceptual process but constitutes it.[10] The fictionalization of the conceptual process brings out the strong affinity between allegory and essay, which share the rhetorical device of prosopopoeia. As William H. Gass puts it, the essay "interests itself in the narration of ideas—in their *unfolding*—and the conflict between philosophies or other points of view becomes a drama in its hands; systems are seen as plots and concepts as characters."[11] It is precisely on account of the dilatory and playful aspect of the essay that the reader comes up with a sense of paradox between Lewis's generic experiment and his ideology of spatial consciousness and language without fuss or mannerism. The reason why *Time and Western Man* is not philosophically convincing is that the authority of its philosophical argument is constantly questioned by the experimental strategies of the essay and the pamphlet.

One significant example of the clash between the generic experiments and the ideology is the inherent contradiction between the temporal character of the essay and Lewis's position on time. Adorno's comments on the function of time in the essay reveal to what extent the genre is a product of modernity. He argues that the essay "shys away from the violence of dogma, from the notion that the result of abstraction, the temporally invariable concept indifferent to the individual phenomenon grasped by it, deserves ontological dignity."[12] It is no coincidence either that repeatedly Montaigne and Bacon are presented as the two fountainheads of the genre. The essay as we know it was obviously born with the modern sense of time with its emphasis on experience. The contradictory nature of Lewis's nonfiction prose becomes blatant: here is an author who extols the values of stasis and timelessness in a medium conceived out of a sensibility based on subjective experience of time.

The fact that the medium of Lewis's nonfiction is at cross-purposes with the message shows that, contrary to a common assumption, the discourse of so-called high modernists is not always and necessarily monological and unequivocal. In fact Jameson goes as far as arguing in favor of a parodic relationship between the fictional and nonfictional components of Lewis's corpus. I would be inclined to support such an interpretation with, nevertheless, major qualifications, which I will present in the next chapter.

If Lewis does not fit Margot Norris's definition of high modernism, and if the generic experiments have a subversive effect, should one see in him a forerunner of deconstruction? I do not think so, precisely because of the contradiction between his credo of spatialization and his experiments with the genre of philosophical discourse. I would suggest that, if one is to look for a means of distinguishing between Lewis and deconstruction, one should not select the presence or absence of experimentation in critical analysis, but rather, the type of relation between experimental form and ideology. In *Les mots en liberté futuristes* (1919), to take another example, Marinetti uses some of the most avant-gardist experiments to express a belief in the greatness of war. There is contradiction because Marinetti does not extol war for its hypothetical subversive effect but for its nationalistic appeal. This implies that the analysis of genre should not be confined to a formal level.[13] In fact the rhetoric and tropes specific to a genre generate meaning and values of their own that may or may not stand in contradiction with the explicit message of a given text. Therefore my inkling is that writers such as Wyndham Lewis may look like budding deconstructionists, but that such categorization is precluded by the discrepancy between the implicit values of the genres of their texts and the explicit ideology of the same texts.

So, if we are not dealing with either a "high modernist" or a deconstructionist, what kind of phenomenon are we faced with? I think that the agon between generic experiment and ideological credo is typical of the cultural and ideological crisis at the core of the modernism I am endeavoring to reclaim. In this respect, Angenot regards the conspicuous role of the pamphlet in the last hundred years as "symptomatic of ideological erosion."[14] It is striking that, whether the pamphlet is written from a right-wing or left-wing standpoint, it remains the expression of intellectuals' frustration within modern society. "Confronted with systems of power, the *clerc,* who is deprived of a stable, institutional status in a lay society characterized by class struggle, expresses in the pamphlet his resentment combined with a phantasm of legitimity." By the same token, the assertive and dogmatic aspect of the voice reveals the fragility of a narrative in crisis, because it is deprived of ideological foundations. "As an unhappy consciousness and strong voice in the text," Angenot writes, "the pamphleteer wants to understand the paradox of his destiny, the misunderstandings of his life, his intellectual solitude. . . . He falls prey to violent certitudes but also to doubt and wavering."[15]

Within this context of cultural crisis, it is therefore not surprising to see Lewis resort to apocalyptism. In *A Bitter Truth* Richard Cork has devoted an entire chapter to apocalyptism in painting before the war broke out in 1914.[16] Picture after picture shows to what extent this apocalyptic trend was prevalent among European painters whose means of expression are all the more revealing as they are visual. Obviously Lewis's own apocalyptism stems from this cultural phenomenon. Time and again Lewis has been hailed as a prophet, be it in the field of politics or that of sociocultural analysis. After World War I his elegy on Western Man had the prophetic renascence of a new world for hypothetical counterpart. At the same time, the apocalyptism of his pamphletic discourse requires that opponents be globalized into a single enemy. Thus Lewis has his Bergsonians, apes of God, partisans of the Great Within, and so forth. The reason why apocalyptism is found in his nonfiction is that it coalesces perfectly with the pathetic and revelatory aspects of the pamphlet. The pamphletic voice does not appeal to the capacity for logical argumentation but to emotion. Furthermore, the truth the voice aims at does not emerge at the end of argumentative process; in typically pamphletic and apocalyptic fashion, it is *revealed*.

Therefore the generic analysis of Lewis's nonfiction brings out the presence of at least two genres with aspects usually associated with literature. Attention to genre in authors who write both fiction and nonfiction is extremely valuable because it allows one to move freely between the two types of writing while suspending thorny and probably sterile questions about authors' intentions. By focusing on the generic identity of the different texts involved, I am able to support my general assumption that, more often than not, a fracture of meaning characterizes Lewis's corpus, and this leads his fiction to contradict his nonfiction. I also hope that such a generic focus makes the point that my term "contradiction" does not involve a value judgement, but that it designates a discursive phenomenon: there is diction and then there is contra-diction.

Furthermore, the interaction between literary and nonliterary genres within a nonfictional context implies that the New Critical and structuralist notion that the modernist text is a self-contained entity is misleading. Indirectly the presence of "literary" strategies in *Time and Western Man* proves that a literary artifact does not exist in an autonomous vacuum since its generic characteristics do emerge in nonliterary contexts. This further implies that, in its attempt to cross generic boundaries, modernism was also working to undermine the notion that art is autotelic or autonomous. This notion has been traditionally associated with modernism whereas it is clear that the early twentieth-century experiments with genre led to a breaking-down of barriers between fields of writing.

Examples of generic hybridization can be taken from the areas of "low" and "high" cultures. For instance, Peter Keating reports that, at the turn of the century, the popular writer Stephen Reynolds practised and coined the new genre of "autobiografiction."[17] K. K. Ruthven points to Pound's use of personae in his critical prose, from the voices of the academic and the reviewer in *The Times* to Wildeanism and phrases of the hillbilly. Also, Pound believed that a poem or an anthology constituted the best critical responses to criticism. Ruthven regards the practice of criticism by anthology as "profoundly authoritarian in its assumption that the very act of selecting this rather than that text needs no justification and is a value in itself."[18] Another way of looking at the problem is to see in this type of anthology a means of demystifying the critical value of scientific objectivity. Ultimately, whether the criteria for selection are stated, the anthology can always be accepted or rejected. Another writer who has blurred the generic lines between criticism and literature is Gertrude Stein. For instance, there is little difference between the reiterative style of "The Gradual Making of *The Making of the Americans*" and that of *The Making of the Americans*.

The modern hybridization of genres can be related to the reaction against the process of specialization that Swift was keen on satirizing in the third book of *Gulliver's Travels,* and that increasingly became visible in the nineteenth century. It is no accident that the symptoms of specialization are recorded by some of the modernists who crossed the boundaries of genre: Ford Madox Ford in *The Critical Attitude*[19] or Wyndham Lewis in *The Art of Being Ruled* (1926). As Todorov argues, the interaction between literary and nonliterary genres within one and the same corpus works right against a nineteenth century that strove to delineate the limits of "Literature." From *Ulysses* through *In the American Grain* to *Doctor Faustus* the trend is unmistakable. The dream of totality may be modernist but this dream is shattered by modernist writing practices.

The despecialization of literature is conspicuous in Lewis's creative texts, which display a more or less "philosophical" or reflective bias. For instance, *The Wild Body* presents itself as a collection of short stories with two essays commenting on the philosophy and literary strategies involved in the short stories. On account of this self-reflexive sensibility, Lewis has been branded as a failed novelist. But rather than seeing in this the sign of failure, one should consider this phenomenon as the sign that modernist texts are characterized by different generic currents that open them to extraliterary contexts. The purpose of the next chapter is to establish the type of transition between Lewis's nonfiction and his fiction at the level of genre and meaning.

3

Genre and Meaning: The Fiction

IN THIS CHAPTER I WILL BE CONCERNED WITH THE READER'S transfer from Lewis's nonfiction to his fiction. In part this transfer corresponds to a generic transformation of a pamphletic discourse to an allegorical. In the nonfiction Lewis uses the genre of the pamphlet to denounce the values and beliefs threatening the ideal of Western Man. In the fiction these values and beliefs transmute into allegorical personifications of ideological cults or "inferior religions."

However, the transfer from the nonfiction to the fiction does not proceed smoothly. The ideological allegory of the fiction is not supported by a narrative authority borrowed from the philosophical beliefs or created within the fictional context. The reason why the narrative is problematic in the fiction is twofold: first, the dogmatism of the pamphlet is undermined by the typically polysemic, dialogical character of allegory; second, the ideological allegory has to compete with a satire of the human species and its inherent absurdities. These absurdities are not ignored in the nonfictional writings: they are stated in order to be supplanted. In the fiction, the same absurdities take over and act as a nihilistic means of depriving the ideological allegory of any utopian or even positive outcome.

On account of this major competition between allegory and satire, Lewis's fiction is located at a crossroads: his allegorical critique of ideologies concurs with the critical projects of authors such as George Orwell, John Dos Passos, or Bertolt Brecht. His satirical critique of the self, reducing the concept of ideology to a cypher, embraces the nihilistic, anti-humanistic trend that created the tradition including Alfred Jarry, Dada, and Beckett. Needless to say the powerful anti-humanistic character of Lewis's fiction stands in blatant contradiction with the humanist ideal of Western Man. This self-contradiction is made possible by the fact that the ideological foundations of Lewis's philosophical writing are fragile to start with. This fundamental elusiveness is precisely revealed in the transfer from the nonfiction to the fiction. I will now proceed beyond this rough and schematic sketch in order to bring out the generic and narrative complexities involved in Lewis's ideological and ontological critiques.

These two critiques, conducted in the fiction, do not proceed according to preset, separate agendas. In practice they interact in the text so that, for instance, a satirical physical portrait will also serve as an allegory of a particular cult. And conversely, an allegory of a particular cult will open up onto an ontological satire of human nature. In effect this means that Lewis's allegory is satirical and his satire allegorical. So it is not my purpose to keep the different genres compartmentalized but, on the contrary, to show how this dynamic of perspectives results in generic interaction.

At a rhetorical and typological level, it is possible to indicate some of the major hinges between the different genres involved in the fiction and the nonfiction. Generally speaking, there is a definite continuity between the essay, the pamphlet, and allegory; all share a concern for conceptualization and creative composition. A kind of cross-fertilization occurs whereby logos and *poesis* interact in the three genres. Thus, by their very nature, pamphlet, essay, and allegory thematize the concept of hybridization. Edwin Honig locates allegory "on the border between religion or philosophy and art, serving to frame significant questions about the nature of illusion and reality."[1] In his historical account of the development of allegory, Jon Whitman argues that by the end of the twelfth century philosophy and rhetoric were engaged in mutual exploration: "the exegetical *distinctio* turns scattered allegorizations into a kind of intricate matrix for rhetorical exploitations, while conversely, the typological lyric organizes the very texture of its language by the categories of scriptural exegesis."[2] In addition, the manichean propensity of the pamphlet undergoes alteration in the shift to allegory, which is a genre characterized by dualistic ambivalence. The shift from pamphletic dogmatism to allegorical ambivalence affects Lewis's expression of the mind-body agon that persists in the two components of his corpus but acquires a different meaning.

As in the pamphlet, in the fiction one finds a critique of ideas and beliefs (*doxa*) translating into an allegory of *idées fixes*. A representative sample can be taken from *The Apes of God* (1930) at a point of the plot when the three conjurors—Zagreus, Ratner, and Margolin—arrive at Lord Osmund's Lenten party. Their knocking at the door is first ascribed to the intrusion of the London Police: "it was surmised that Phoebus ... was at grips with the Law-and-Order dragon—though in spite of the deference due to their champion this Theoretic Underworld still shook in its criminal shoes, its Edgar Wallace teeth never ceased to chatter, its Potemkin heart was in its throat.

The World that had become fashionably Underworld wilted deliciously, at the bare prospect of wholesale detection: half-amorously it fluttered at the shadow of Authority."[3] The capital letters are pointers to the allegorical context in which a satire of cults or inferior religions develops.

Another work exemplifying the shift from a pamphletic satire to an allegorical is *The Childermass,* which can be read as an independent work, but whose reading is arduous if not mind-boggling without reference to *The Art of Being Ruled* or *Time and Western Man.* The narrative is concerned with child cult that in *Time and Western Man* Lewis defines as "Utopia" (70). In part 8 of *The Art of Being Ruled* he projects the vision of a society peopled with "Neuters" or sexless children taught to remain irresponsible and allergic to rational consciousness. The switch from the ideological critique of Lewis's pamphlets to *The Childermass* as well as his whole fiction is one from the analysis of a meaningless world to the creation of one. Angenot points out that "the valueless and therefore meaningless world contemplated by the pamphleteer is burlesque, infantile and atrocious; arbitrariness masquerades as wisdom. . . . The world of imposture is perceived as a lugubrious carnival."[4] We have here a succinct summary of the typology characterizing the trilogy of *The Human Age* or *The Apes of God.* In addition, the major trope of the world-upside-down typical of the pamphlet translates into the Lewisian creation of a dystopia or inverted utopia whereby heaven is actually hell, and artists the apes of creators.

The generic intratextuality of Lewis's corpus is worth underlining because it contributes to the identification of an allegorical typology in his fiction. In her theory of allegory,[5] Maureen Quilligan identifies the text that the allegorical narrative cites as the "pretext." For instance, *The Divine Comedy* has the Bible for pretext. In Lewis's case, one has an additional, one might say, internal pretext to the extent that the text quoted belongs to the same corpus as the quoting text. Thus *The Human Age* is characterized by external and internal pretexts: the Bible, Dante, Milton, as well as Lewis's nonfictional, especially political writings. Although Quilligan does not make the point, one could say that allegory partly consists in a vast quotation of some given pretext. The quotation is always dynamic because it consists in an act of interpretation. In Lewis, the internal quotation is inaccurate or distorted because the allegorical representation in his fiction is not in keeping with the ideas or principles of the nonfiction. The quasi-perfect illustration of such a contradiction is the juxtaposition of the essay "Physics of the Not-Self" and the play *Enemy of the Stars,* published in a single volume in 1932.

Both works are the products of revised earlier texts: the play was first published in the *Blast* of 1914, while the essay was originally published in *The Chapbook* in 1925. Of the two, the play has undergone extensive revisions whereas the essay remains substantially unchanged. A few pages long, the essay aims at working out the philosophy of the intellect in social, ethical, and linguistic terms. Philosophy is said to give "freedom from the obscenities of existence" (*CPP,* 201), and the body is indicted as the "great public road of private fraud" (*CPP,* 198). By contrast, the play represents the self steeped in the obscenities of existence and enslaved by the will. The beginning of the play stages the allegorical birth of a chthonic race slowly emerging out of the earth, or what looks like a "HUT ROLLED HALF UPON ITS BACK, DOOR UPWARDS, THE CHARACTERS GIDDILY MOUNTING IN ITS OPENING" (*CPP,* 144).[6] With its indirect yet implied link to the project of Western Man and spatializing truth, the essay is an expression of Lewis's nonfictional logocentric discourse. As such and in its virtually unchanged form, it functions as a prolepsis or pretext to the 1932 revised version of the play. The relation between the pretext and the allegorical play, however, is agonistic. Thus the simultaneous publication of the two in the same volume is a local manifestation of the kind of agon occurring in the general corpus at the level of meaning and genre.

The agonistic effect of contradiction is triggered because the transfer from the nonfiction to the fiction has a destabilizing impact on the philosophical authority of Lewis's nonfiction. Although allegory ensures continuity between his pamphlets and his fiction by personifying the *idées fixes* of his critique, it simultaneously undermines the dogmatic certitudes surfacing in his pamphletic writing. Indeed, the generally recognized indirectness and linguistic duality of allegory forces the narrative into dialogism and ambiguity. Debates among critics often refer to Quintillian's definition of allegory as saying one thing and meaning another. Critics such as Quilligan object to such a definition arguing that the allegorical text is not governed by hierarchical levels of meaning but by polysemy working itself out through the narrative. Whitman has a fine way of overriding the problem of definition by saying that allegory is "outspokenly reticent, proclaiming that it has a secret," and that the basis for its technique is "obliquity."[7] Thus a narrative like *The Vulgar Streak* presents itself ostensibly as a realistic novel or, even for some, as a worthless potboiler. And yet the narrative lends itself to an allegorical reading that makes its transparent realism but an appearance.

A distinction has to be made between the dialogism of the pamphlet and that of the fictional narratives. The dialogism of the pamphlet indicates the presence of discourses that the pamphleteer undertakes to criticize. But this critique implies a set of beliefs that pulls the pamphlet towards monologism. By contrast, the dialogism of allegory works against the dogmatic voice of the pamphlet and the set of beliefs that is responsible for the personifications of ideologies and cults.

The same destabilizing effect can be detected in Lewis's visual art, the oblique character of which is conspicuous: from the visually enigmatic plates of *Timon of Athens* through the mystifying figure of *The Sibyl* (1926; Michel, pl. 89) to the intricacies of *Magellan* (1927; Michel, pl. 89). This allegorical dimension also accounts for the narrative tendency of his painting which emerges in works such as *The Crowd* (1914–15; Michel, pl. VI), *Departure of a Princess from Chaos* (1936–37; Michel, pl. 107) or *La Suerte* (1938; Michel, pl. 129). By the same token, the allegorical obliquity of this visual art should prevent any facile interpretation of it as an exemplification of Lewis's nonfictional beliefs.

The destabilization of the nonfictional dogmatic voice is best seen at the rhetorical level of prosopopoeia, which, as was seen in the previous chapter, lends a poetic character to the pamphlet and the essay. In the guise of personification, prosopopoeia becomes one of the chief devices of allegorical narrative. Whitman's etymological definition of personification shows to what extent it is close to that of prosopopoeia: "the word 'personification' is a composite of the Latin words *persona*, meaning 'mask' or 'person,' and *facere*, meaning 'to make.' This term corresponds to the original Greek composite *prosopopoiia*, which was transliterated as *prosopopoeia*."[8] In Bernard Dupriez's *Dictionary of Literary Devices*, each term is given a separate entry, but the two definitions are very similar, at least as far as the fundamental mechanism is concerned. Personification is defined as "endowing inanimate objects or abstractions with life and human characteristics"; and prosopopoeia is the "presentation of absent, dead, or supernatural beings, or even inanimate objects, with the ability to act, speak, and respond."[9] In addition, both personification and prosopopoeia are concerned with two levels of technique, one involving the narrative voice, the other involving characterization. I will first consider the level of narration.

Lewis's art of narration includes only two works in which the narrators are involved in the plot of events: Ker-Orr in *The Wild Body*, and Snooty in *Snooty Baronet*. The rest of the works are either narrated by an external narrator, or they take the form of dramatic dialogues. That Lewis wrote two plays, *The Enemy of the Stars* and *The Ideal*

Giant (1917), that his first long piece of writing involves actors as characters, and that the latter half of *The Childermass* reads like a drama are certainly no accidents. This and his narrators' gift of the gab indicate that his narration has performance and mask for chief characteristics. While his narration has been repeatedly described as the bastion for omniscient monologism, the theatrical aspect of his narratives can be shown to undermine the dogmatism of his pamphlets.

The Revenge for Love constitutes the best example of a narrative, the effect of which is to weaken what is preconceived as the Lewisian ethos. The narrative clout of the novel derives from its remarkably sustained use of free indirect speech. The technique is often erroneously equated with the stream of consciousness: in fact, free indirect speech points to the artificial process of narration while retaining a mimetic function by reproducing the idiolect of a given, socially defined character. The technique is therefore one of obliquity and, to borrow Browning's formula, gives "truth broken into prismatic hues."[10] This implies that, first, the utterances cannot all be ascribed to the author; and, second, that the narrative is submitted to a constant process of fragmentation.

Before offering any further comment, I will provide two examples of the technique in *The Revenge for Love*. The first is concerned with Victor Stamp's special idiom: "A very hell of a lousy situation, he granted you it was that. It seemed like somebody's hoodoo. . . . Yes, he was jammed on a lee-shore this time right enough!"[11] This is Stamp reflecting on his life as an exiled Australian artist, as he tries to produce a picture. Each term has been carefully chosen to signify the background of colonial Australia. The other example is concerned with Stamp's wife, Margot, who towards the end of the novel decides to save her husband from a plot to use him as decoy for arms contraband: "How much she loved this aimless thing! But she was Nature mourning for the mate of her youth. She was the wind sighing on the wart-leaves for its existence among the glacial peaks. . . . She was the sigh on the last rose, and the whisper of the last lily" (*RFL*, 360). The idiom characterizing Margot derives from her adulation of what Lewis considered maudlin romanticism. Her speech takes the form of lyricism, which in other places the narrative parodies by distorting quotations from Tennyson's *Maud*.

The narrative technique is invaluable because it exemplifies what, in *The Concept of Modernism*, Astradur Eysteinsson calls "the dialectical relation of modernism and realism."[12] The narrative of Lewis's novel allows for a dialectic between experimentation with the pragmatic function of language and exploration of the authority of narration.

It has been argued that the ethos of the novel is anti-Marxist because the technique of free indirect speech is mainly concerned with an anticommunist discourse.[13] This is giving Lewis's narrative short shrift. The above two examples alone indicate that the breadth of application of the narrative technique is much wider. An exhaustive analysis of the narrative would demonstrate that the technique is in fact uniformly applied from one end of the ideological and political spectrum to the other. It is this comprehensiveness that makes the narrative a realistic novel; however, the parcellization of social reality into a multiplicity of individual idioms constitutes the modernist character of the novel.

However, there is more to it than free indirect speech, which, it turns out, functions within an allegorical context. The possibility of interpreting the characters of *The Revenge for Love* as allegorical personifications of *idées fixes* is apparent in the Margot example, especially in the second sentence of the above quotation: "But she was Nature mourning for the mate of her youth." The capital letter implies the allegorization of romanticism as an abstract concept to be represented and parodied. A full-blown example of allegorical mask or personification is located at the end of the novel when, held as a prisoner in Spain, Hardcaster is informed of the Stamps' death: "Swollen with an affected speechlessness, Percy proceeded to give a sculpturesque impersonation of *THE INJURED PARTY*" (*RFL*, 380). The difference between Margot's "Nature" and Hardcaster's "*INJURED PARTY*" is that the latter is a deliberately chosen mask or parodic pose, whereas the former is the sign of ideological alienation. The point here is not to whitewash the novel of any ideological bias, but to reestablish a sense of balance and bring out the fundamentally dialogical character of Lewis's narrative even and especially in the case of a political narrative. Unless one decides to fall silent in order to mute any ideological bias, dialogism remains a dialectical means of recognizing ideological limitations while still clinging to one's credos.

Beyond the ideological tenor of the different idioms involved, what is of capital importance is that the ethos that governs the satirical creation of these idioms is questioned in a fundamental way. Considered from an allegorical viewpoint, the narrator of free indirect speech functions as prosopopoeia and, more precisely, as a personification of the narrative function: the narrator puts on the linguistic mask or makes himself the mouthpiece of the character whose ideology is to be presented. What takes the wind out of the narrative sails is the fact that the narrative process functions only as a rhetorical trope, not as a means of asserting "truth" emanating from an authoritative oracle. This role of prosopopoeia endows Lewis's allegory with a self-critical function that is absent from the mere personification of *idées fixes*.

The critique of the narrative authority recurs in at least two other works. In *The Apes of God*, Zagreus provides Dan his disciple with an "encyclical," which he himself received from his mentor Pierpoint. An excerpt from the epistle is quoted and becomes part of the narrative. For the reader familiar with Lewis's nonfictional works it is clear that the positions defended in the epistle coincide with those of the nonfiction: postwar wealthy bohemia is accused of aping and diminishing the "real" artist; democratic society is seen to have a levelling effect on culture; partisanship is advocated at the expense of impersonality. The encyclical seems to function as the fulcrum of the satire conducted in the narrative.

What should also be underlined is the fact that the encyclical functions as prosopopoeia: Pierpoint is absent from the narrative and never intervenes as a character. The encyclical is therefore a device to endow an absent character with a voice. This case of prosopopoeia is further elaborated in part 9, "Chez Lionel Kein Esq.'" where a debate between Zagreus and Kein develops. The reader is told that Zagreus's argumentation is in fact based on a rehearsal of Pierpoint's arguments. Again, Zagreus's impersonation of the shadow character is an elaboration of prosopopoeia. Zagreus is only one type of ventriloquist: in the latter part of the work, Blackshirt alias Starr-Smith fulfills the same role by "broadcasting" Pierpoint's political ideas.

Both the encyclical and Zagreus's impersonation are means of thematizing the role of the author in the text. Pierpoint represents the elusive yet pervasive origin of the narration. At some point, Melanie the painter refers to him as a painter turned philosopher, modeling himself upon Whistler. The self-referential nature of the description is conspicuous. In part 11, "Mr. Zagreus and the Split-Man," Ratner's and Zagreus's costumes for the Lenten party are made according to Pierpoint's description. In other words, the description of Zagreus's costume corresponds to Pierpoint's statement, which makes him the writer of *The Apes of God*. Pierpoint is therefore a synecdoche for authorship, while it is likely that the "book of words" Zagreus is reported to carry hidden in his pocket is *The Apes of God*.

Yet the fact that this narrative origin is ventriloquized by mouthpieces such as Horace and Starr-Smith also questions the authority of the encyclical and the characters' reliability. It is said of Pierpoint that he has a "microphone-personality" (*AOG*, 401). By definition he is invisible and metafictional: if he were to appear, then the Lewisian distinction between art and life would collapse, and he would become an object of satire. For the sake of the principles spelled out in the encyclical, Pierpoint must remain a narrative ghost. This implies then that the authorship and ethos of *The Apes of God* are threatened by an equally spookish status.

The same thematization of narrative authority recurs twenty-four years later in *Self Condemned*. At the end of the first part of the novel, the historian René Harding visits his disciple Rotter who reads him an article he wrote presenting Harding's views of history. Again, the "article" becomes part of the narrative and can be shown to present views coinciding with some of Lewis's nonfictional positions. What prevents one from seeing the article as a simple transposition from nonfiction to fiction is the fact that it functions as a recognizable quotation. Like the encyclical, the article is a case of prosopopoeia whereby Lewis's conception of history is "voiced" or "aired." However, what makes the quotation a pastiche is its rhapsodic psittacism. Hence the disciple is called Rotter. Gérard Genette refers to a case of self-parody in Proust's *La Prisonière,* where a character delivers a speech sounding like a typical Proustian sample.[14] Genette argues that the caricatural and satirical function of the speech is indicated by its uncalled-for virtuoso-like quality. The same analysis applies to Lewis's use of the encyclical in *The Apes of God* and of the article in *Self Condemned*.

Yet, it is precisely the verbatim character of these pastiches that leads one to question the apparently self-parodic function of the texts. Yes, the encyclical and the article may be self-parody but, by the same token, nothing in the texts prevents them from being read as the statements of belief. The beliefs are parodied; nonetheless they are spelled out. From the wider perspective of Lewis's career in the thirties, the notion of self-parody has to be confronted with the fact that *The Apes of God* was published at the beginning of the decade that saw the application of the ideals of *The Art of Being Ruled* and *Time and Western Man* to the political situation of the days. How does one square an experimental, self-parodic fictional text with political pamphlets entrenched in the belief of the politics of the intellect?

My assessment of such passages is that they are both parody and credo. Such an ambivalence could be regarded as a flaw only if unity and coherence of meaning are deemed to be the sole criteria for evaluating a literary piece. What seems to me more important is that the persistence of the credo indicates what Edward Said refers to as the "worldly" mark of a text.[15] Self-parody never totally erases Lewis's credos; instead, it establishes a tension between belief and self-criticism. The credos point at the ideology of Lewis's fiction, and this ideology originates in the nonfictional component of his corpus.

I will now consider how prosopopoeia functions at the level of characterization in Lewis's fiction. The ubiquity of this trope in his narratives derives from the fact that his dualism of mind and body leads him to define the self in terms that coincide with the definition of prosopopoeia as the presentation of absent, dead, or inanimate objects with ability to act, speak, and respond. Thus in "The Meaning of the Wild Body" the root of the comic lies in the belief that men "are all *things,* or physical bodies, behaving as *persons*" (*CWB,* 158). The part of the self that is physical matter is what for Lewis makes the self dead or absent. Prosopopoeia is therefore the main trope of an ontological satire based on the premise that as thing the self has no identity. The several examples the author uses to support his definition of the comic confirm the importance of the rhetorical figure:

> If you saw (to give another example of intelligence or movement in the 'dead') a sack of potatoes suddenly get up and trundle off down the street . . . you would laugh. A couple of trees suddenly tearing themselves free from their roots, and beginning to waltz: . . . a lamp-post unexpectedly lighting up of its own accord, and immediately hopping away down to the next lamp-post, which it proceeded to attack, all these things would appear very 'ridiculous'. (*CWB,* 159)

Incidently Lewis shares prosopopoeia with a major popular art of the twentieth century, and that is the cartoon.

His creation of a thing behaving as a person draws on the three recurrent metaphors identified by John Holloway.[16] These are the self as thing, machine, and animal. An example can be taken from a posthumously published sequence to "Morpeth Olympiad" originally published in the 1915 *Blast.* In the sequence, "The Countryhouse Party, Scotland," Cantleman reports his observation of another member of the party: "Leo's body is a sluggish colony of massive blond segments. . . . Those are worms that are his arms—also his legs. I regard him as a gigantic annelid. His body is probably a red-blooded earth-worm, white at the extremities of the segments."[17] The series of metaphors, first triggered by the word-play on "sluggish," has the cumulative effect of categorizing Leo as worm or slug. Part of the remaining narrative rests on the slug behaving as a person or as Leo.

Another general effect of prosopopoeia accounts for the compelling intensity of a great deal of Lewis's prose. Indeed the trope can produce a sense of hallucination or "delirious exaltation"[18] by evoking imaginary things. The character of Humph in *Snooty Baronet* is a case in point. The role of prosopopoeia is to transform the publicity agent into an enormous chin. The expressionistic description of his meeting with the Baronet—the shuffling against the wall, the silent blank

staring, the Baronet's paralysis with repulsion—all these correspond
to the sense of hallucination that the rhetorical trope is expected to
produce. In another passage concerned with disgust at the Wild Body,
Ker-Orr observes a sexual minuet between the two protagonists of
"Beau Séjour" (1927), Carl and Mademoiselle Péronnette: "what she
suggested to me was something like a mad butcher, who had put a
piece of bright material over a carcase of pork or mutton, and started
to ogle his customers, owing to a sudden shuffling in his mind of the
respective appetites. Carl on this occasion behaved like the hallucinated customer of such a pantomime, who, come into the shop, had
entered into the spirit of the demented butcher, and proceeded to
waltz with his sex-promoted food" (*CWB*, 62). The description is
complex because it involves at least two figurative levels. On the one
hand, a female dancer is compared to a butcher and a male dancer to
a customer. On the other, the female dancer is the object of rhetorical
prosopopoeia as *she* is also the "carcase" of meat covered with a piece
of bright material—dancing. If the passage is not exalting, it is certainly delirious.

Side by side, one also finds in the Lewisian narrative the typical
use of prosopopoeia for the surreal animation of objects. There is the
often quoted example of the Vallet restaurant in *Tarr*, the described
commercial expansion of which stands in synecdochic relation to human appetite. Or there is this surrealistic description in *The Apes of
God*: "—a chain, a stool, clothes hanging like a carcass in a stall gaping
and sagging—handless, footless, and without head" (333). What
Lewis's versatile use of prosopopoeia effects is the blurring of the
outlines of subject and object, which his nonfictional discourse pronounced anathema.

From a generic viewpoint, his use of prosopopoeia for the definition of the self has a significant impact on the historical evolution of
allegory. In his definition of the trope, Dupriez notes that it is a
"figure of elevated or 'sublime' style."[19] A thing is elevated to the
status of person, which implies that "person" as a concept stands at
the top of an evaluative hierarchy. It is this character of the trope
that contributes to the equally elevated style associated with allegory.
However, Lewis's use of the trope occurs within the context of the
avant-gardist, anti-bourgeois crusade against the liberal concept of
"man." The antihero of his narratives is the product of this recurrent
use of prosopopoeia, which has a bathetic effect on the sublime style
of allegory. The reason why Lewis's allegories are concerned with
cults or inferior religions as opposed to spatializing truth and spatial
intellect must be directly attributed to the prosopopoeia of his satirical characterization, which robs allegory of its hierarchical system of

meaning. In what follows, I will use "personification" as a case of prosopopoeia within an allegorical context, while I will reserve the use of prosopopoeia for the satirical context. The distinction may seem hair-splitting but benefits the analysis by showing to what extent the Lewisian narratives oscillate between allegory and satire.

In his analysis of the nineteenth-century novel, Henri Mitterand argues that the realistic narrative does not consist only in a mimesis of "History" at the political, institutional, or factual level, but also in a mimesis of manners or ways: "ways of moving and speaking, dressing, eating; ways at work, in bed, at the party, or at death; ways of telling stories or of leading an argument. . . . What is social reality, what is a group, a category, a class, or a given period but the sum and system of these behaviours?"[20] Although aiming at a universal, ontological indictment of the self, Lewis's satirical technique heavily draws on narrative techniques of realism. For instance, the introduction to the characters of *The Wild Body* emphasizes this combination of realism and satire: the stories include an innkeeper who "rolls between his tables ten million times in a realistic rhythm that is as intense and superstitious as are the figures of a war-dance" (*CWB*, 149–50); or a Breton dancer who "circles round [his wife] with gestures a million times repeated" (*CWB*, 150). Although of quasi-cosmological scope, the satire requires the rendering of the "realistic rhythm" and daily "gestures" to be effective.

By the same token, these elements of realistic satire can convert into elements of modern allegory. For instance, in the description of Agnes in *The Revenge for Love* as golf-player and lover of fake antiques, whose speech includes recurrent words such as "pukka," and whose financial status does not match her social aspirations, one can see the realistic satire of post-war colonialism. Yet simultaneously, the same elements of characterization can be shown to constitute the allegorical components of personification of say, "colonialism-in-the-thirties." The mechanical recurrence of the word "pukka" and explosions of mirth characterizing Agnes then function as signs of an allegorized cult or *idée fixe*. From the point of view of meaning, the switch from satire to allegory panders to the two general interpretations that have divided the Lewisian critique: Lewis as a satirist of human absurdities versus Lewis as a satirist of ideologies. The ambiguity is not a reflection of critical biases only, but also stems from the narratives whose equivocal character is testified to by the dual meaning of the Lewisian prosopopoeia: the self as thing behaving like a person, or the self governed by an *idée fixe* or ideology.

So, at a time when modernists were supposed to be exploring psychical depths, Lewis practiced an allegorical type of characterization corresponding to the flat character of E. M. Forster's description. But then is "modernism" uniquely concerned with a characterization of depth? D. H. Lawrence, who saw salvation in the principle of the quick of self, was also attracted to the notion of *idée fixe*. In "Democracy," posthumously published, he evokes a modern allegory: "the whole human will pivots on some function, some material activity, which then works the whole being: like an *idée fixe* in the mental consciousness."[21] Similarly, Bergson is simultaneously the philosopher of *durée* and the theoretician of comedy as mechanical and obsessive action. The modern character of allegory in part derives from its tendency to collapse into absurdist comedy with its nihilistic implication for the definition of the self. Kafka's *Metamorphosis* (1912), Orwell's *Animal Farm* (1945), or Ionesco's *Rhinoceros* (1960) illustrate this modern generic hybridization of allegory and comedy.

Lewis's mechanistic absurdism—clearly a feature of his satire—combines with what Angus Fletcher has identified as the "daemonic agent" of allegory. "If we were to meet an allegorical character in real life," he writes, "we would say of him that he was obsessed with only one idea, or that he had an absolutely one-track mind, or that his life was patterned according to absolutely rigid habits from which he never allowed himself to vary."[22] I have quoted from Fletcher at such length because his terms of definition almost overlap with those Lewis uses in "Inferior Religions" (1928) to introduce the characters of *The Wild Body*. Lewis's emphasis on will and the wildness of the body also coincides with the daemonic energy Fletcher ascribes to the allegorical agent. Nor is it a coincidence that in "Cantleman's Spring-Mate" the chief protagonist's war-camp companions should be referred to as A, B, C, and D. This mode of characterization derives from the process of abstraction, which reduces allegorical agents to their bare essentials.

Fletcher describes the temporally rigid daemonic agents as "visual icons," devoid of growth or change. Thus the allegorical plot tends to be uniform: a quest or a battle. Either Christian journeys in search of Celestial City, or titanic angels vie for the control of Heaven. *The Childermass* and its two sequels are based on such archetypal plots. The first half of *The Childermass* is concerned with Pullman's and Satters's wandering among the flatlands in search of the Bailiff and his celestial city. *Monstre Gai* and *Malign Fiesta* are concerned with titanic confrontations between the Devil's army and God's angels. Battle reappears in as disparate works as *Enemy of the Stars* between Arghol and Hanp and in *The Red Priest* (1956), in which Augustine Card engages in boxing matches one of which proves lethal to his opponent. Allegorical psychomachia, however, does not have to take place at a physical level only, but can also take the form of dialogue, stychomythia, or debate. The shift from the physical level is illustrated by the titanic aural contest in *Monstre Gai*,[23] or the fight between Arghol and Hanp, following their verbal messages and counter-messages. From a more general viewpoint, the latter half of *The Childermass* rests on the linguistic psychomachia between the Bailiff and a succession of interlocutors who are eliminated when their opposition becomes too articulate.

At the same time, many a plot of Lewis's fiction can be read either in picaresque or in detective terms. The picaresque plot is a realistic transmutation of the allegorical quest or journey. In *The Apes of God*, for instance, Dan can be interpreted either as the *eiron* of an allegorical quest supervised by his mentor Horace Zagreus, or as a naïve witness exposed to the follies of a social class in a loosely connected picaresque series of episodes. As for the detective plot, it emerges in the first long narrative, *Mrs. Dukes' Million*, and reappears in *Snooty Baronet*, *The Revenge for Love*, and *The Vulgar Streak*. What allows the translation from allegory to detective novel is the enigmatic character central to the definition of both genres. One should, however, point out that novels such as *The Revenge for Love* or *Self Condemned* present themselves as non-parodic bildungsromans in which Hardcaster and Harding evolve during the course of the narrative. This type of temporality contradicts the rigid, non-evolving temporality of the allegorical plot. But if the growth of the character often corresponds to a breakaway from ideology, it does not offer a liberation from ontological absurdity.

Quest and psychomachia do not account for the entire specificity of an allegorical plot. Indeed, allegory shares the quest with romance, and the battle with the epic. In her analysis of great traditional allegories such as *Piers Plowman, Roman de la Rose*, or *The Faerie Queene*, Maureen Quilligan brings out the rhetorical specificity of the allegorical plot. She selects wordplay as a recurrent feature of allegory and as "the disposition to generate narrative structure."[24] For instance, *The Childermass* is characterized by puzzling episodes that borrow their fantastic dimension from allegory. One episode is concerned with Pullman's and Satters's fantastic walking across an eighteenth-century picture. By the time they reach the end of the picture, they are squeezed by the diminishing angle of perspective in the background of the picture. Here the plot develops out of taking perspective literally instead of as a drawing technique to achieve effects of verisimilitude. Another example of allegorical plot motivated by pun is found in part 12 of *The Apes of God*, which is concerned with a Lenten party. In a gossipy lecture to Ratner and Dan, Zagreus draws a satiric portrait of his hosts, known as Lord Osmund and Lord Phoebus. Simultaneously, Margolin (as one of the party conjurors) is shown throwing "Lightship Safety Matches" at Lord Osmund's nose. The capital letters do not refer to a specific brand of matches only: they also function as allegorical indicators of a plot consisting in shooting shafts at targets of satire.

The rhetorical aspect of Lewis's allegorical narratives is reinforced by the emblematic character of proper names and of titles. A title such as *The Childermass* is a direct pun on the two components of the word: democratic society consists in a mass of children, which corresponds to the denunciation of Peter-Panism of *The Art of Being Ruled*. At the same time, the title directs the reader to one of its pretexts: the Bible. Lewisian protagonists herald their allegorical status with their names: Cantleman is the leader of the herd; the anagram of Tarr's name identifies him as the embodiment of an aesthetic principle; Pullman is a man of time and therefore of movement; Stamp and Cruze personify the will; in *Monstre Gai,* the name of Sentoryen combines the ambivalent nature of the centaur with the neologism "yen" used by Lewis to designate woman. In each case, the emblematic character of the name is directly related to the type of action developing in the allegory.

In Fletcher's typology of allegory, style is discussed in connection with the "cosmic image" or "*kosmos*" that "signifies (1) a universe, and (2) a symbol that implies a rank in a hierarchy."[25] The second part of the definition is also associated with secondary meanings of ornament or sartorial symbolism. Therefore the genre of allegory, which rests on the twin principles of creation and creativity, leads to the creation of a fictitious universe and of a style that chiefly relies on effects of texture. The texture of Lewis's writing has long been noted and, from Hugh Kenner through John Russell and Fredric Jameson to Bernard Lafourcade and Paul Edwards,[26] successful analyses of his texts have centered on his style as opposed to the creation of macrostructures. This common practice of a minute type of analysis is certainly no coincidence and indirectly confirms the fundamentally allegorical character of the textuality of Lewis's writing.

However, Lewis's use of allegory does not entirely corresponds to Fletcher's typology. In particular, basic elements of allegory that inform his writings undergo a process of devaluation. For instance, the "ornamental" character of allegory is conspicuous in the recurrence of symbolism such as the talisman, insignia, and astral representation. In Lewis, astral symbolism merges with emblematic naming as in "Cantleman's Spring-Mate," where the mate's name is Stella, or in "The War-Baby," where Lutitia's villa is called "Mars." One finds an

example of allegorical insignia in *The Childermass,* where the enigmatic signs of the Bailiff's banner are described in great detail. In
The Apes of God a long passage is devoted to the description of Zagreus's coat designed by Pierpont for the Lenten party. Such a description corresponds to what Fletcher identifies as the allegorical
"hieroglyphs of dress." This hieroglyphic characteristic is a synecdoche for allegorical texture, which, Fletcher writes, "is 'curiously inwrought,' worked in ornamental detail."[27]

And yet this astral and ornamental symbolism fails to foster a sense
of allegorical sublimity. Although Lewis's style spins an elaborate,
textual sense of creativity, it fails to deliver a cosmological sense of
creation. Thus, in "Cantleman's Spring-Mate" the sexual act between
Cantleman and Stella is represented as an act of anthropophagy and,
in *Enemy of the Stars,* Arghol's and Hanp's downfall is illustrated by
the drawing of one prostrate figure and of another collapsing beneath
an isolated star (Michel, pl. 94).

Detail is another element that functions as a generic hinge between
allegory and Lewis's satirical realism. As Eysteinsson reminds us, detail is the cornerstone of the realistic effect of comprehensiveness.
Lewis's central scene of the party or banquet in *Tarr, The Apes of God,*
or *The Revenge for Love* fulfills the realistic aspiration to totality that
is, however, frustrated by a narrative running amok with fragmentary
close-ups, or slipping into the ornamental miniaturization of allegory.
In particular, Lewis's prose displays what Fletcher refers to as the
mosaic, paratactic aspect of allegorical textuality.[28] Several features of
his syle contribute to the fragmentation of his sentences among which
are the dash, the colon, hyphenation, dislocation, and apposition.
The following paratactic passage describing Arghol in *Enemy of the
Stars* combines apposition with the dash: "mask stoic with energy
(mind cleaned off slick, stripped for action—body become brain)"
(*CPP,* 179). Syntactical dislocation and hyphenation, which dislocates
words as the dash dislocates clauses, characterize the following passage: "His mind, that iron-throated mastiff with the big blank bay,
he flings off as it sets up its death-howl" (*CPP,* 180). A good example
of paratactic use of the colon and of its twin, the semicolon, is found
in the description of Kreisler's rape from the victim's viewpoint: "The
figure talked a little to fill in an interval; it had drawn: it had suddenly
flung itself upon her and done something disgusting: and now it was
standing idly by the window, becalmed, and completely cut off from
its raging self of the recent occurence" (*Tarr,* 194). So what we have
is the ornamental style of allegory, the modernist detailing of which
neither contributes to the creation of a hierarchical universe, nor fosters the sense of social comprehensiveness.

The use of parataxis is not unique either to Lewis or allegory. In his modernist manifesto, Eugeni Zamyatin advocates parataxis: "Syntax becomes elliptical, volatile; complicated pyramids of periods are dismantled and broken down into the single stones of independent clauses."[29] The dash reappears in the writings of as disparate authors as Gertrude Stein and Arthur Cravan, the dadaist editor of *Maintenant* in Paris (1912–15). Cravan's self-portrait reads as follows: "Confidence-man—sailor in the Pacific—muleteer—orange-picker in California—snake-charmer—hotel-thief—nephew of Oscar Wilde—lumberjack—ex-boxing champion of France—grandson of the Queen's Chancellor (England)—chauffeur in Berlin—etc."[30] In Lewis, the ancestor to the dash is the mathematical sign $=$, which he sprinkled in the 1918 version of *Tarr*. This stylistic experiment can be found in Marinetti's linguistic collages dated 1912, which are supposed to illustrate "numerical sensibility," the function of which was to achieve "geometrical and mechanical splendour."[31] As for the colon, it also appealed to the modernist sensibility of Pound for whom, Sanford Schwartz reports, its use gave the impression of "superposition."[32] However, although these stylistic features keep cropping up in other modernists, they strikingly combine and recur in Lewis's whole writing career. That they appear in an allegorical context is therefore no coincidence. Indeed, they add to the curiously inwrought texture of Lewis's narratives, which, as hyphenation indicates, draw on miniaturization.

Eysteinsson argues that today the survival of realism depends more on the type of narrative convention than on the use of detail testifying to the authenticity of the narrative.[33] It can be argued that the modernist use of realistic detail is directly responsible for the destabilization of nineteenth-century type of realism. It is a truism that *Ulysses* is replete with details of observation. At the linguistic and experimental level, it is the detail—that is the unit—that is predominant: Stein's analytical combinatory of linguistic units is a case in point. From a pictorial viewpoint, the fact that the limits of the canvas often coincide with the boundaries of the picture suggests that the picture is a detail of a larger yet elusive totality. From Picasso through Mondrian to Riopelle, pictorial representation is often characterized by a centrifugal movement preventing/evoking a sense of completion or self-containment. However, fragmentation and the potential anarchy of detail lie right at the core of the realistic tradition. Hence George Orwell once characterized Dickens as the writer of the "*unnecessary detail*" and of the "wonderful gargoyles."[34] This also implies that the referential function of realistic language was in jeopardy from the start: not enough or too much detailing would equally fail the test of realism as discourse of totality and presence.

Lewis's stylistic practice stands in total contrast not only to Verlaine's injunction to wring the neck of eloquence, but also to his own theoretical support of a prose without fuss or mannerism. This contradiction led him to rewrite *Enemy of the Stars* and *Tarr* in what he intended to be a less flamboyant, more accessible prose. In *Satire and Fiction*, Lewis argues that *The Apes of God* exemplifies the clear, visual prose of the Great Without. And yet the work is stylistically ambiguous: the prologue is written in a characteristically inwrought style, while the remaining parts of the narrative are written in a relatively clearer prose. Lewis's modernism lies neither in his aesthetic claim for a language of communication unhindered by mannerism nor in the highly ornamental texture of his allegorical narratives, but in the contradiction between the aesthetic claim and the artistic practice. His satire of self, be it ontological or sociological, requires a physical or social body to start with. To this extent his prose remains fundamentally deictic. At the same time the object of description or of ideological analysis is dealt with obliquely with allegorical texture spinning out of a stylistic cocoon. The description of Bestre's body illustrates the particular tension between texture and deixis:

> His very large eyeballs, the small saffron ocellation in their centre, the tiny spot through which light entered the obese wilderness of his body; his bronzed bovine arms, swollen handles for a variety of indolent little ingenuities; his inflated digestive case, lent their combined expressiveness to say . . . things; . . . His tongue stuck out, his lips eructated with the incredible indecorum that appears to be the monopoly of liquids, his brown arms were for the moment genitals, snakes in one massive twist beneath his mamillary slabs, gently riding on a pancreatic swell, each hair on his oil-bearing skin contributing its message of porcine affront. (*CWB*, 78–79)

The deictic thread runs throughout the itemization of the body; but this thread is spliced with a series of chiefly reifying and animalizing metaphors, the function of which is to present a thing or animal behaving as a person. The effect of the prose is not to offer a clear, realistic description of Bestre's body; instead the descriptive reference to a hypothetical yet powerfully sexual body has to be disembedded from an allegorical texture, where parataxis is created by means of semicolons, apposition, dislocation, and hyphenation. This paradoxical sense of obscenity and elusiveness derives from the "elliptical effect" that Mary Ann Caws attributes to the modernist representation of the body: "seen entire, the body seems to say nothing; seen naked, it seems to spark no story. Seen in part, it speaks whole volumes; seen veiled, it leads into its own text."[35]

Nor does the use of apparently transparent prose guarantee untrammelled access to reality. *The Vulgar Streak* is a good example of an unadorned yet allegorical text. Its general allegorical message is summarized by Vincent's statement that he strove "*to get on top*" (*VS*, 174). The narrative is concerned with the polysemic implications of the statement. From a literal viewpoint, Vincent tries to ascend to the top of the hierarchical ladder; from an allegorical viewpoint, he tries to maintain himself above matter and body. The allegorical dimension of the text plays upon the sociological and ontological meaning of "materialism." The novel can therefore be read as an allegory of the self's attempt to rise above matter with social structure functioning as allegorical, polysemic vehicle.

The Vulgar Streak is symptomatic of the evolution of Lewis's allegorical approach that is visible from *The Apes of God* onwards and that culminates with *The Human Age*. The phenomenon of linguistic impoverishment of his texts, underlined by Russell,[36] derives from a shift in allegorical strategies. Indeed, the allegorical character of the later texts has less to do with stylistic texture and more with polysemy. To this extent, Lewis's later narratives herald Beckett's ascetic yet allegorical texts.

I will postpone my analysis of his final allegories until part three, in the context of a political interpretation of his writings. So far, my analysis of his allegorical narratives has confined itself to the surface of the text. However, the obliquity of allegory lends itself to a psychoanalytical interpretation of narratives by an author who displayed scorn for Freudian analysis. No doubt the risk of running into a pothole or of hitting a false bottom is high, but my purpose is to provide elements that will turn out to be fundamental to the analysis of Lewis's aesthetics and politics.

4

Man and Woman

IN THE FIRST THREE CHAPTERS OF MY STUDY I HAVE ENDEAVORED to show that a monolithic reading of Lewis's texts is made impossible by the fact that the different parts of his corpus do not add up to a cohesive message. This lack of semantic cohesiveness I regard as a fundamentally modernist aspect. The absence of such cohesiveness is most conspicuous in the transition from the nonfiction to the fiction, whereby Lewis fails to create in fictive terms the vision of philosophical totality and stability to which his nonfictional texts aspire. What the transition from the pamphletic essay to the satirical allegory registers is the vast ideological bankruptcy that the Western world underwent at the turn of the century, and that increased with cataclysmic events such as the First World War and the 1929 financial crash. Lewis's modernist use of allegory indicates a fall from hierarchy and sublimity that affected both the type of vision and the terms of creativity.

I suggest that chief among the factors responsible for this loss of creative sublimity is the slow yet perceptible downfall of the father figure and of patriarchal values that were challenged most conspicuously by the suffragette movement. The loss of sublimity in Lewis corresponds to the disappearance of a *kosmos* with its traditional paraphernalia of patriarchal insignia and functions. We are still reeling from this collective and psychological phenomenon. From Jacques Lacan's psycho-linguistic association of the symbolic system with the Law of the Father to the postmodernist orphans haunting the pages of Pat Barker's *The Man Who Wasn't There* and Peter Ackroyd's *English Music,* the search for the dead Father remains compelling and will not cease.

Although the present chapter consists in a detailed psychoanalytical speculation on Lewis's response to the loss of the father figure, the argument stems from the general framework I have just sketched. In particular, Lewis's approach to this sociocultural predicament is typically modernist: his texts both attempt to assimilate a disinteg-

rating tradition and proceed to ram against the same tradition. I analyze his endeavor to recreate a patriarchal hero in chapter 10 within
the context of his political statements, while in the present chapter I
concentrate on the impact of the absent father on his statements on
man and woman in society. Chapter 4 and chapter 10 are therefore
complementary.

Psychoanalyses of texts range from Freud's pioneering essays on
Leonardo and Dostoievsky to Lacan's interpretation of Hamlet and
of "The Purloined Letter," as well as Julia Kristeva's analysis of Giotto
and Céline, and Wayne Koesterbaum's analysis of male writing cooperation between Eliot and Pound.[1] All four enterprises have in common the general subject-matter of psychoanalysis, but the four
enterprises do not necessarily share the same premises concerning the
relationship between psyche and text.

During the last thirty years, academic psychological analysis has
been dominated by Lacanian methods, or methods deriving from
Lacanian writings, some of whose fundamental concepts include the
equation of the Law of the Father with symbolic organization, phallic
symbolization with penis lack, and the unconscious with linguistic
structure. These concepts have been used in counter-reaction to literary analyses that, following a nineteenth-century tradition, saw in
texts the transparent inscription of the author's psyche. The Lacanian
"revolution" consists in giving back to Caesar what belongs to Caesar;
that is, giving back textuality to texts.

The price for this necessary revolution has been the bracketing of
the subject, and more precisely the textualization of the subject. For
instance, it is remarkable that most of Lacan's theoretical statements
rely on no case history of any patient of his. Either the cases are
Freud's famous patients who have entered the Freudian canonic texts,
or they are literary characters such as Hamlet. This textual emphasis
results from the conjunction of two powerful breakthroughs: one is
Freud's shift from a biological model to a psychological, the other is
the theoretical elaboration of structuralist and poststructuralist Saussurean linguistics.

Despite the hegemony of such an approach, there have been signs
of resistance. One very common type of pure opposition to psychoanalysis sees in it, and rightly, an attack on the humanistic Cartesian
subject. But there are other movements of resistance that are even
more challenging because they develop within discourses and practices of psychoanalysis while maintaining a critical distance from
them. The main stumbling-block for these movements of resistance
is the privilege granted by theory to language. Progressively the con-

stitutive role of language has come to be perceived as a formidable system of determinism or a prison-house, to use a famous formula.

The over-determination of language in the psychoanalytical account of the subject or subject-as-language has two effects. One is the removal of context from the analysis, and the other is the truncation of the particular for the sake of conceptual totalization. The absence of contextualization has led to the silencing of political, sociological, and cultural factors in the production of texts. Thus it is no coincidence that the 1980s saw the expansion of "cultural studies," the function of which is to foreground the cultural and social identity of texts. Furthermore, in keeping with the dogma of the death of the subject, Lacanian theory and its epigones have logically evacuated anything that smacks of biography. In fact, this particular type of psychocriticism has consisted in the erasure of *bio* so as to let *graphy* speak for itself.

This theoretical erasure was done for the sake of conceptual totalization, which Lacan's famous formula—the unconscious is a linguistic structure—encapsulates. In considering the signifed as a mere effect of the signifier, Lacan reduces the subject to a linguistic totality cut off from any empirical ontology. In fact, if there is any ontology in Lacan, it is of a linguistic type: "It is the world of words that creates the world of things."[2] This self-sufficient, autarcic fortress has lost some of its formidable air in the recent years. In North America, critical psychoanalyses of texts have appeared that either explicitly or implicitly reject linguistic totalization as an inevitable premise.

Thus critics like Peter Brooks practice "formalist" psychocriticism with the proviso that the textual, rhetorical character of this criticism cannot be based on the premise that the human being is to be bracketed. In effect, Brooks sees psychoanalysis as a derivation from self and life. In his analysis of symbolic homosexual male intercourse in male collaboration over texts, Wayne Koestenbaum not only uses a Freudian methodology and terminology, but also explicitly rejects any temptation to erase the biographical and concrete level of psychoanalysis. Searching for a method that does not conceive the author as textual autonomous production of meaning cut off from specificity, Colin MacCabe argues that Stephen Heath's decision to ignore the biographical significance of the signifier "cane" in Orson Welles leaves the analysis of his cinematography incomplete. In contrast to Stephen Heath, Shari Benstock does not hesitate to establish a direct link between Aubrey Beardsley's graphic conflation of Oscar Wilde and Salome on the one hand and, on the other hand, Wilde's self-identification with Salome as biographically documented by a photograph taken in Paris.[3]

The sense of contradiction that one might derive from MacCabe's or Brooks's approaches could only be caused by a dogmatic belief that the primacy of language in our being precludes any existential, phenomenological, perceptual, biographical, or historical reference. In fact, this sense of contradiction would stem from a binary opposition between text and non-text. However, MacCabe's reference to Welles's signifier "cane/Kane" and Benstock's reference to the photograph of Wilde posing as Salome point to a much more complex relationship between text and non-text, whereby the text is already in the biographical and the biographical is always in the text. In other words, if the biographical constitutes an origin of some sort to the text, this origin is already mediated by signs and representation. This is the reason why Alan Durant's distinction between a thematic, biographical psychoanalysis and a formal, linguistic psychoanalysis is not very helpful.[4] If one takes for granted that all of our experience is always and already combed by language, then a thematic psychoanalysis is bound to be linguistic and formal. Thus the intermediacy of texts, photographs, and paintings does not authorize us to evict the biographical from critical analysis.

The snag of theoretical totalization is very accute in psychoanalytical criticism. As Derrida remarks, Freud was quite aware of this snag and emphasized the individuality of each dream as opposed to the elaboration of a totalizing dictionary of oneiric symbols.[5] By emphasing the particular dream, Freud implicitly emphasized the particular dreamer and his/her individual use of dream language. Willy-nilly, the "subject," "agent," or "biographical origin" surface again. In this respect, MacCabe's distinction between Barthes's concept of the death of the author and the cinematographic French *nouvelle vague*'s recognition of the author as means of asserting the "specificity of the codes that went to make up the cinema"[6] reinforces the contrast between a totalizing approach and one that shatters totalities by raids into specificity.

The precedence of totality over specificity leads to the type of criticism that Peter Nicholls offers of Lewis's critique of the blurring of distinctions in modern culture. Thus, Nicholls writes that "the doubling and symmetry within [Lewis's] narratives testifies to the inescapable specularity of desiring relations, to the narcissism which he locates as the structural compulsion of democratic (or communistic) societies for which the other must always prove to be the same."[7] At no point does Nicholls examine the political context and ideological charge of Lewis's statements on democratic (is it the same as communistic?) societies. My point is not to invalidate Nicholl's theoretical approach: theories are always lurking beneath the surface of commentary. Rather, this theoretical application fails because, faithful to its totalizing reflex, it neglects to examine the specificity of the text.

It seems to me therefore that today the task of psychocriticism is to maintain a dialectical relationship between the biographical and the representational. Texts cannot be regarded as the direct transcription of the artist's mind and cannot be analyzed at the expense of their imaginary, artificial aspects. The object of psychocriticism is not to make abstraction of writing in order to get access to the real stuff; rather, it is to interpret a construct that is the only piece of representation available to the reader. Psychocriticism functions insofar as there is text. In addition, texts cannot be reduced to a spontaneous overflow of powerful emotions. Instead, premeditation, play, self-consciousness, camouflage, and blindness are at the heart of the writing activity and shape the process of reading.

Psychocriticism constitutes one form of reader's response to these textual strategies that are never gratuitous and are always meaningful. Brooks point out that texts are always addressed to someone, and that they therefore function within the context of communication between narrator and reader, which the narrative structure sometimes symbolizes as in the case of Conrad's narrator Marlowe.[8] In this respect, the reader's situation is the same as the analyst's: they both try to reconstruct a psychological pattern that can be deciphered only by signs and representations.

However, the fundamental difference between reader and analyst is that the reader does not have access to the author as human being. The validity of psychocriticism is curtailed by the fact that no response will be elicited from the author by the psychocritique. In fact, the artist has a privilege that s/he shares with no patient, which is one of noncommittal silence. Thus the work of art neither confirms nor denies. Brooks sees the relation between text and psychocritic as one that "involves a willingness, a desire to enter into the delusional systems of texts, to espouse their hallucinated vision, in an attempt to master and be mastered by their power of conviction."[9] What Brooks here voices is the rhetorical appeal of the text and the strategies of pathos the author uses more or less consciously to transmit his or her message. The psychocritic is the reader who responds to the seduction of the text. This seductive strategy has a purpose that Lacan expressed in a general, neo-Hegelian theory of recognition of self that applies to the specific situation of the textual exchange taking place between author and reader. "Man's desire," Lacan argues," finds its meaning in the desire of the other, not so much because the other holds the key to the object desired, as because the first object of desire is to be recognized by the other."[10]

However, Brooks's notions of mastery look outlandish to me; instead, I see in the seductive strategies of a text the writer's means of negotiating the psychological process of unveiling and exposure. These strategies are used to mitigate the apocalyptic moments of personal truth, and the act of representation is a means of involving the reader in the process of self-exposure. The reader is necessary to ensure recognition of apocalyptic truth by means of representation. So if Brooks is right in referring to the power of conviction the text strives to generate, I am not persuaded by the notion of the reader's attempt to master and be mastered by the text. Psychocriticism is closer to a case of maieutic process, or midwifery, the function of which is either to attend the delivery of a new consciousness or helplessly to record its abortion.

If the psychocritic has no direct access to the author's response to the analysis, and if textualized reports are the only biographical elements available, what is going to bail out this enterprise? Brooks's answer is quite interesting: in the process of reading, the critic produces interpretive hypotheses. What determines the validity and plausibility of these hypotheses is their capacity to "produce more text," to generate "previously unperceived networks of relation and significance, finding confirmation in the extension of the narrative and semantic web."[11] My psychological interpretation of Lewis's texts is not meant to be genetic to the extent that I do not try to gauge all of Lewis's writing by it. At the same time, I would argue that my interpretation is valid insofar as it produces more text, that is to say meaning, particularly in connection with Lewis's political writings.

To grasp the particular psychological idiom of Lewis's writings, one needs to take account of the social, political, and cultural language out of which his own vocabulary evolved. I cannot pretend to be exhaustive, let alone comprehensive, in this area. However, the obvious starting-point is the sociocultural discourse of the fin de siècle in Britain as analyzed and documented by Elaine Showalter.[12] The last twenty years of the nineteenth century were characterized by the twin phenomena of the progressive social liberation of women and the medicalization of homosexuality as sexual deviance, as well as its legal definition as social delinquence. Both phenomena were perceived as threats to heterosexuality upon which the patriarchal notion of masculinity depends to perpetuate itself. This social crisis generated sociocultural phantasms that both associated feminist suffragettes with Uranism or lesbianism and viewed the male homosexual as the blurring factor of gender definition and boundary.

Lewis's discourse on gender emerged out of this sociocultural matrix. Born in 1882, Lewis grew up in the midst of the questioning of Victorian values that, as Lyn Pykett observes, constituted a context for a whole generation of writers from H. G. Wells, Ford Madox Ford, and E. M. Forster to May Sinclair, Virginia Woolf, and Rebecca West.[13] Pykett is particularly useful in bringing out the type of cultural language that developed in response to these new social currents. Specifically she quotes from Otto Weininger's *Sex and Character,* the first English translation of which was published in 1906. Weininger's representation of gender identity is based on an implacable binary opposition between male and female: while the male is on the side of consciousness, the female lies on the side of the unconscious; while form is the signet of man, matter is what woman wallows in; while woman is at the mercy of chaos, the masculine genius succeeds in shaping chaos thanks to his access to comprehension by means of universal memory.[14] Male, female, man, woman, form, matter, chaos, and masculine genius are some of the building blocks of Lewis's statements on gender.

An introduction to these statements can begin with a few quotations from *Tarr,* in which the tendency is strong to shove woman into matter and keep her there. For Tarr, the "sexual sphere seemed . . . to be an average from which *everything* came, from it everything rose or attempted to rise. . . . God was man: the woman was a lower form of life" (*Tarr,* 327). The uncommon use of the definite article before "woman" indicates a vague echo of Nietzsche, who no doubt would have referred to *das Weib.* But besides Nietzsche, one can also hear Freudian overtones in the emphasis on sexuality as the alpha of human nature. It is on this basis that Tarr distinguishes between man and woman. This distinction coincides with the mind-body agon: "everything started female and most so continued: a jellyish diffuseness spread itself and gaped upon the beds and bas-fonds of everything: above a certain level sex disappeared, just as in highly-organised sensualism sex vanishes. On the other hand, *everything* beneath that line was female" (*Tarr,* 327). The implicit line between the female zone and the male is important because it adds another ideological dimension to the dualistic antinomy of the Wild Body and the intellect. The female does not have access to the upper level and is therefore confined to the Wild Body.

What should be our assessment of Tarr? Should one dutifully see in him a purely fictional creature cut off from its author and creator, or should one see him as a straight Lewisian mouthpiece? Again, it seems to me that the answer will not be found in *Tarr* only. Lewis's position on the gender question is complex and needs to be tracked down in the different areas of his corpus.

Passages can be selected to show that on the theoretical level Lewis was able to grant woman what was then regarded as freedom and emancipation. Thus marriage is considered as slavery, whereas abortion and prostitution are "signs and instruments of freedom rather than despotism, exactly indeed as the conventional feminist would assert."[15] Yet the notion that some animals are more equal than others insidiously creeps in. For instance in chapter 6 of *The Art of Being Ruled*, the idea that man and woman are intellectual equals is accepted. But Lewis adds the proviso that a superficial difference exists, whereby woman's specialization is sex. In other words, and as in *Tarr*, woman is governed by the inferior religion of the Wild Body, it is her *idée force*. With one hand Lewis gives woman freedom, which he takes away with the other.

Significantly the general line of Lewis's argument represents woman as threat and man as perpetually striving to assert his identity. For instance, he makes a valid point when he argues that feminism is utilized both to weaken the father's authority within the family and society and to provide cheap labor on the work-market. The father-principle has been destroyed at the microcosmic level of the family only to be recreated at the macrocosmic level of the state: "A kind of gigantically luxurious patriarchate is what democracy and monster industry together have invented" (*ABR*, 201–2). But when it comes to the analysis of feminism itself, the spectre of the Wild Body reappears ominously. In his opinion, feminism does not aim at equality but at domination and the creation of a matriarchate. The possibility of a matriarchal society represents a threat in Lewis's vision, and one can go back to 1917, when "Cantleman's Spring-Mate" was published, to grasp the nature of this threat: "all women were contaminated with Nature's hostile power and might be treated as spies or enemies. . . . So [Cantleman] approached Stella with as much falsity as he could master" (*BB*, 310). A matriarchate would amount to the art of being ruled by woman, that is to say, the emissary of nature and the Wild Body.

Lewis also argues that his use of "masculine" and "feminine" does not carry sexual or biological connotations, as the terms can interchangeably be applied to both man and woman. Yet one wonders why Lewis chose these words. Their neutrality is questionable since his own definitions of "woman" and of "feminine" more often than not coincide. The feminine is defined as follows: "More uniquely alive to the things of the moment; more docile and mercurial; more burdened with and swayed by the tidal movements of the unconscious—finally, more *unconscious*, less 'intellectual'" (*ABR*, 251). Here is Tarr on the female once more: "a jellyish diffuseness [that] spread itself and gaped upon all the beds and *bas-fonds* of everything" (*Tarr*, 327). In both cases, the defining characteristics are formlessness, the unconscious, and the flux. It is obvious that, despite the author's argument to the contrary, "female" and "feminine" are synonymous in his vocabulary.

It is also plain that Lewis reserves specific connotations for each lexical category. If the feminine and female connote formlessness, the unconscious, and the flux, by implication the masculine and male connote form, consciousness, and stasis. Symptomatically, the masculine connotations are implied rather than spelled out. This in itself is a sign of the precariousness of traditional values that reached back to a pre-Darwinian, pre-Freudian, and pre-industrial era. Although a sociocultural explanation of the sort I provided at the beginning of the chapter helps us understand what happened to these values, it does not provide the particular circumstances that surrounded the production of Lewis's individual corpus. I will therefore analyze Lewis's gender allegories with a view to bringing out psychological patterns or traces that, I assume, crisscross his texts. If, as Freud originally claimed, the unconscious manifests itself through language, then oblique and enigmatic allegory seems to be a perfect medium for unconscious manifestations.

Lewis's demotion of woman can be related to the imperative psychological need to assert an identity for oneself. The distinction between man and woman is of paramount importance in his writing because it was lacking in his own life. From the age of eleven onward, Lewis developed under the exclusive influence of his mother without a father as a counterpart. Thus the parental mirror was exclusively female and feminine. One can even detect a double absence of the father: physically he was no longer part of the family; in addition, identification with the male principle was simply out of question since it corresponded with the father who was the object of bitter accusations. Identification with the father implied the transference of the father's guilt onto the son for having deserted the mother. Lewis's drastic and disparaging distinction between man and woman derives from this lopsided identification with the mother figure. The male principle in him is not the result of a process of education but, on the contrary, an act of wilful assertion. However, the male principle is an unstable affair, always jeopardized by the castrating influence of the mother. The fact that the mother retained her power over the son is illustrated by Lewis's rejection of his father's invitation to study at an American university and by his profound distress on his mother's death.[16] In *Blasting and Bombardiering* he goes as far as making his mother's death during the postwar pneumonia epidemic the incentive for the study of Western Man:

> Parents who have lost the apples of their eyes in wars and who mourn them extremely, are apt to experience a hostile feeling thenceforth for the members of the nation they hold responsible for their death. . . . I, sustaining a loss the other way around, had not the consolation of feeling a slight coldness for the Kaiser. Mine was, momentarily, a more abstract vendetta. (*BB,* 189–90)

Yet, following a psychological logic, Lewis made Herculean efforts to set himself free from the maternal influence that stifled a part of his personality.

There is no doubt that the author could look back at his past writings and examine them with irony and distance. The process of such self-awareness is miraculously preserved in the rewriting of "The Crowd-Master," first published in *Blast* 2 (1915). There are two other versions of this short text. One, never published during Lewis's lifetime, is in *Unlucky for Pringle,* edited by C. J. Fox and Robert Chapman; the other is in *Blasting and Bombardiering* (1937). With its protagonists, Blenner and Multum, the first version rests on the embryonic device of the double. The second version was probably written after 1922, for one finds a description of Leo Makepiece Leo in terms similar to those used for the description of Bestre in a story published that year. The chief difference between these two versions and the third consists in the degree of detachment between the author and his protagonist. In the third version, the story reads like a miniature bildungsroman of three chapters written from an ironic viewpoint. I shall take the third version as the main basis for textual interpretation and refer to the other two versions as necessary or relevant.

As is often the case with Lewis, war in his fiction is the pretext for the analysis of other phenomena. The actual subject of the three chapters in *Blasting and Bombardiering* is not so much the First World War as the allegorical genesis of the self, with war as synecdoche for the Wild Body. Three stages can be distinguished in Cantleman's development. First, in Scotland comes the news that war has broken out, and Cantleman's state of ignorance is brought out. In the following passage one perceives a portrait of a Lewisian self back in 1914, when *Blast* was first published: "Celebrated for minor violence, too, was *he,* a rough Bohemian—he savoured violence for its own sake, as a coarse joke, or the crepitation of a chinese cracker. He was not a man of blood. . . . He was a suffragette" (*BB,* 1937, 70). Second,

Cantleman experiences an initiation on the train from Scotland to London. Third, now initiated, Cantleman dives into the vortex of London crowds stricken by war-psychosis. The three versions are characterized by the same theme—that is to say, the quest for gender identity.

In the 1937 version war is a means of identification with the father, and therefore with the masculine principle. A patriarchal genealogy is established linking Cantleman's forebears to the imperialist tradition associated with Clive and Outram. In the second version the oedipal identification with the father is rejected when it is said that Cantleman "would never be a soldier, since his father had been one: so why consider war?" (*UFP*, 47). In the first two versions war exerts fascination on Cantleman, who does not see through it as an inferior religion satisfying the need for action and violence, but responds to its glamour of responsiblity, martiality, and authority. This fundamental blindness to the true nature of war, which is brought out by the ironic narrator of the third version, remains unanalyzed in the first two versions where Blenner/Cantleman experiences an "innate military exultation" (*Blast 2*, 95/*UFP*, 49) when war breaks out. Paradoxically, war brings about the creation of a self along the lines of the masculine principle. In the third version, the function of the journey from Scotland to London is to initiate Cantleman in the masculine principle as a principle of the intellect. The goal is a masculine self, which no longer draws on the Wild Body and action for its authority.

The survival of the masculine principle depends on its distinction from the feminine. The psychological process underlying the journey to London aims at creating a dividing line between two antinomic principles, which, ultimately, originate in the parental figures. The passengers on the train constitute the members of a *kosmos* reflecting Lewis's vision of prewar English society: one recognizes the upper classes in the influential traveller, the middle-class bourgeoisie in the officers, the lower classes in the slum-youths and the "masses" (*BB*, 1937, 74). As an artist, Cantleman is not a member of the class system, and the model for self-creation turns out to be the figure who symbolically can set himself free from social straitjackets: the sailor. The sailor is selected to personify rational consciousness in contrast to the feminine excitment of the crowd: "The Crowd-proof Jack Tars were the first break in the continuity of the Crowd-spirit Cantleman had met with since the war began blowing up" (*BB*, 1937, 79).

Side by side with the sailors' compartment is the women's, to which Cantleman decides to move. His change of compartment can be interpreted as another symbolic attempt at self-identification: his change is from the masculine compartment to the feminine. Here is an account of this rather transparently Freudian scene: "he would sleep better among the vegetative shapes of the women. He forced two grunting bodies apart and joined in the female seance" (*BB*, 1937, 74). This regressive desire for the womb is not thoroughly fulfilled; it leads to disgust, as Cantleman experiences qualms at the sensation of heat from the body of the neighboring woman. The identification with the mother and the feminine principle is also rejected in a scene witnessed by Cantleman. From the train, he observes a young reservist from York bidding farewell to his family. The lasting image of this scene is not concerned with the father, whose role is passive, but with the mother, "whose sarcastic grin and fixed eyes, and her big body with one shoulder hunched up—almost a grace, like a child's trick—as her eyes wandered, were not easily forgotten. . . . she was the unhappy child—not he—whose doll was being stolen" (*BB*, 1937, 78). In this mother-son relationship, the need to escape from the mother's influence is most conspicuous. Within this context, going to war is tantamount to identifying oneself with the masculine principle and to claiming independence from the mother whose doll one no longer is.

It is this detachment from the feminine that Cantleman's experience of the crowd reproduces. Intoxicated by the news of an imminent war, the London crowd becomes a vast body moving vortex-like across the metropolis. In the midst of the crowd the protagonist is put to proof. First he fails as he feels enthusiasm, but eventually his "detachment" is said to be "complete" (*BB*, 1937, 81).[17] Cantleman has achieved self-control and maintains a distance between himself and the crowd described in the following terms: "The 'great historical event' is always hatching; the Crowd in its habitual infantile sleep. Then the appointed hand releases the clutch, the 'great event' is set in motion: the crowd rises to meet the crash half awake and struggling, with voluptuous spasms. It is the Rape of the Crowd" (*BB*, 1937, 81). The simultaneous presence of literal and figurative levels of meaning; the allegorizing capitalizing; the prosopopoeial function of the crowd; the mosaic style created by parataxis and colon or semicolon; the metaphor to represent fate: all these features combine to create a cohesive allegorical context for the representation of the feminine principle as negative model of passivity and hysteria.

This allegorical context is sustained by extended metaphors or long conceits. Since the crowd-master is the sailor, the crowd is the ebbing body of waters, "aimlessly flowing through these torpid coils" (*BB*, 1937, 84). As a collective body, it feeds on the Bergsonian flux of Lewis's analysis in *Time and Western Man*. Vortex-like it is sex and war, Eros and Thanatos in one. Cantleman's experiment, however, does not lead to the assertion of the crowd-master at the still centre of the vortex. His visualization of Lady Hamilton in "tight-fitting bathing drawers" (*BB*, 1937, 86) drags him down below Tarr's dividing line between the female zone and the male. From the reader's viewpoint, the conclusion to the story is ambiguous: is Cantleman derided and is therefore the principle of detached consciousness implicitly relinquished? Or is not Cantleman's sexual desire a little too loudly trumpeted?

The elusiveness of the masculine principle as static point of intellectual detachment is also apparent in *The Childermass*, where the characters are under the sublunary influence of the feminine principle. Pullman, the protagonist, does not personify the masculine principle but its decline. The masculine principle is in fact embodied by two other characters. One is Barney, the other Macrob the Scot. They are complementary as Barney represents the physical and concrete aspect of man, whereas with Macrob the intellect is predominant. Barney is a figure of pugnacious resistance as he knocks down an opponent who called him a sissy. The allegorical dimension of the character is evident when he is described as a "blue-eyed lion of the slums . . . [with] the haughty carriage of the youthful coster-male" (*CM*, 187–88). In his lethal confrontation with the Bailiff, Macrob becomes the Phineas of mass culture, tormented by the harpies of the swooning, feminine crowd or "herd of nan-men" (*CM*, 215). His death is the allegorical destruction of the masculine principle that in Lewis's *kosmos* never survives.

From a Lacanian standpoint, this destruction presents an interesting puzzle. Peter Nicholls provides an interpretation of the art of satire in Lewis by stating that satire "supplements its object not by breathing new life into it but by 'murdering' it as surely as, in Lacan's words, 'the symbol manifests itself as the murder of the thing.'"[18] The aim of Lacan's statement is to free language and the symbolic of material origins as well as to make desire a symbolic expression. But there is another murder involved in the process: the Lacanian subject's entrance into the Symbolic system coincides with the oedipal murder of the Father as "author of the Law." So, to some extent, the Name-of-the-Father coincides with oedipal, symbolic parricide: the former requires the latter, and vice versa.[19] If we push this interpretation to its logical conclusion, then Lewis would be embracing the Symbolic order and revelling in the Law of the Father. No wonder then that his texts prompt critics such as Ann L. Ardis into feminist analyses.[20] However, this type of interpretation goes right against Fredric Jameson's remark that, contrary to D. H. Lawrence's, Lewis's ideological sytem does not rest on the typical opposition between phallus and non-phallus. From the start, Lewis's phallocentricity was undermined by a relentless satire of the representation of the male body and culture, as is exemplified by *Sunset among the Michelangelos* that depicts Schwartzeneggerian males engaged in physical rituals (1912; Michel, pl. 6). At the same time and in contradiction to the physicality of these overmen, the Lewisian agon between the masculine principle and the feminine principle is based on the dematerialization of "man" who is systematically associated with the intellect. Thus a solid line is created that divides the masculine intellectual level from the feminine physical level.

Nicholls's and Jameson's divergent interpretations create a puzzle that can be solved in the following terms: Lewis's satirical art of spatial petrification should be regarded as an absurdist and nihilistic response to the vapidities of both our unconscious and our cultural ideologies. In other words, nothingness would substitute itself to the phallus. This interpretation runs throughout Bernard Lafourcade's analyses of Lewis's texts.

The curious thing is that none of these interpretations taken separately brings a satisfactory answer to the gender question in Lewis. On the one hand, feminist criticism responds to the undeniable misogyny of some of Lewis's writings, which seems to indicate the presence of a patriarchal author; on the other, Jameson and Lafourcade respond to the fact that there is obviously something missing, which is confirmed by Lewis's repeated attack on the fetishistic rituals of a phallocentric culture.

An interpretation of this Lewisian indeterminacy may start with a detour toward sexual anarchy. Lewis's precarious gender system includes a third component that is going to wreak havoc with the author's apparent dualistic antinomies between man and woman. This third component is the ambiguous figure of the male homosexual also referred to by Lewis as the shaman or invert. Homosexuality he regards as a process of feminization that brings about the downfall of Western Man:

> In the levelling, standardization, and pooling of the crowd-mind, as the result of a closer organization from above and greatly increased pressure on any irregularities of surface or temperamental erection, it is the masculine mind that tends to approximate to the feminine rather than the other way round. This is inevitable, seeing that the masculine is not the natural human state, but a carefully nurtured secondary development above the normal and womanly. (*ABR*, 186)

This feminization is supposed to entail the death of the father and the destruction of the traditional family cell.

One can encapsulate Lewis's view of male homosexuality in a syllogism: the feminine is the unconscious, non-intellectual Wild Body; the male homosexual is feminine: therefore the homosexual is the unconscious, non-intellectual Wild Body. Also, the male homosexual is the man who has not succeeded in outgrowing the state of childhood. He is the perpetually unweaned child. The close connection between woman and child recurs in Lewis who sees the child as "sexless" "but so preponderatingly feminine as almost to merge in the mother-figure on which it is dependent" (*ABR,* 184). *The Childermass* partly owes its title to its characters: a nightmarish crowd of nobodies whose principle of identity is anonymity. No division between male and female exists, and everything has been reduced to the jellyish diffuseness of the feminine.

The talismans of the Bailiff's parodic *kosmos* signify the threatening domination of the feminine principle: these are the "doric palmets and figures from idalionic amulets of fecundity" and "a phoenician mask of Astarte, equine, with retreating forehead, the protruding lips isolated into a separate, heavily-functional, feature" (*CM,* 125–26). A passive moron and a *sub persona infantis,* Satters is singled out as a demonic agent of the feminine crowd. The relationship between Pullman and Satters is based on the blurring of gender roles:

> Satters bursts with his great flesh-gauntleted fist into the ladylike aperture between Pulley's coat-sleeve and ribs. It bursts in like a bomb. The ponderous thing, with its crawling energy and heat, conveys to the slight body, in whose side it has lodged itself, the sense of parturition. Heroically weighted with it the pregnant Pulley stoically advances, with responsible measured tread. (*CM,* 75)

The dividing line between genders is first blurred by the homosexual stance of the two characters. It is then emphasized by attributing to Satters a male role and to Pullman a female. Characteristically, the female role is not only sexual but also maternal as Satters's penetration "into the ladylike aperture between Pulley's coat-sleeve and ribs" turns into a "sense of parturition."

The link between a passive, homosexual crowd and the domination of the matriarchal principle is one of the main allegorical concerns of *The Childermass.* The Bailiff sides with the enemy of Western Man, and in Lewis's terms, that is time. Thus the Bailiff is Cronos, who not only castrated his father Uranus, but also ate his children. Because of this castrating function, the Bailiff is responsible for the slaughter of the innocents or for the "childermass."

Both in *The Art of Being Ruled* and *The Childermass* Lewis ascribes the shamanization of Western society to the French revolution, which saw the downfall of figures of authority. This psycho-historical analysis takes the form of an allegory where Pullman turns into a prosopopoeial dog for the concept of male homosexuality, and where a mythical beast, which has Milton's diabolical "Cerberean mouths" for allegorical pretext, stands for domineering matriarchy. First Pullman exclaims:

> "I consider *the father* a side-show a mere bagatelle—they are like the reason, overrated and not essential at all, that is the fathers—the male at all if it comes to that."
> He laughs, clearing up the atmosphere. Exit Fathers like a cohort of witches, turning tail at sight of the bristling righteous phalanx of incestuous masculine matrons, with hittite profiles, hanging out like hatchets just clear of the chest, Eton-cropped, short stout necks firmly anchored in asthmatic lungs, with single eyeglasses, and ten diamond corking-pins representing the decacerephorous beast of the deliverance. They guard the child-herds. Revolutionary cockades bouquet'd with spatulate figleaves, symbolic of absolute divorce anti-family son-love and purple passion, dissimulate their abdominal nudity. Pulley barks fiercely: he is the gelded herd-dog. He barks at the heels of the Fathers, bearded despotic but now despatched. (*CM*, 92)

Lewis then proceeds to describe the fathers. As in the above passage, the descriptive principle is inversion so that there is a transference of feminine and maternal characteristics to the masculine:

> Enter unobserved at the other extremity of the stage a small select chorus of stealthy matronly papas. They applaud as one man, community-singing the national anthem of the New Babel jazzed. . . . Sweetly hand-washing they stand aside, retiring Big Businessmen. Featuring as their spokesman, a supershopwalker offers meat-pale sunkist fleshings of celanese silk stuffed with chocolates, crossword-puzzles, tombola-tickets for crystal-sets, and free-passes for war-films, to the million-headed herd of tiny tots of all ages but one size. (*CM*, 92)

Through this process of feminization, Lewis provides an explanation for the devaluation of masculine, Western values such as intellectual consciousness for the benefit of the Wild Body and its basking in the unconscious. In *The Art of Being Ruled*, it is clearly stated that homosexuality is part and parcel of the war waged against the intellect, and its four weapons are listed as follows:

> (1) the propaganda *for* sensation; (2) the propaganda *against* the intellect;
> (3) the imitation of the intellect, and of the things of the intellect, by all

that is most deeply committed to pure sensation; and (4) the movement to merge cleverly these opposites and pretend that they are one, forcing what has outstripped the human sensational average to return on its steps and put itself at the service of what it had laboured to transcend. (*ABR*, 245)

The Lewisian equation between the antinomies of male and female on the one hand, and of intellect and sensation on the other, is here to be found in unequivocal terms. Male homosexuality is anathema because it breaks down the bona fide barriers between mind and body that Lewis strives to maintain.

The author presents his views on homosexuality as the result of his study of "the consciousness of homosexuality." Yet one is allowed to wonder how objective this study remains, particularly with regard to the fact that the discussion of the phenomenon recurs with compelling insistence. It is dealt with not only in *The Art of Being Ruled* and *The Childermass,* but also in *The Dithyrambic Spectator* (1931), *Hitler* (1931), and *The Doom of Youth* (1932). The theme also reappears in *The Apes of God* (1930), *Self Condemned* (1954), and the last two volumes of *The Human Age* (1955). From a psychoanalytical and, one might even add, from an allegorical viewpoint, the theme of homosexuality recurs like a demonic obsession.

Characteristically, Lewis displays an ambivalent attitude towards psychoanalysis. In *The Art of Being Ruled* he satirizes the discipline by dubbing it "the highly spiced incestuous pastry of Freud" (63); yet, in the same work, he does not hesitate to apply a Freudian reading to the phenomenon of male sexuality. Betraying a deep interest in the rite of passage from adolescence to adulthood, he writes: "It is natural that at this juncture, faced with the often very unnerving and disagreeable tests which accompany initiation, a certain percentage of boys should shrink from crossing this bridge to *responsibility* and *manhood*. The 'spoilt child' would no doubt much rather stop with its mother" (*ABR,* 302). I suggest that a link exists between Lewis's own difficult rite of passage to manhood and his obsessional concern with homosexuality.

That the author's division between the masculine principle and the feminine might be connected with repressed homosexual desire in himself will no doubt sound preposterous or unacceptable to some. But there are elements in his work that support the following assumption: male homosexuality is perceived as a threat because it represents the son's feminizing identification with the mother, which kept haunting the Lewisian psyche. What I propose is a chiefly speculative and limited attempt to interpret these elements. One assumption underlying this speculative study is expressed by Freud: "What decides whether we describe someone as an invert is not his actual behaviour, but his emotional attitude."[21] I realize that Freudian theory is not beyond questioning, but I believe that a Freudian account remains helpful especially in the case of repressed homosexuality, which, for historical, social, and cultural reasons, Freud was actually faced with. Another assumption is that, although all psychological aspects in a work of art are not necessarily attributable to the artist who created it, the recurrence and persistence of the same type of psychological features can be assumed to indicate a pattern belonging to the artist's own psyche.

To begin with, it should be underlined that there exists no definite theory of male homosexuality. This indeterminacy is best brought out by Kenneth Lewes, whose study remains one of the most comprehensive and perceptive analyses of the different approaches to the question.[22] Concerning his controversial study of Leonardo da Vinci, Freud points out that "the particular process we have singled out is perhaps only one among many, and is perhaps related to only one type of 'homosexuality'."[23] In 1962, Wiedeman could still write that there "is no agreement that a specific libidinal fixation accounts for inversion in the male."[24] For instance, there is no consensus concerning the stage at which homosexual tendencies develop in an individual. Wiedeman argues that sexual identity is acquired during the pre-oedipal phase, within the first three years of childhood. Yet his view is that homosexuality should not be ascribed to a single cause: it "is the result of the total development of the individual."[25] Similarly, for Leon Saul and Aaron Beck, pregenital drives represent only one mode of explanation. On the other hand, there is the psychoanalytical school stressing the exclusive role of the pre-oedipal stage in the development of homosexuality.[26] As far as Lacan is concerned, he makes the mystifying, if predictable, statement on homosexuality: "Male homosexuality, in accordance with the phallic mark that constitutes desire, is constituted on the side of desire, while female homosexuality . . . as observation shows, is orientated on a disappointment that reinforces the side of the demand for love."[27]

There used to be the theoretical question of whether to define homosexuality as sexual perversion or gender modification. This debate led the American Psychoanalytic Association to remove homosexuality from its list of perversions and diseases. Not all agreed with the decision and, although the removal seems sound enough to me, I will nevertheless draw on both camps of the debate because, beyond ideological quarrels, some analyses can be found to be complementary. The scientific community has recently claimed to have discovered a "homosexuality gene" with special link to the mother, which would cut short the debate on perversion or modification. However, even if we assume genetic origin, one has still to deal with the historical, cultural, sociological, and psychological factors that may turn homosexuality into a "problem."

These questions are far from being otiose in the context of Lewis's biography written by Jeffrey Meyers.[28] We know that the separation of his parents when he was eleven was experienced as a shock, and we also know that, in his case, the phase of puberty, which psychoanalysis regards as a reawakening or intensification of the oedipal complex, took place while the father was absent and while the mother took over the task of educating her son. Little is known of Lewis's very early years other than the author's own ambivalent recollections. Either childhood is represented as an American Golden Age, or, as in *Rude Assignment,* the father's martial influence is bitterly resented. Lewis reports that at eight he was a "war-chronicler," creating war stories on paper that he then stitched together. This in part explains why the war theme in Lewis's fiction appears well before World War I, but it also shows that, like money, war is a key word in his conception of relation to the father.

In the general psychoanalytical texts on male homosexuality, three characteristics are recurrently debated. First, there seems to be a general agreement on the preponderant role of the mother. This perhaps lopsided explanation emerged very early both in Freudian and Jungian psychology.[29] Both in 1910 and 1922, Freud elaborated his theory of male homosexuality on the basis of "a very intense erotic attachment to a female person, as a rule [the] mother."[30] The potentially homosexual male child does not identify himself with the father because the latter is simply absent. Freud goes on:

> The child's love for his mother cannot continue to develop consciously any further; it succumbs to repression. The boy represses his love for his mother: he puts himself in her place, identifies himself with her, and takes his own person as a model in whose likeness he chooses the new object of his love. . . . He finds the objects of his love along the path of *narcissism,* as we say.[31]

The decisive factors of both the over-influential mother and the absent or indifferent father are also stressed by Freudian followers such as Wiedeman, Saul and Beck, and Pasche. Socarides summarizes the different emotions involved in the male homosexual's latent attitude towards his mother:

> In the mother-child unity one can discern (i) a wish for and fear of incorporation; (ii) a threatened loss of personal identity and personal

dissolution; (iii) guilt feelings because of a desire to invade the body of the mother; (iv) an intense desire to cling to the mother which later develops into a wish for and fear of incestuous relations with her; (v) intense aggression of a primitive nature toward the mother. (33)[32]

I propose to use these five points as a guideline in my attempt to understand Lewis's relation with the mother figure.

The wish for incorporation into the maternal body appears very often in Lewis's fiction. One of the symbols of this desire is the room that keeps recurring from the early Wild Body short stories to "The Room without a Telephone" (1951) and the "Room" of *Self Condemned*. From a biographical viewpoint, the end of Lewis's stay on the continent coincides with his return in 1908 to England—that is, the mother. It is on his return that Lewis writes *Mrs. Dukes' Million*, a manuscript that indicates a collaboration between mother and son.[33] The fear of incorporation and personal dissolution are expressions of the same problem. To be incorporated is to lose one's distinctness. Lewis's first long narrative blurts out the self-identification with the mother.

Indeed, it is very likely that Royal-Fane's impersonation of Mrs. Dukes is an unconscious creation of the phallic mother, gathering mother and son into one. It is probably no coincidence either that the expression of this primal symbiosis should reduce the son figure to a mask or prosopopoeia:

> Before getting into bed, Mrs. Dukes looked at herself from several different points of view in the glass. It was Mrs Dukes' face, her mask, but not her eyes. . . . A moment afterwards, although her swathing still remained on, it was no longer Mrs Dukes' head on the body. With fair hair cut short, and death-white clean-shaven face stood Ernest Nichols. (*MDM,* 48)

The analogy between this impersonation of the Mother and the "Portrait in Two" in chapter 9 of *Twentieth Century Palette* is remarkable.[34] In the latter chapter Evelyn Parke, the protagonist, is asked to paint the portrait of Alice, the mother of his friend Harry Symes. The day comes when Evelyn "unveils an extraordinary double amalgam based on multiple exchanges (the mother wears her son's tweed, the son wears the mother's tiara, etc.)."[35] Both this portrait and the impersonation Royal/Mrs. Dukes present the same parodic and grotesque unity of the phallic mother. Ahstarte or, in Hebrew, Ashtoreth, is a divinity traceable to the Babylonian goddess Ishtar who personifies both fertility and maternity. In *Enemy of the Stars,* the spectators are presented with the vision of a "black and herculean . . . bearded Ashtarte—

epicene divinity of an iron tribe of spartan habit" (*CPP*, 161). Besides the satirical allegory of shamanized Western Man, the androgynous figure could also be regarded as a particularly striking reappearance of the phallic mother.

The ever-renewed attempt to maintain watertight compartments, the description in the first number of *Blast* (1914, 141) of modern egos locked in promiscuous, siamese relationships, the dividing line between male and female, all these indicate an ideal of personality resisting dissolution and amalgamation. In a very perceptive analysis of the relation between art and life, Parker describes the Lewisian predicament:

> The artist . . . has the choice—a crucial one in Lewis's early writings—between consuming Nature or being consumed. Nor was the choice confined to the sphere of art. Any close contact with Life presented the same alternatives: masterful exploitation or self-immolation to a monstrous Nature. As "Cantleman's Spring-Mate" and "The War-Baby" show, all the hunger of Nature can be found in the female sex.[36]

Does one not detect behind this monstrous, consuming, hungry Nature the overpowering, all-too-loving maternal body? Once the maternal body becomes threatening, then the symbolism of protection becomes one of claustrophobia. "Junior," an unpublished story written in the fifties, dramatizes the dread of the maternal body. Although the title refers to the birth of John Leslie's son, it also refers to Leslie and his relation to the mother-figure. Female friends pay a visit to his wife Perdita and her newborn, and in a surrealistic moment, Leslie's attitude is described: "he heard a woman precipitately approaching. His first instinct was to hide behind the curtains. Instead, he flung himself down on a sofa, his face buried in his hands. At least she should not kiss him!" (*UFP*, 110). The rest of the story relates how Leslie abdicates his paternal position and literally flees from his wife, whose body has become maternal.

In his summary of the homosexual's feelings towards the mother, Socarides mentions "guilt feelings because of a desire to invade the body of the mother." It seems to me that Lewis's texts hardly exhibit any sense of guilt. Jameson argues that in his theory of non-moral satire, Lewis succeeds in repressing guilt for persecuting the victims of his satire.[37] But one could equally argue that the rejection of an ethical viewpoint encourages one to consider satire at a more primitive level. The truth of the unconscious is made to prevail at the expense of ethics. So, instead of guilt, what one sees is an upsurge of two fundamental emotions: disgust and aggressivity, which motivate not only the attitude towards the mother but also Lewis's satire. In "Junior," the expression of disgust is unequivocal and is found in an extraordinary description of the prenatal situation:

> In his imagination, [Leslie] reduced the entire company to foetuses. A small dark wriggling monster. Then he knew that there was a piscine phase of the foetus—and he could visualize them all, at that stage of life; collected in a tank. As a little fish, he could see himself glassily eyeing Perdita. The sharp-sighted are apt to be granted this fundamental vision of the human, in the moments immediately succeeding procreation—the female adoration of the just-born abortion, striking a spark. (*UFP*, 110)

Leslie as fetus eyeing Perdita: this is the son in his relation to the mother. Beneath the comic vision of a collection of fetuses lies the dark brooding of a mind disgusted by flesh. In the process the son has become a monster, Perdita's Caliban. The story is all the more important as it shows the shift from disgust for the mother to a universalization of disgust for humanity:

> [Leslie] had ceased to confine himself to the horrors inseparable from the female state. He . . . considered the whole field of eyes and noses, of nails stuck along the tips of our extremities, of bad smells and nice smells, the clowning of the intellect, its somersaults into religion and into non-religion. Indeed, everything you could think of, male and female, mental and physical, to use the popular dichotomies. (*UFP*, 114)

Lewis's nihilistic sense of the grotesque is fully present in this very condensed statement and could be said to be fueled by the initial disgust for the maternal body. His "violence" originates in the loathing of the body.

Violence against the mother figure is not incompatible with love for the same. Indeed the relationship with the mother is ambivalent as she is both loved and hated: for a loving mother can also be perceived as a castrating one. Pasche interprets the feelings of the overprotected child as follows: "the mother treats her son like a penis that she herself does not possess, either because she could not obtain it from her husband, or because she was not gratified by it. . . . It is not enough to say that he is castrated, he is the organ of replacement of a being which repairs itself at his expense."[38] This psychological situation is transparent in Lewis's relation with his mother. Does he not share his erotic adventures in letters to his mother from continental Europe?[39] The mother is everywhere present and intruding, be it in matters of laundry that Lewis sends from France or in matters of the heart such as the love affair with Frieda from which Mrs. Lewis rescues her son. Although affectionate with his mother, Lewis must have suffered from being the "doll" of this smothering passion.

In response to my argument, one could counter that Lewis's aggressivity is not directed at the mother, but at the father. In his interpretation of "A Soldier of Humour," Lafourcade defends such a thesis.[40] I do not think that this interpretation contradicts mine. As puzzling as it may be, it is quite conceivable that Lewis's aggressivity had both parents as targets, hence perhaps its intensity. The most blatant case of parricidal violence is found in Kreisler. In the first chapter of *Tarr* it is expressly underlined that his tribulations originated in his confrontation with and rebellion against his father. Financially dependent on his father, Kreisler desperately waits for the letter that would solve his problems. On his awakening, the first thing he does is to let his eye search for his father's letter under the door, but only anger can fill the vaccuum left by the absent letter: he "had stared menacingly as he found nothing there" (*Tarr*, 78).

However, violence towards woman is no less conspicuous and consists of beatings, murder, or rape: Brobdingnag beats and almost kills his wife; Beresin batters an African woman; Kreisler rapes Bertha; in *Monstre Gai* women in the Yenery are exterminated; and in *Malign Fiesta* a woman is thrown to goat-men to be raped and eaten alive. But there is also a reverse pattern whereby woman is also the aggressor. This is the case in *Enemy of the Stars*, where Hotshepsot attacks Arghol; in *The Revenge for Love*, where Cruze's attack on Hardcaster is vicariously enjoyed by Gillian; and in *Monstre Gai*, where the chief of the Yenery turns out to be an aggressive, masculine virago.

So woman appears as both victim and aggressor. That this dual role is associated with the mother figure is best exemplified in *Self Condemned*. Commenting on Lewis's stay in Canada during the Second World War, Lafourcade regards the series of watercolors entitled *Creation Myths* as evidence that his experience of Canada was something other than "painful desolation."[41] And yet *Self Condemned*, supposedly drawing on Lewis's Canadian experience, reads like an "immense bad dream," to borrow Kenner's description.[42] Indeed the story is nightmarish because it is concerned with a confrontation with something Lewis carried in the luggage that is his unconscious.

Self Condemned reads like an allegory with two levels of meaning. At the literal level, the novel is the story of René Harding after his decision to relinquish his career as a historian in England and to set sail across the Atlantic to start a new life in a pioneering country. At the figurative level, the novel tells a secret tale of rebirth that can take place only by erasing the past and cutting loose from the motherland. The first part of the novel is partly devoted to depicting the relationship between mother and son: they are "allied in a very special union" (24) and are the two parts of a single whole. René says to his mother: "I am in two halves, one half of which is *you*" (17). Mother and son are in love with each other: "She patted and caressed his hand, and he almost danced in his chair with pleasure, like a big dog that is caressed. He arched his legs in a rampant attitude, his toes beating for a moment a quick tattoo" (*SC*, 24–25). However, this complicity is destroyed by the mother's parting shot: "You are not by any chance *a fool*, my son?" (26). So the mother is both adored and feared. It is this ambivalence that governs René's emotions for the great bulk of the novel.

It is also on the archetypal maternal figure, standing like a huge ominous totem at the beginning of the novel, that the rest of the female cast is based. All the other female characters can be seen as paler, parodic versions of the mother figure. And what is most striking is that almost all of them are subjected to some type of aggression.[43] The symbolism of blindness recurs in the second and third part of the novel, and encourages one to think in oedipal terms: Oedipus kills his father and sleeps with his mother. Hence he loses his sight as a form of punishment. However, in *Self Condemned,* the actual subject of the psychological plot is not parricide but matricide. From Mrs. Harradson through Mrs. McAffie to Hester, it is the maternal body that is the target of aggression.

The novel seems to present two conceptions of love: one is asexual, the other sexual. Helen the sister is supposed to illustrate the former, while Hester is the useful commodity. A paler version of the mother, the sister actually contributes to a phantasy of incest, as when René states to Helen: "You have always been what I love best in the world" (*SC*, 139). The reason why sexual love between Hester and René is reified is that such a means of alienation is necessary to prevent disgust from arising. For love between Hester and René is also incestuous. It is the function of part two to reveal the phantasmic nature of their relation. A sharp contrast is established between the debased sexual relation between Hester and René in the first part of the novel and, in the second part of the novel, Hester's "almost maternal love" for René—as John Holloway puts it.[44] In this respect, the second part is profoundly ironic. René has been divested of his public identity and stranded in the material microcosm of the Blundell Hotel, only to be reunited with the mother figure from whom he fled. Hence the relationship, previously hyper-sexualized, becomes asexual, and the sense of unity reappears: "we are one" says René to Hester (*SC*, 239). This statement contains the seeds of the final tragedy of the last part of the novel, which turns out to be the repetition of the first part as well.

René's allegorical quest for a new land is not crowned by the rebirth of a new self. Or rather, the rebirth is tragic and ironic because one is never born *ex nihilo*. Hence Re-né is self condemned. Just before leaving England, he bids good-bye to Helen, whose symbolic fall anticipates Hester's death. In both cases, what is represented is the mother's death or the ultimate attempt to jettison the overwhelming passion of a loving mother; hence the "Testament of Mothers":

> one's old bitch of a mother was a figure one approached with reverence, because she had given birth to one. . . . though indeed she had only loaned her belly for the pre-natal drama. She is always supposed to be awfully fond of Me because of her having permitted all this to go on in the spare-room she's got down there, for Little Strangers. Often one hears of 'her bowels yearning' for the one-time occupant of the spare-room. The fact of course is that, except for the extent to which she may be influenced by the stream of waffle she had to consume on the subject of her 'love,' she must feel what most landladies do about their lodgers. (*SC*, 142)

Although here one is made to understand that the mother does not feel any natural love for her child, one can also decipher the passage by inverting its message: although the tenant of my mother's spare room, I do not owe her any rent. So in the third part of *Self Condemned* René once more endeavors to set himself free by becoming financially independent. This corresponds to a disenfranchisement from the mother figure, whose function is then to claim her debt. Hester's obsession with a return to England, the motherland, defeats any attempt at disenfranchisement. In this psychological context, Hester's death is the performance of matricide, and this terrible yet necessary act of transgression accounts for the violent, destructive emotions undergone by René.

These oscillate between love and hatred for his deceased wife. The positive memories are those of unity where mother and son, wife and husband are one: "The Hester he saw at present . . . had become as much part of his physical being as if they had been born twins, physically fused—or better, one might say, for physical amalgamation would be unpleasant, identical twins" (*SC*, 376). On the other hand, once dead the mother returns to haunt the son. She becomes the "graffito woman" (gr-affie-to) to which Hester's mangled body is compared. The unity is desacralized. In a double act of accusation, René violently rejects Hester's blackmailing "act of insane coercion" (which makes him the eternal debtor) and the false sentiments of love created by the Mother (*SC*, 391–92). In both cases, René cancels the debt of love: "He now regarded his graffito with the scorn which would be meted out to some unmasked impostor" (SC, 392). The intensity of the latter part of the novel derives from the psychomachia between the graffito as matriarchal principle and a self striving to be reborn, disenfranchised, and masculine. The failure to achieve self-hood is conveyed in the metaphorical description of René's brain: "The constant sense of loneliness ended, in the white silence, as a necessary ingredient of the white silence, which was all that was desired—the negation of the visual. . . . at last consciousness ebbed quietly away, and René lay in a dreamless sleep, alone in this place dedicated to silence, totally removed from life" (SC, 372–73). The white silence finally provides the sought-for relief of tension, releasing René from the dislocating agon between the masculine and the feminine.

A second recurrent characteristic of male homosexuality in psychoanalytical theory and observation is sadism (and its counterpart, masochism), which, according to Saul and Beck, is a castrating drive. This mixture of aggressivity and endurance of pain is certainly not absent from the writing of Lewis, who attended Rugby where, as he reported to Marshall McLuhan, "he was the first Rugby man to receive six beatings by a prefect in one day."[45] In Self Condemned one can also read that the Christian gentlemen from Rugby "would learn to smite people hip and thigh, and to exact an eye for an eye, and a tooth for a tooth. The canes of the prefects, as well as those of the masters, would harden this Christian Gentleman-in-the-making in other ways" (SC, 108). Sadomasochism is already a recurring feature of Lewis's earliest writings such as "Les Saltimbanques" (1909) and "Brobdingnag" (1911). One finds it fully-fledged in "The French Poodle" (1916), "Cantleman's Spring-Mate" (1917), and "The War-Baby" (1918). In Tarr, one can read the telling story of a schoolboy taking masochistic pleasure in having his hand jabbed by a neighbor's penknife: "This boy had seemed to wish to see his hand a mass of wounds and to delect himself with the awful feeling of his own black passion" (Tarr, 125). In addition, Kreisler's hatred is directed at Soltyk three times: the victim is twice hit on the face, and then shot at a seriocomic duel. In Enemy of the Stars, Arghol endures mysterious beatings from a no less mysterious uncle or half-uncle; irrationally, Snooty Baronet shoots Humph both in the mouth and the anus;[46] and Hardcaster is a victim twice in The Revenge for Love: he is first shot in the leg by Alvaro who also enjoys frightening Josepha, and he is sadistically beaten by Jack Cruze, who hammers away at his stump, the latter being an obvious phallic symbol, especially at

O'Hara's party where it protrudes, surrounded by keen female admirers.

Then there is the nightmarish representation of the sexual act as an act of cannibalism. Whether this motif is the expression of sado-masochism or the exorcism of a traumatizing primary scene, it remains the fact that it recurs in Lewis's works with painful obsession. The canine aggression of cannibalism is best seen in the series of *Tyros* that were painted in 1920–21. Characteristically situated between figurative art and abstraction, pictures such as "Self-Portrait as a Tyro" (Compton, pl. 116), represent toothy males figures.

Within a fictional context, Lewis uses the traditional substitution of food for sex. For instance, the relationship between Tarr and Anas-tasya is described in culinary terms, and a long scene of orgy develops before the two are said to spend the night together. The substitution of food for sex is completed when, on the occasion of his first meal of oysters, Tarr is said to kiss Anastasya's "salt wet eating lips" (*Tarr*, 310). In *The Wild Body*, Lewis actually identifies this substitution as the "shuffling ... of the respective appetites" (*CWB*, 62). In this respect, cannibalism in Lewis is based on such a shuffling of the appetites, but with the eating appetite gone wrong.

"Cantleman's Spring-Mate" (1917) can be regarded as an arche-typal text where from a positive act of assimilation, sex switches into an act of cannibalistic aggression. Stationed in a military training-camp in Southern England during World War I, Cantleman makes love to Stella the country girl: he "grinned up towards [the nightin-gale] as he noticed it, and once more turned to the devouring of his mate. He bore down on her as though he wished to mix her body into the soil, and pour his seed into a more methodless matter, the brown phalanges of floury land" (*BB*, 310). From Carl and Mademoi-selle Péronnette's erotic dancing, through the Baronet's devouring of his waspish mate, to Hardcaster's endless mouthering of Gillian's lips the consumption of the sexual partner remains a standard feature of Lewis's representation of sexuality.

His last works do not indicate any final, atoning representation. If anything, the sexual act as an act of cannibalism reaches a degree of paroxysm never expressed before. In *Malign Fiesta*, the last volume of *The Human Age*, it is reported seriocomically that in hell French cooks are spared torture because their skills are in demand among the elite: "Sammael rather frowned on this, as it savoured of indul-gence, and it was better to deny oneself these delicious sauces. *Sauce Hollandaise* to him smelt of sin" (*MF*, 353). The substitution of food for sex is all the more powerful as the elite of Angel City is supposed not to take part in sexual activity. The switch from sex as food assimilation to sex as cannibalism is recorded in the description of Sammael's execution of the female Sinner witnessed by Pullman. The internal "pretext" to the allegorizing description is *The Diabolical Principle*, published twenty-four years earlier, in which Lewis satirizes the Paris-based magazine *transition*. It is particularly striking that his satire of Lautréamont's *Lay of Maldoror* anticipates the description of the execution. I will quote from *The Diabolical Principle* first, then from *Malign Fiesta*:

> wild animals drag naked snow-white virgins across moonlit mountains, tearing their tender flesh upon the jagged rocks and leaving a trail of blood.[47]
>
> [Sammael] flung the door open, getting bitten in the hand by one of the ravening beasts. There burst into the car the fearful stench, there was a scarlet flash of sexual monstrosity, the whining and snorting of a score of faces—the beasts leaping on one another's backs, so that several appeared to be about to spring onto the roof of the car.—Scores of sinewy arms terminating in claws shot into the car, and snatched the woman out of it. . . . She lay there, a raw and bleeding mass—even her face seemed to have been devoured. The arm had been laid bare at the top, and the bone was visible. (*MF*, 372 and 378)

The excerpt on Lautréamont is parodic: Lewis scoffs at the decadent mannerism. By contrast, the fictional excerpt is much more ambiguous, as it also strikes a thematic, obsessive chord: copulation turns once more into an act of anthropophagous aggression. The body and its diabolics is no longer an external object of satire; it has become the destructive Antagonist within the self.

A third recurring characteristic in certain examples of *repressed* male homosexuality is paranoia. The hypothesis of a link between paranoia and homosexuality was put forward by Freud both in 1911 and 1922. Paranoiac symptoms appear once homosexual desire is denied free expression and fulfilment. Paranoia is a means of warding homosexual desire off by creating delusions of persecution. Here is a description of the psychological process:

> The mechanism of symptom-formation in paranoia requires that internal perceptions—feelings—shall be replaced by external perceptions. Consequently the proposition "I hate him" becomes transformed by *projection* into another one: "He *hates* (persecutes) *me*, which will justify me in hating him." And thus the impelling unconscious feeling makes its appearance as though it were the consequence of an external perception: "I do not *love* him—I *hate* him, because HE PERSECUTES ME."[48]

As with any other psychological disorder, there occurs a "detachment of the libido from people—and things—that were previously loved."[49] This libido is not free-floating, it becomes attached to the ego, which in the process becomes larger than life. The end result consists in a regression to the narcissistic stage.

Kreisler, Lewis's first major fictive creature, is gnawed at by paranoia. The text is unequivocal: as he observes Soltyk and Anastasya walking in the street, his "sense of persecution seized him in a frenzy of suspicion" (*Tarr,* 121). A story like "The Man Who Was Unlucky with Women," unpublished but written in the fifties, combines intense feelings of disgust and contempt for woman with a sense of persecution. Richard Dean's relation with his wife is disrupted as she betrays him twice by having love affairs. On the second occasion, his wife's illicit lover is provoked into battle by Dean who, however, is easily defeated by his swifter, more experienced opponent. What is Dean's motivation for fighting with the man? Although he is presented as a jealous and suspicious husband, his fight is obviously not motivated by love for his wife, whose sexual promiscuity and shared "lush red sex-fruit" (*UFP,* 160) he finds repellent. It is as if the woman's unfaithfulness were a pretext for expressing hatred and disgust. On the other hand, the mechanism of transforming the object of love into an object of suspicion could be said to underlie the relation between Dean and the man. If such is the case, then the fight with the lover has no other symbolical function than providing physical contact of an illicit nature.

What reinforces this interpretation is that the rest of the story relates how Dean trains himself as an agile boxer for no other apparent reason than that of emulating his sexual competitor: "[he] would pick a fight whenever there was an opportunity, and knock down a variety of people in all parts of London. He avoided conversation, he did not reproach his victim first, but just weighed in with his spectacular agility" (*UFP,* 167). The externalization of homosexual desire into an opponent appears vividly at the conclusion of the story when Dean is attacked by a fierce dog while fighting with a man: "From a ghastly cavity in Dean's neck the blood poured out, and before very long it was apparent that he was not able to defend himself against this new type of aggression" (*UFP,* 168). The aggressive, life-threatening dog could be seen as symbolizing a repressed desire perceived and endured as a threat to one's masculine ego.

It is uncanny that this story presents similarities with Kate Lechmere's account of her relation with Lewis, brought to an end by her defecting to T. E. Hulme. Like Dean's opponent, Hulme wins Kate Lechmere away from Lewis, who "had an actual fear that he might be supplanted by another at the Rebel centre." Like Dean, Lewis displays a "suspicious and jealous nature." The same contempt for the unfaithful woman and the show of aggressivity towards the competitor are both reported as well. Lechmere explains that "some mornings he would arrive in a very excitable state and rapidly pace up and down the studio calling me a 'bloody bitch'"; and she describes "Lewis rushing down Picadilly and accosting Hulme . . . crying out 'What are you doing to me?'"[50] Both Lechmere and Lewis report that Hulme would have suspended Lewis upside down on the park railing. As Meyers points out,[51] Lewis was a tall man, which makes this feat quite improbable. However, Lewis chose to keep this image in *Blasting and Bombardiering* (36), and what is significant is that its symbolism is one of inversion.

"The Man Who Was Unlucky with Women" is also contemporary with *The Red Priest,* published in 1956, and "Creativity," an unpublished short story edited by Lafourcade in *Blast* 3 (1984). In both texts the same pattern of jealousy and suspicion on behalf of a woman occurs and leads to a physical fight between the protagonist, who is either a husband or a brother, and the sexual rival. Augustine Card is obsessed with boxing and eventually kills a fellow priest. In "Creativity," Simon challenges his sister's fiancé and is eventually killed by a fierce dog.

Meyers's assessment of Lewis's legendary paranoia is inconsistent. Concerning the feud between Lewis and Roger Fry, he rightly remarks that even paranoids have real enemies. Yet he also asserts that "Lewis could not have led . . . a carefully organized and intensely productive existence if he were paranoid and suffered from persecution mania."[52] But, it seems to me, organization and production are not incompatible with manias, they simply belong to different compartments of the same self. At the same time, Meyers is prepared to document Lewis's intense feelings of "suspicion." He reports Lewis's notorious habit of sitting against a wall and his use of the Pall Mall Safe. When Meyers does dwell on the paranoiac displays, he offers four explanations. The first is to relate Lewis's feelings to his feuds with the Bloomsbury circle. The second is to say that the same feelings originated in a postwar trauma.

At first sight, these two reasons seem quite plausible and fair. However, they are defeated by Meyers's own report. In chapter 3 of his biography one reads that Lewis "could be aloof, defensive and hostile"; and in chapter 2, Augustus John is reported to complain about Lewis's "malignity, quarrelsomeness, suspicion." These two chapters deal with the 1902–12 period in Lewis's life, that is to say, before the war and before the Bloomsbury feuds started. In a third explanation,

Meyers suggests that Lewis liked to pose as an artist who had a lot of enemies. However, one can also wonder whether repeated postures of paranoia do not actually function as a symptom as well.

Meyers's fourth explanation consists in the following: "The severe and degrading poverty that he suffered during his entire adult life accounts in large measure for Lewis's suspicious character and hostile behavior after the War."[53] The question of money is very interesting because in Lewis's texts it has a powerful symbolic meaning and function that go beyond the author's financial difficulties to express a psychological type of reality. In *Tarr* this symbolism, already gestating in *Mrs. Dukes' Million,* is initiated in the description of Kreisler's feeling towards woman who for him is a "Pawn-shop, in which you could deposit not your dress suit or garments, but yourself, temporarily, in exchange for the gold of the human heart and any other gold that happened to be knocking about" (*Tarr,* 100). So, an equation between gold and love is established.

As Levenson notes, most of the affective relations in the novel can be conceived of in terms of triangular configurations.[54] For the sake of concision and efficiency, I propose to visualize these configurations and bring out the symbolic function of money:

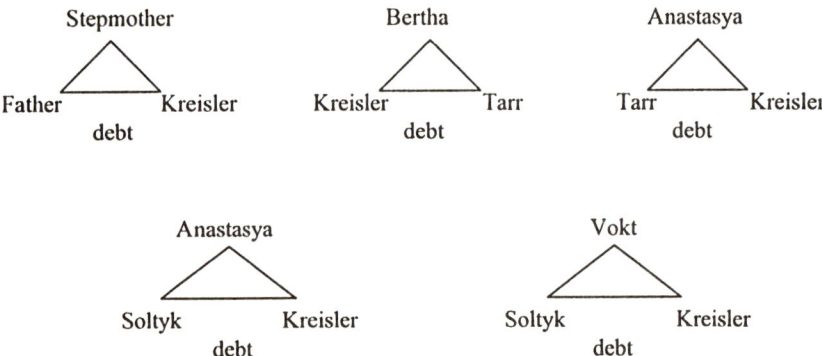

The first triangle is the archetypal trinity of the oedipal complex. The four other triangles are all superimposed on this *ur*-triangle. The stepmother was actually destined to Kreisler the son. However, the father as the rival marries the fiancée. Therefore to love the fiancée amounts to incest, as she has become the mother. At the same time, the father's marriage is resented as an act of robbery. Although the father is the son's creditor, he is fundamentally indebted to the son.[55] The second triangle shows how the shuffling of partners is still underpinned by the same symbolism of debt. Kreisler becomes a parodic version of the father or "a vast Magog of Carnival, an antediluvian puppet of fecundity" (*Tarr*, 93). Although Kreisler seems to be robbing Tarr of Bertha, Tarr is indebted to Kreisler for getting him rid of Bertha. Thus Bertha alias the fiancée alias the mother is spurned twice as she is both discarded by Tarr and raped by Kreisler. The attachment to the mother turns into disgust or aggressivity.

With the third triangle, a new distribution occurred. Tarr becomes the father and robs Kreisler of Anastasya. So Kreisler is once more the frustrated son. Tarr is therefore indebted to Kreisler, as is noted by Jameson.[56] Tarr reimburses his debt to Kreisler by adopting his child and marrying Bertha. Anastasya the fiancée is idealized, although she is also perceived as a natural threat. Tarr and Kreisler alternatively assume the roles of father and son but, while Tarr is either an artistic begetter or competing sibling, Kreisler is consistently portrayed either as a parodic father or incompetent sexual rival. In both cases the father figure is either diminished or derided. As Kreisler's double Tarr *is* the father of Bertha's child. Yet this paternity is rejected and transferred to Kreisler, whereby the father figure is reduced to a puppet of fecundity.

The fourth triangle is another parodic version of the first and represents Kreisler's misinterpretation concerning Soltyk and Anastasya, whom he mistakes for lovers. His logic is that of the pawnshop: an exchange of money occurs between the two as Soltyk is Anastasya's art agent. Paul O'Keeffe argues that Soltyk and Kreisler are doubles.[57] I think that they are more accurately described as sexual rivals. Soltyk is a father figure and a competitor apparently robbing Kreisler of Anastasya. He is therefore indebted to Kreisler. The fifth and last triangle reveals what lies beneath appearances. Soltyk remains a father substitute and rival, and Kreisler the son, while Vokt is the object of desire or fiancée substitute. Although it is tempting to see Vokt as a father substitute,[58] he does not fit the pattern because Kreisler has *free* access to his "purse"—that is, until Soltyk robs him of Vokt. So while the four other triangles are based on a heterosexual mode of relationship, the fifth is a homosexual trinity. This is confirmed by Kreisler's explicit homosexual desire for Soltyk at the duel, as noted by O'Keeffe.[59]

Through Vokt and Soltyk, it is the heart of the mother that is at stake. This is implied by the statement that after Kreisler's death, the father is paying the bills left by his son. For, ultimately, it is the father who is indebted to the son from whom he stole the mother. Kreisler is finally victorious on the threshold of death in his prison cell, the maternal symbolism of which is conspicuous. The "*liebhaberei*" (*Tarr*,

292) of the cell, Kreisler dies with a "numbing and nondescript feeling" for his (step)mother. Kreisler finally encounters peaceful unity with the maternal body though death, and therefore the dividing line between male and female created by Tarr is surreptitiously transgressed.

The pattern of repressed homosexual desire in Lewis's texts is therefore not lacking. His obsession with the homosexual question becomes an oblique expression of an obscure, anxious desire. Such a psychoanalytical explanation would then shed light on the function of the allegorical line dividing the masculine from the feminine as a means of preventing any identification with the female Wild Body. The danger of any sexual ambiguity is avoided by removing the masculine identity from the sexual level to the intellectual or nonphysical. However, at this stage one can cast doubt on such a theory. Indeed, was not Lewis's fear of persecution fostered by external events? As is shown by Meyers's biography, Lewis *was* the toy of people's resentment or manipulation. Why should one attribute the sadomasochism of his characters to his own psyche? And finally, why should Lewis's deep attachment to his mother, which is unquestionable, necessarily imply homosexuality?

With the latter question one reverts to point (iv) of Socarides' description of the homosexual attitude towards the mother: "an intense desire to cling to the mother which later develops into a wish and fear of incestuous relations with her." This desire is one of the basic components of the oedipal complex and is not unique to the homosexual experience. Otto Rank sees faithfulness to the mother as the cornerstone of the Don Juan legend:

> the characteristic Don Juan fantasy of conquering countless women . . .
> is ultimately based on the unattainability of the mother and the compensatory substitute for her. . . . [The fantasy] involves the deeply-rooted biological wish for the exclusive . . . possession of the mother, as once experienced in the pleasure of the prenatal situation and forever afterward sought as the highest libidinal satisfaction.[60]

There is an undeniable Don Juanesque characteristic to Lewis's multiple feminine conquests. But how is one to interpret these conquests? Is this an endless, forever frustrated search for the mother, or should one see in them a self-perpetuating attempt to bolster a fragile masculine self-image? Otto Rank himself indicates the potential homosexual tendency of the Don Juan figure on account of this attachment to the mother.

If, indeed, the work of art neither confirms nor denied truth of an empirical nature, then the questions posed above will never receive satisfactory answers. The critical challenge is to resist the temptation to treat texts as cognitive propositions concerning the author's psyche. As interpreter, the critic of Lewis's text has no option but to "produce more text," to recall Peter Brooks's argument, and to keep weaving the semantic web out of his/her textual speculation. If "confirmation" of my hypothesis concerning Lewis's representation of repressed homosexuality is to be sought for, it is by discovering further patterns of meaning in seemingly neutral texts such as *America, I Presume* (1940).

The work is typically Lewisian in that it stands midway on the frontier between essay and fiction. On the one hand, it is concerned with a sociocultural examination of North America; on the other, it deals with a secret journey back to one's origins. Chapter 16 is at the heart of such psychological preoccupation, as it relates an "accident [that] took place mostly in the bowels of the earth."[61] This accident affects the life of an ostentatiously masculine protagonist, Major Corcoran, who is invited by the Warden to visit "Brunswick Hall" at a major university.

In his biography Meyers identifies Brunswick Hall as Hart House, the Men's Union of the University of Toronto, and the Warden as Burgon Bickersteth. Meyers summarizes an accepted interpretation of this episode of *America, I Presume:* "Lewis noted that the Warden used to spend all his summers with the Hitler *Jugend;* and suggested that he took an unnatural, not to say homosexual, interest in the naked athletes who disported themselves under his benign authority."[62] The most obvious statement in chapter 16 supporting such a reading is: "I realized that [Brandleboyes] had seen the same things that I had seen, in spite of his official detachment. I began to understand why he was a little mad" (*AIP,* 243). This is Corcoran commenting on the Warden. One should avoid the trap of regarding Corcoran as a reliable narrator because, in fact and perhaps unwittingly, chapter 16 reveals that Corcoran, who has seen the same things as the Warden, is a "litle mad" as well.

The irrational, uncanny aspect of the visit becomes evident when the two characters go to a little chapel enhanced by a system of electrical lights. As the Warden toys with the system, the light goes out and, moving in darkness, the two men collide. With his elbow, the Warden hits the Major's forehead: "I rubbed with my forefinger the bump immediately above my eyeglasses. It might have been my eye" (*AIP,* 239). It could be argued that the scene functions as a dramatization of Lewis's increasing ocular problems that eventually led to his blindness. But this reference to the eye has voyeurism for its counterpart.

Guided by the Virgilesque Warden, the Major proceeds through the different levels of a chthonic, Dantesque universe. Chapter 16 is actually concerned with a descent into hell and with a fascinated exploration of the Wild Body: "The passages were cellarish; large and hot. A dull thumping came from behind the door" (*AIP*, 239). The lower the two men go, the hotter the atmosphere grows. The object of the Major's voyeurist expedition is the Wild Body. The first group he watches (without being watched) consists of six "lumpy youths . . . in milling pairs, slogging each other with six ounce gloves" (*AIP*, 239). Next is "a blaze of athletic flesh; I found beneath me two pairs of dazzlingly naked young gentlemen, with the bulging breasts with birdsnests in the middle, and bulbous calves . . . and bright red shoulders . . . that heaved and undulated in the arc-lit court" (*AIP*, 240). The Major is secretly bewitched. Here he is in a phantasmic, sadomasochistic mood: "one was compelled to think of swords plunged into those heaving shining bodies: of those eyes rolled up in death, as vanquished they sank upon the sand of the circus. How much better than bulls! (my mind ran on): a boy bleeding to death in the arena" (*AIP*, 241). How can one ascertain that the Major himself does not fall prey to the delirium of the dithyrambic spectator? On the contrary, everything seems to point at the lack of control. As he watches naked young men swimming, he reports: "My head was swimming. I wiped my forehead and my bump above the eyeglass began to throb" (*AIP*, 242). Is not this aquatic scene, with which the Major entirely empathizes, suggestive of the homosexual yearning for primal, maternal unity through narcissistic love in a body of waters and in the depths of warm yet oppressive matter?

Grabbing at the Platonic branch, the Major hastens to lift himself out of this miasma: "I yawned. The reality was disappointing. I had been looking at shadows upon the walls of a cave" (*AIP*, 244). The world of the Wild Body does not constitute reality; instead, reality is the product of the intellect, it is fundamentally Socratic. However, this Socratic reality is stubbornly elusive in this chapter of *America, I Presume*. Although he is supposed to have seen through the "American Idea," the Major does not escape from the cave of matter easily. The dream framework of the allegorical narrative becomes accentuated, and the Major's return to the surface of things takes on an even more surrealistic aspect. He and the Warden encounter two policemen whose authenticity is uncertain. As the Warden opens a door, the Major is dealt a blow in the chest, and his emergence out of the depths of the building into open space reads like a violent birth as he gasps "like a deep sea fish flung up by a marine earthquake upon dryland" (*AIP*, 251). The return to common reality does not correspond to the triumph of consciousness.

No longer a psychopomp, the Warden, who has been identified as a homosexual, acts now as a persecutor compelling the Major to visit an endless series of rooms, and driving him to the verge of breakdown: "'*Stop* here!' I almost screamed. And I went off into a spasm of insane laughter, which at once changed into a fit of coughing, as laughter often will with a chain-smoker" (*AIP*, 253). This orgasmic fit of laughter provides a momentary release of tension, and the Major falls asleep in a bedroom looking like a ship's cabin. In this primal, maternal vessel, the Major experiences a peaceful state of repose or "glorious coma" (*AIP*, 254).

At some point during his visit, Corcoran offers the following analysis: "It was not just hot dogs and hamburgers, skyscrapers and G.Men. Walt Whitman was more fundamental to America than they were. I had, in this machine of a country, got down to the *Leaves of Grass*" (*AIP*, 242). Whitman is repeatedly referred to by Lewis. He is discussed in *The Art of Being Ruled* and *Paleface*. Above all, Lewis parodies two poems by Whitman in a short story, "The Yachting Cap," published the same year as *America, I Presume*. The two poems are "Facing West from California's Shores" and "Out of the Rolling Ocean the Crowd."[63] Lewis's hero is a vagrant whose name is Kipe. He is described as a simpleton, displaying childish enthusiasm for the waves of the ocean. Lewis's parody of Whitman's celebration of nature and communion with the maternal ocean is based on a commentary from *Paleface*:

> Walt showed all those enthusiastic expansive habits that we associate with the Baby. He rolled about naked in the Atlantic surf, uttering "barbaric yawps" . . . in an ecstasy of primitive exhibitionism. . . . A freudian analyst specializing in inversion or perversion would have said . . . that he was certainly the victim of a psychical "fixation," which incessantly referred him back to the periods of earliest childhood.[64]

So Kipe is depicted as a child or big baby wrapped in "a cocoon of rags" (*UFP*, 147), grovelling on the sand, and playing with a cap in the waves. Kipe is the symbolic child wearing his father's cap and diving into the maternal body of the ocean. Naturally, this communion is given short shrift as a big wave strikes him down. While "The Yachting Cap" is an allegorical exegesis of homosexuality, chapter 16 of *America, I Presume* is an equally allegorical enactment of homosexual attraction: at the end of his visit Corcoran signs the visitor's book with the name of Walt Whitman.

What has all this got to do with Lewis? A lot, I think. The psychological link between the Major and the author is indirect, and I will try to bring it out. The Major's signature acknowledges the homosexual or, in Lewisian terms, the feminine side of his psyche. His other half is his wife Agatha, in an oblique reference to Agatha Christie. What is most important is that Agatha functions as the Major's alter ego. This is alluded to comically when the Major attributes the best parts of his narrative to his wife's cooperation. Furthermore, a brief analysis of Agatha's portrait allows one to argue that Corcoran's alter ego or other half is closely related to an aspect of Lewis's own biography which finds expression through a series of surrogates and displacements. Here is her portrait:

> Agatha's father was an American, who had not a drop of English blood, but who would water at the eye if you showed him a watercolor of Kent. He took the little Agatha to Great Britain when she was six. She became a young Englishwoman, went to Roedean, and pushed herself into the front rank of detective story writers by the age of twenty-nine. (*AIP*, 52)

It is fairly easy to transcribe this story back into its original, biographical idiom: Lewis's move to the Isle of Wight with his family, his years at Rugby, and his emergence as an avant-gardist (by the age of thirty-two). Corcoran goes on:

> But her father returned to America, having divorced her mother in routine American style. For he was a routine American in his aggressive sex-life. He paid for Agatha's schooling. . . .
> Agatha had the good taste to prefer England as a place of residence, but she remained an American at heart—half aborigine, half Roman. The American relations soon ceased to correspond. American divorce is like death. Then there is the "unplumbed, salt, estranging sea." A week of ocean travel plus divorce, with its recriminations, rapidly turned into a stranger the little girl who had been left to grow up in England, while her big swaggering he-man poppa went rolling back to Nineveh, N.Y. with a new Mrs Morgan, and settled in Philadelphia where he died. (*AIP*, 52–53)

This passage reads like a self-analysis and a review of major past events: the parents' divorce, the decision to stay in England, and the father's remarriage and death. What also stands out is the endurance of a painful trauma for which a ruthless father is made responsible. Lewis's account of Agatha's life is actually autobiographical. She is both the abandoned, yearning child in Lewis and the creative self in the Major. Her psychological function is to bring out the Lewisian repressed self-identification with the "feminine" principle that, in Corcoran, leads to the manifestation of latent homosexual desire. Corcoran, Agatha, Whitman: this metonymic chain of identification is potentially endless and is at the core of the Lewisian conception of the self.

The last great work to dramatize the problem of male self-identification is *The Human Age* (1955), which adds two more sequels to *The Childermass*. What makes *The Human Age* a Kafkaesque work is the allegorical dimension of its narrative that implies, among other things, that the depiction of physical torture is not to be taken literally. Or rather, the physical is at one remove, the product of a mental, phantasmic hell. Milton's *Paradise Lost* provides an allegorical pretext to Lewis's last major work. In particular, the lines "The mind is its own place, and in it self / Can make a Heav'n of Hell, a Hell of Heav'n"[65] are relevant to *The Human Age,* the place and action of which are symbolic of a state of mind. This allegorical level is suggested by Hachilah, whose narrative function is to point at the "pretext" and dream framework of Lewis's allegory. While showing the Punishment Cells to Pullman, Hachilah states: "it must be remembered that we are in a symbolical, as it were—not a real world. These people, these Sinners, have their being, to some extent, in something like a painted existence. The tortures, like those of the figures in the Inferno of Dante, are of nightmarish kind—it is as if they dreamed" (*MF,* 410). The Bailiff's mother, the Punishments Cells, and Hachilah himself constitute the allegorical paraphernalia necessary to the narrative, nothing more. The inferno of *Malign Fiesta* is outlandish because it originates in the Wild Body from which the Lewisian self is alienated. The Bailiff's mother is another example of the castrating figure and an archetypal representation of the old hag. Her house is described as "the towering antechamber to the domesticity of an ogress" (*MF,* 330), in which Pullman experiences anxiety and claustrauphobia. Sadomasochism also finds almost too obvious expression, especially in the case of the "Sodomite" on display in the Punishment Cells. In *Monstre Gai,* Pullman feels persecuted by Sentoryen and his homosexual proposal. Homosexuality is referred to as "riding the Centaur," and the name of Sentoryen is obviously an amalgamation of Centaur and yen, the latter term designating woman who in the narrative lives in the "Yenery." The centaur belongs to a deep-seated, personal mythology as witnesses *The Centauress,* which Lewis painted twice in 1912 (Michel, pl. 5 and 6). Finally Pullman shares Corcoran's voyeurism as he explores the homosexual red-light district.

In his endeavor to create a Human Age, Sammael the puritanical Devil encourages procreation among the angels. However, creation in Sammael's new age is parodic as the transition from the angelic state to the human is sexually ambivalent. As the Devil and his fiancée kiss, the following reaction is triggered: "The cheers were hysterical. There were men and women at the side of the car, locked in burning embraces. Pullman saw many angels embracing one another—either from want of a woman or homosexually, Pullman did not know" (*MF*, 515). Thus genesis coincides with a sense of confused reality and ambiguous gender identity.

The temptation is strong to see a direct link between Lewis's sense of ontological spuriousness and the spuriousness of his masculine figures. Neither Sammael nor Pullman are emasculated; instead, their masculinity amounts to simulacrum and disguise. Parading with his fiancée, Sammael acts "very 'gay cavalierish,' waving his right hand, laughing with the utmost grace, bending down devotedly,—an elegant comedy, in short" (*MF*, 530). The whole of *The Human Age* presents either homosexuality as *the* mode of sexuality, or heterosexuality as an act of pretence and violence. The masculine hero turns out to be a poseur, while his procreative capability is indirectly questioned. Sentoryen mischievously asks why Pullman's offspring on earth never looked like their father. Although described as a "masterful creature" and a "man of heroic cast" before his visit to the homosexual sex shops, Pullman is nevertheless a "puppet of fecundity," to use the terms applied to Kreisler. It therefore befits him to organize the carnivalesque, malign fiesta to celebrate the Devil's betrothal, which turns into a black mass of the Wild Body. In Lewis carnival not only expresses the grotesque omnipresence of the body, but also the paradoxical spuriousness of the self. Because of this simultaneously bombastic and euphemistic nature of the self, Lewis's ontological vision oscillates between a reality replete with visual information and a reality of false bottoms.

The psychomachia between the masculine and the feminine therefore begets three conceptions of the self. One is androgynous and is represented by Major Corcoran's feminine alter ego. Another is phallocentric and finds full expression in the heroes of Lewis's allegorical politics, which I discuss in chapters 9 and 10. Yet another is the mask, represented by Pullman and Sammael, but also Snooty Baronet or Vincent Penhale. In Lewis simulacrum partly yet significantly derives from the psychological imperative to treat identity as an exercise in camouflage and illusionism. Psychological androgyny, phallocentrism, and simulacrum—these are the three poles of Lewis's implicit discourse on sexual anarchy. The relevance of gender identification in Lewis's reflexion on self and creativity I will endeavour to bring out in the second half of the next chapter, which ushers in an analysis of the author's philosophy of art.

Part Two
Aesthetics

5

A Genealogy of Impersonality

As INDICATED IN CHAPTER 1 OF MY STUDY, LEWIS'S OUTLOOK partly derives from a philosophical tradition that claims the experience of the objective world as a main constituent in our dealing with "reality." This belief in the objective existence of things is not specific to Lewis. Philosophical movements such American pragmatism, represented by Peirce, William James, and Dewey took empirical reality as the basis for their theoretical elaboration. From a British viewpoint, histories of philosophy tell us that the turn of the century saw a rebellion against what was conceived as Hegelian idealism, notably in the texts of Bertrand Russell and G. E. Moore. To our jaded philosophical palate, Moore's "A Defence of Common Sense" (1923) may seem archaic and naïve. And yet in its claim for the unquestionable existence of the empirical world regardless of logical and causal connection with mental facts, the article certainly indicates a tremendous interest in reformulating the tradition of empiricism.

The modernists took part in this task of reformulation. Although their positions on the issue were not identical and did not result in a clearly definable school of thought, their attempt to establish the existence of *some* object in *some* terms is ubiquitous. The introductory chapter to *Modernism* by Malcolm Bradbury and James McFarlane constitutes the consecration of a theory of modernism that ignored the modernist search for the object by emphatically defining the modernist work of art as an autotelic, self-referential, autarcic, or self-contained entity. For instance, the two critics claim that modernism is associated with "the coming of a new era of high aesthetic self-consciousness and non-representationalism, in which art turns from realism and humanistic representation towards style, technique, and spatial form in pursuit of a deeper penetration of life." They further maintain that modernism "tends to have to do with the intersection of an apocalyptic and modern time, and a timeless and transcendent symbol or a node of pure linguistic energy." It is curious and worth underlining that such a view has been sustained by not only different but also antithetic schools of criticism: the same view prevails from Irving Howe who freed poetry of "the dross of matter and time" to Terry Eagleton for whom the modernist work betrays its fetishism by parading as an "autonomous, self-regarding, impenetrable . . . arte-fact, in all its isolated splendour."[1] For Eagleton the price for this anti-commodifying strategy is its isolation from political forces that might transform the capitalist status quo.

However, these theories of modernist self-reflexivity do not take into account a modernist aesthetic of the object recorded by different modernist authors in critical essays, but also implicit in fictional and poetical contexts. A great deal of modernist aesthetic has as its premise a relation of intentionality between subject and object, which means that the artwork, be it writing or painting, is underpinned by an aesthetic of openness to the world out there. Undoubtedly Lewis's statements on art belong to this modernist tradition, and a steadfast search for the object can be observed throughout his career from *Blast,* where abstraction is declared not to be able to escape from representation, to *The Writer and the Absolute,* the premises of which are "the paralysis induced by the unreal—our nature's rootedness in *fact.*"[2]

One of the best examples of the modernist aesthetic of the object is found in the famous theory of impersonality usually associated with T. S. Eliot's 1917 essay "Tradition and the Individual Talent." The fact that this theory and its variants constitute a process of dematerialization of writing is only half of the story. At the core of this theory lies the belief that by means of the dematerialization of the self, the object would be laid bare. Matter is to be negated for matter to be reborn, pure and objective.

However, the claim that modernists were engaged in the search for the object does not obliterate the other claim that they were simulta-neously interested in the reality of mental facts regardless of logical and causal connection with the empirical world—to revert Moore's formula. The point of my argument is not to prove the theory of modernist autotelicism wrong. Rather, it is to bring the "self-referential" aspect of modernism in dynamic relation with its empiri-cal aspect. In typically self-contradictory fashion, modernism both suscribed to and counteracted the tradition of empiricism. Signs of anti-empirical, Nietzschean perspectivism in modernism can be traced back to discourses such as dandyism, which emphasize the illusionis-tic, artificial character of art. In the second half of this chapter I will use Jessica Feldman's study of dandyism, *Gender on the Divide,*[3] as a theoretical framework to analyze the modernist discourse on dandyism, which stands in contradiction to the objectivist theory of impersonality.

Rather than churn out yet another study of impersonality, I propose to establish a genealogy of the concept that displays similarities with the postmodernist notion of the death of the author. Thus a certain type of continuity between the two periods exists, although it does not prevail. While both currents of thought extol impersonality, their purposes for doing so diverge. For modernism the author will be impersonal so that the object is revealed by language; for postmodernism the author dies so that, already free of the object, the signifier can finally jettison the subject. This discrepancy is noteworthy not only for the sake of the genealogy of impersonality, but also for the canonization of modernism to which postmodernist theory has eminently and sometimes ominously contributed. Indeed, on account of its over-semiotization of art, text, and culture, postmodernist theory has systematically ignored or misrepresented the modernist aesthetic of the object.

Wyndham Lewis's and T. S. Eliot's ideas on impersonality are usually viewed as radically antithetic. On Eliot's 1917 belief in the "progress of an artist [as] a continual self-sacrifice, a continual extinction of personality,"[4] Lewis remarks that art "can be used . . . as a perfectly good litmus paper for many an acid test, without involving a pretentious 'depersonalization' of the artist . . . the 'artist' remains just Mr. This or Mr. That—and we observe that he is a seething mass of highly *personal* fine-feelings."[5] This rebuttal, written in 1934, contains key words and key concepts that will keep recurring in the history of twentieth-century criticism. These are the reference to the comparable function of art and science, the identity of the artist or "name," and the question of pathos and internal self. Lewis's opposition to the idea of impersonality is invaluable, not because he sustained it, but because it introduced a sense of contradiction and ambiguity in the debate. His defence of personality stems from his materialist vision of life. In 1927, he maintained that it is "actually as impossible (as it is undesirable) for an artist to be 'impersonal' as it is for a 'tree' to be neither an oak, nor a birch, nor a pine, nor any known tree, but the abstraction 'tree.' . . . Artistic creation is always a shut-off—and that is to say a *personal*—creation."[6] While Eliot creates a division between the man who suffers and the man who creates, Lewis depicts Shakespeare as a man who suffered *and* created. His tragic characters are "much more mirrors held up to his tired and baffled mind than they were the mirrors of any nature that he objectively could know" (*LF*, 160). Lewis's rereading of Shakespeare derives from the twentieth-century conception of the self: the artist is characterized by multiplicity and heterogeneity, and his characters are in search of *one* hypothetical author.

However, what is equally significant in Lewis is the desire to cut off the self from material origins and to achieve the state of the not-self which he equates with pure intellect. This credo drives him to self-contradiction. In "'Detachment' and the Fictionist," published the same year as *Men without Art* (1934), he argues that "the handling of the material of art or of science—of *fact*, in other words—does 'detach' a man from his personality (composed as the latter is of race, class, period and the rest)" (*CHCC*, 227). Thus Eliot's conception of literary history as "simultaneous order" and Lewis's self-detached fictionist require the bracketing of the historical, political, and national self. Some kind of ideational or transcendental self hovers above the miasma of life: anywhere out of the world! But then, in a spirit of reversal typical of modernist aesthetics, in 1937 Eliot gave a further twist to the debate. In his review of *The Lion and the Fox* he declares that the "detached observer, by the way, is likely to be anything but a dispassionate observer; he probably suffers more acutely than the various apostles of immediate action. . . . The future of the detached observer does not seem to me very bright. Perhaps it never was."[7]

Eliot's and Lewis's reflexions on the author betray the same restlessness concerning the self. Their modernist rejection of subjectivity coincides with a flight from self towards "object" which can be observed in other writers. In 1934 Pound made the object a condition for knowledge and meaning: "A general statement is valuable only in REFERENCE to the known objects or facts."[8] The same quest is expressed by Bergson whose influence on modernism can be traced down to Pound's definition of the ideogramic method in *Guide to Kulchur*. Bergson wrote: "Were . . . detachment complete, did the soul no longer cleave to action by any of its perceptions, it would be the soul of an artist such as the world has never yet seen. . . . It would perceive all things in their native purity: the forms, colours, sounds of the physical world as well as the subtlest movements of the inner life."[9] Clearly the issue of impersonality is only the tip of a huge philosophical iceberg. Ultimately the question of reality and its origin is at stake. Bergson's description of the world as perceived by the artist gives birth to an apprehension of reality in all its purity and directness. Attending this search for objective reality were all the predictable snares of falsehood and solipsism. Thus the debate on Berkeleyism was revived in the pages of *The Egoist:* the object becomes spurious because it has its origins in the self. Hence the modernist paradox according to which the threat of solipsism begets the truth of the object. For Hulme the perception of object by subject is achieved by means of poetry as "a visual concrete [language] . . . [which] always endeavours . . . to make you continuously see a physical thing, to prevent you gliding through an abstract process."[10] Wallace Stevens's "The Snow Man" (1923) can be read as an illustration of Hulme's prescriptive formula. The emotional self is annihilated to make room for the expression of perceptual reality or what is. In 1929 Eliot defines the subject according to the object, as in the following: "Andrewes's emotion is purely contemplative . . . his emotion is wholly contained in and explained by its object."[11]

The modernist striving towards objectivity also combines with the frequent use of scientific metaphors and comparisons. It is significant that in 1910 T. Sturge Moore stood for the Flaubertian cause of impersonal art and proposed the following parallel: "The object of science is to determine the conditions that play the part of immediate causes in respect to phenomena. Art discovers those conditions in respect to certain highly pleasurable emotions and sensations."[12] Three years later, in *The Egoist,* Pound substituted an assertion for the parallel: "The arts, literature, poesy, are a science, just as chemistry is a science. The subject is man, mankind and the individual."[13] Not only does Eliot describe the creative process in chemical terms, he also coins a new formula: objective correlative. Naturally, knowledge always involves processes of objectification, but here the objectifying process of art acquires a programmatic ring. Indeed, from Pound's poetry as science to Italo Calvino's author as "writing machine," the program remains the same. It is an arresting thought that the art and creativity of the twentieth century should be simultaneously marked by Freudian exploration of psychical depths and by artistic fascination with prisms, surfaces, and windowpanes (of the Orwellian make).

That we are indeed dealing with a program and not merely figures of speech is worth underlining. In the decade when "The Waste Land," *Ulysses,* and *The Wild Body* were published, I. A. Richards turned criticism into a scientific activity. This is made possible because he first cancels the distinction between art and life: "When we look at a picture, or read a poem, or listen to music, we are not doing something quite unlike what we are doing on our way to the Gallery or when we dressed in the morning."[14] A poem becomes another object of experience and can therefore be submitted to scientific description and analysis. Hence the mental event involved in dressing in the morning or in looking at a picture consists in a stimulus and ends in an act. It is defined as an "impulse." The good is redefined as the satisfaction of "appetencies," while criticism "is the endeavour to discriminate between experiences and to evaluate them."[15] As for the self, it is defined as "a system of interests."[16] To describe psychological processes, Richards systematically resorts to objective correlatives. The reader is invited to visualize memory as "a solid with a large number of facets upon any one of which it can rest."[17] Or the mind is compared to a system of magnetic needles stimulated by powerful magnets and constantly readjusting themselves. And of course the distinction between scientific, verifiable statements and poetic pseudo-statements implicitly applies to Richards's own critical practice.

What in these modernist claims begins to hatch is the postmodernist full-fledged Copernican decentering of the humanist self. Both endeavors have as background Nietzsche's obituary on the death of God. However, while Eliot's artist was born out of the historical matrix of literature, Barthes's scriptor was "born simultaneously with the text. . . . there is no other time than that of enunciation and every text is externally written *here and now*." Thus Barthes furthers the modernist dematerialization of the historical self, and this allows him to foreground text and signifier as "objects" of analysis: it "is language which speaks, not the author," Barthes writes in 1968, "to write is, through a prerequisite impersonality (not at all to be confused with the castrating objectivity of the realist novelist), to reach that point where only language acts, 'performs', and not 'me'." The hot-air balloon of Anglo-Saxon modernist self-referentiality never entirely takes off because more often than not it is weighed down by a material belief in the object. However, once the object has been been spirited away and with it its referring agent, then the author can finally expire. Barthes's poetics of impersonality is whitewashed of any sign of chaotic humanity. The "scriptor no longer bears within him passions, humours, feelings, impressions, but rather this immense dictionary from which he draws a writing that can know no halt."[18]

By 1967 Derrida had seen through the logocentric traps of structuralism. Commenting on the French structuralist critic Jean Rousset, Derrida brings out the structuralist privileging of a general, mathematical, spatial theory over the study of an individual given work or over the monography of an author.[19] Here my intention is not to develop an analysis of structuralism along the lines of the Derridean infinite play of signifiers accumulating supplemental meaning by substituting for the absent centre a chain of signs without transcendental signifed. Rather, "reading over the shoulder" of Derrida can be a means of understanding the continuities and discontinuities between modernist impersonality and postmodernist impersonality. In particular, the Derridean critique of structuralism is an efficient means of analyzing the desubjectification that underlies the death of the author.

Lewis, Eliot, Richards, and Barthes all contributed to what in 1925 José Ortega y Gasset dubbed the "dehumanization of art." Ortega's statements on twentieth-century art display all the characteristics mentioned above. Poetry is described as "the higher algebra of metaphors," and Mallarmé, to whom Barthes also refers, is perceived as a precursor of ghostwriting. His verse is said to muffle "all vital resonance" and to present the reader with "extra-mundane" figures. Ortega then asks: "what business has the poor face of the man who officiates as poet? None but to disappear, to vanish and to become a pure nameless voice breathing into the air the words—those true protagonists of the lyrical pursuit. This pure and nameless voice, the mere acoustic carrier of the verse, is the voice of the poet who has learned to extricate himself from the surrounding man."[20] Such a statement and its specific terminology are symptomatic of a thinking destined to prevail in the latter half of the twentieth century. Does not Ortega share his dream of dehumanization and its tropes with Foucault who in 1969 imagined that after the death of the author all "discourses, whatever their status, form, value, and whatever the treatment to which they will be subjected, would then develop in the anonymity of a murmur."[21] Foucault also views writing as a process of depersonalization, and the skeleton in the cupboard makes another appearance: "the mark of the writer is reduced to nothing more than the singularity of his absence; he must assume the role of the dead man in the game of writing."[22] The prescription of writing as a posthumous activity suggests a new definition of criticism: repeated acts of necrophilia. All the concepts I have just analyzed reappear in Blanchot's *The Space of Literature* (1955). In order to reach the rarefied, anonymous space of literature where only the endless, Beckettian murmur of language persists, the writer has to "die": "The writer . . . is one who writes in order to be able to die, and he is one whose power to write comes from an anticipated relation with death."[23] Death of the self is both the condition for writing and its purpose. There is little doubt that Blanchot influenced Barthes and Foucault. However, and although preceding both, Blanchot turns out to be the most extreme of all three. Situated beyond mathematical objectivity and turning a blind eye on the world of things, language in Blanchot aspires to pure, self-reflexive autonomy.

With his rejection of a hermeneutic definition of writing, with his emphatic pragmatism and thought of the "outside," Foucault meets modernist objectivism more than halfway. However, his determination to give primacy to the field of enunciations as opposed to that of matter indicates a discontinuity worth underlining. In Foucault the enunciable and the visible stand side by side in watertight compartments: there is no connection between words and things. The linguistic experiments of *Enemy of the Stars* (1914), Dada, and *Finnegans Wake,* or the stylistic compositions of Gertrude Stein and Raymond Queneau, all these show that the Saussurean principle of convention was not the privilege of theory. At the same time, the exigencies of the self kept prodding this world of enunciations. In this respect, D. H. Lawrence should not be seen as the writer who missed the experimental train. His vision of depths stands in the shadow of the modernist linguistic experiments. While in *The Order of Things* (1966) Foucault maintains that the chasm between "the being of man" and the "being of language" cannot be "erased," James Joyce chooses to express Stephen Dedalus's first sexual experience by means of a specific comparison: "[Her lips] pressed upon his brain as upon his lips as though they were the vehicle of a vague speech."[24] This prefigures *Ulysses* with Molly's linguistic flux and Bloom reading the newspaper while defecating. Foucault shares with Robbe-Grillet a world of surfaces, planes, and serialization. During an interview with Paul Rabinow,[25] Foucault expressly rejects polemics as an intolerable means of approaching ideas. He characterizes polemics as a language of gesticulation, and reports discarding polemical books after a glance at the first page. This reads like an act of censorship against an idiom considered tainted. His utopic theoretical discourse would therefore exclude Lewisian satire, the language of the gesticulating Wild Body. In Lewis the experiment with language does not proceed smoothly. The visible intrudes upon the enunciable and shatters the dream of an autarcic world of signs.

Preceding the modernist objectivist approach to language stands the Aristotelian linguistic circuit according to which the identity of the author is determined by the relation between words and that to which they refer. In his *Poetics* Aristotle ruminates over the fact that both a poet and a scientist versified their material and that no distinction was made between the two: "and yet Homer and Empedocles have nothing in common but the metre, so that it would be right to call the one poet, the other physicist rather than poet."[26] What determines Aristotle's process of identification is the object of discourse.

The earlier part of the twentieth century saw the development of a post-Aristotelian genealogy of impersonality that culminated with the postmodernist death of the author based on a paradox: the modernist drive towards objectification has resulted in the postmodernist disappearance of the object. The death of the object derives from the death of the emotional, impure self. A disembodied self has no access to things. T. E. Hulme alluded to this when he wrote: "All poetry is an affair of the body—that is, to be real it must affect the body."[27]

With Barthes and Foucault, subject and object have been eclipsed, and one is left with a discourse that rules as a self-referential, supra-historical system (Barthes), and in constant flux (Foucault). Up to his *History of Sexuality,* Foucault insisted on studying cultural documents at the expense of the great texts of philosophy: he draws on the anonymous murmur of the past centuries in order to analyze what made possible a mode of thinking particular to a period. Foucault's archeology is thus a systematic and methodological endeavor at deper-sonalization. The hegemony of "discourse" derives from the chasm between the "being of language" and the "being of man," and fore-closes any Aristotelian exploration of the relation between language, subject, and object. What remains puzzling is that, although Foucault asserts the existence of this chasm, he nevertheless refers to such things as "events" or "facts." Derrida leveled the same type of criticism at the whole structuralist enterprise. In the context of his reading of Lévi-Strauss's anthropology, he argues that, although structuralism presents itself as the critique of empiricism, it nevertheless resorts to empirical writing based on empirical proof.[28] In this respect, Fou-cault's thought can be visualized as a chiaroscuro world with subject and object lost in the penumbra, while light flows from signs as from neons in the night.

In fact the structuralist inconsistency concerning the referential function of language and its relation to the world of things points to another difficulty. In 1961 Foucault published his major study *Mad-ness and Civilization,* in which he sets himself the task of writing the history of "madness itself." This formula is what catches the attention of Derrida, who argues that by definition writing a history of madness is to expel it into rational objectivity. Madness cannot be told and cannot tell itself. Repeating Foucault's own words, Derrida states: "'Madness is the absence of *oeuvre.*'"[29] Since writing is on the rational side of the looking-glass, a text cannot be told from the original site of madness or the irrational. We have here the ultimate paradox of this genealogy of impersonality that in its final stage consists in not only eliminating subject and object, but also in doing away with language and writing, which thwart access to some pre-logocentric origin from which the "author" would be exiled.

Furthermore, Foucault's ideal of a vast, anonymous murmur jeop-ardizes the feminist call for a recognition of gender difference. The death of the author might spell the death of gender for the sake of an asexual, homogeneous, nameless discourse—unless, of course, one wishes to regard all questions of gender in merely linguistic terms. The fact that postmodernist theory of the signifier does not "speak" to all is strikingly illustrated by works such Marcia Ian's *Remembering the Phallic Mother.* In the occidental postmodernist retreat into the signifier, Ian sees the fetishistic cult of the phallus, substituting a totalizing signifier for the lack of the signified, that is to say, substituting "representation for that which it represents."[30] That a male bias also impoverished the modernist reflexion on impersonality is ironically brought out by Stevens's "The Snow Man." At a time when feminism has gained theoretical recognition, the use of "himself" in the penultimate line of the poem stands out, and so does the title. These words give an unintentional twist to the quest for impersonality. Although dead or thawing, the author remains gendered.

The self reappears in a modernist theory silently competing with the theory of impersonality, and often manifesting itself as a practice. Indeed it is worth noticing that modernists holding theories of impersonality were also distinguished dandies: Eliot, Joyce, and Pound all embodied this combination. This dandyism is not just an atavism of nineteenth-century Beau Brummellism. As Jessica Feldman has shown in *Gender on the Divide,* it constitutes a double discourse on gender from a male viewpoint and on the creative principle. It is also striking that dandyism is a modernist phenomenon: there is no dandy in postmodernist theory, and this for a very good reason. The dandy is the product of social conventions that establish a forceful division between the genders. Modernism both belonged to and destabilized this context by means of the figure of the dandy. Postmodernism has no need for the dandy because the gender question has been reformulated by two cultural movements: feminism and gay culture.

While the theory of impersonality sustains the search for the object, dandyism fosters the Nietzschean, perpectivist, interpretive approach. From Baudelaire's essay on makeup (1859) to Stencil's "eight impersonations" in Pynchon's *V.* (1963), masquerade and artifice remain central to the nature of modern art. Dandyism is the element that pulls away from the objective world and that cuts free from history and materiality. As Feldman puts it, "artificial, polished surface—cultural arrangments—[the dandy] announces as primary, as constitutive of self. I am what I choose to appear to be."[31] This in a nutshell is the philosophy on which the character Tarr is based. The anagram making up his name indicates that the artist is born simultaneously with art: Tarr = art. Tarr actually proclaims that the artist's first act of creation is to create himself.

Feldman regards the successful dandies as writers "'on the divide' . . . who manage to escape, by the energies of genius, the prison of dichotomous gender." However, other elements in her theory lead one to infer that the dandy's discourse is also characterized by a sense of unresolved tension rather than "escape." In particular, she argues that "military in bearing and discipline, the dandy is also fragile and whimsical as a butterfly."[32] I emphasize this aspect of Feldman's theory because it functions perfectly within Lewis's dualism, which, as was shown in chapter 4, coincides with gender division. It is within the context of her analysis of nineteenth-century French artist Barbey d'Aurevilly that Feldman brings out the self-contradictory nature of dandyism. Barbey made contradiction a principle of creativity: "Just as his life as a dandy contradicted his life as an artist, he would contradict himself deliberately and fundamentally. . . . When Barbey's contradiction and antithesis reached a heightened pitch of energy, they would become paradox."[33] This principle of self-contradiction surges in Lewis's *Code of a Herdsman* with the often quoted injunction: "Contradict yourself. In order to live, you must remain broken up."[34]

This principle of contradiction as principle of creativity also characterizes Lewis's very discourse on gender and creativity. For instance, he regards Shakespeare as a "feminine genius . . . [who was] receptive; he was the type almost, of 'the artist' . . . he was the *ideal spectator*, we could say. But he was not, in consequence, without personality: the spectator in question was very much moved" (*LF,* 149). In *Snooty Baronet* (1932), the same view is held. Reluctantly the Baronet acknowledges that "woman has a monopoly of those rudiments of expansive emotion which constitute the beginnings of art" (38). Yet two years later, in *Men without Art* (1934), the description of Henry James "as a creative artist [who] was led into the field of his predilection, which was a twilit feminine universe—of little direct action, and of no gross substance at all" (123) sounds hardly complimentary. It actually endorses Tarr's conception of the female artist as "*parvenu*" (*Tarr,* 215). However, in *The Hitler Cult* (1939), Lewis reverts to an androgynous conception of the creative principle as he argues that the "genus 'artist' is volatile, nervous, prone to emotional excesses. With that other type-form, the 'feminine,' the artist has much in common."[35]

Such an oscillation may have strictly philosophical origins: the definition of the creative principle in feminine terms functions at the expense of the equally important search for the object. But it may also have more personal, psychological causes: the definition of the creative principle in feminine terms represents the threat of destabilizing sexual anarchy, since in Lewis the feminine and the homosexual are equated. The powerful link between gender as principle of creation and gender as principle of creativity emerges in an autobiographical sketch Lewis wrote: "My mother's and father's principal way of spending their time at the period of my birth was the same as mine is now: my mother painting pictures of the farmhouse where we lived, my father writing books inside it."[36] In *Mrs. Dukes' Million*, Lewis's novel of origins, a process of allegorization is already at work whereby Royal and Fane, who impersonate Mrs. Dukes, are archetypal figures of Lewis's dual genius. In chapter 2, "The Portrait," Royal is introduced as painter, while in chapter 11 Fane is referred to as a romantic poet. In the last chapter of the novel, Fane is said to be "still a poet, only now instead of being a poet in prose, he was a poet in paint. This is after all no more a dislocation of terms than the other" (*MDM*, 365). Art seems to be defined as a point of conjunction of antinomies such as father and mother, masculine and feminine, and writing and painting.

The play with gender identity is recorded in some of the photographs taken of the author. I am thinking in particular of the two portraits of Lewis as soldier and as avant-gardist that are reproduced in *Blasting and Bombardiering*. The irony is that the softness of expression occurs in the military context, whereas the hard look characterizes the avant-gardist's portrait. And then, there is the hat. In Lewis's iconography of self-portraits, that hat has a code of its own. Although hats are usually associated with masculinity and phallic representation, the Lewisian pictorial hat is ambivalent. It is either the pointed, aggressive hat of *Mr. Wyndham Lewis as a Tyro* (1920–21; Michel, pl. 74); or the bell-shaped, soft-rimmed hat of *Self-Portrait with Hat* (1930; Michel, pl. 99). Although Lewis is reported to have encouraged his vorticist colleagues to wear non-bohemian, plain suits, the hat seems to have survived the injunction and can be read as a remnant of the discourse on gender implicit in dandyism.

The play with the hat is no coincidence either, for it belongs to the sartorial topos of dandyism underlined in Feldman's theory. *Tarr* displays a sartorial code from Tarr's self-designed coat and Anastasya's bespangled, extraordinary costume to Butcher's Oxford tweed, Bertha's flesh-revealing gown and, most importantly, Kreisler's *frac*. The object of mad obsession, the *frac* takes on allegorical dimensions. The fact that Kreisler cannot recover his *frac* from the pawnshop to join Fraulein Lipmann's bohemian party indicates his failure to lift himself out of nature and create himself.

The factor undermining the dandy philosophy is of course sexuality, instinct, whatever determines the self materially. This is the reason why dandyism is a discourse on gender. This is also the reason why woman, sex, and death are major preoccupations of *Tarr*. Kreisler is like the grain of sand grinding a smooth mechanism to a halt. His accidental murder of Soltyk and his rape of Bertha point at a body rebellious to dandyist self-creation. Tarr's philosophy of the "lonely phallus" (*Tarr*, 20) stems directly from the dandy's discourse. For the dandy, Feldman writes, "physical love is vulgar and ugly. Erotic victory disgusts him, because it means losing a vital, composed isolation. If the dandy is cold and pure, why not 'mate' him with his own kind: a statue. The statue will not metamorphose into life, because the dandy's impertubability freezes all movement."[37] It is therefore no coincidence that when Tarr discovers Anastasya waiting for him in his studio, she should be described as a white statue bathing in the moonlight. Anastasya was partly conceived as the objet d'art of Mallarmé's aesthetics. The name of the character derives from a line in Mallarmé's "Prose" (1884): *"Elle dit le mot: Anastase! né pour d'éternels parchemins."*[38] When Tarr declares that art "is identical with the idea of permanence" and that "soft, quivering and quick flesh is as far from art as it is possible for an object to be" (*Tarr*, 312), his position is fundamentally Mallarmean. Lewis may also have been influenced by Théophile Gautier's *Mademoiselle de Maupin*. Feldman offers a summary of its conclusion which is strikingly similar to the conclusion of *Tarr*: "After dividing a night of love between Rosette and d'Albert, she leaves forever, preventing erotic victory from degenerating into the futility of repetition, the vulgarity of satiety."[39] The function of the Kreisler-Bertha or Sorbet-Bertha alliances is to underline the inescapability of repetition and vulgarity.

The dandy therefore represents the possibility of subverting the material determinism of the self. In the context of Lewis's corpus, the dandy is the anti-figure of the self as defined in "The Meaning of the Wild Body." The shift is from "a thing behaving as a person" to "a person behaving as x." In other words, dandyism turns the dehumanizing prosopopoeia of "The Meaning of the Wild Body" into the creative mask of an aesthetic of impersonation. In this respect, dandyism and the modernist mask of Richard Ellmann's description coincide.[40] It is no coincidence that Pound's *Mauberley* and *Mrs. Dukes' Million*, whose illusionism has been demonstrated by Hugh Kenner, should have been written in the wake of Oscar Wilde's theoretical texts that combine dandyism and mask. Impersonation can be observed as a constant principle of creativity in Lewis's career. Even in *Self Condemned*, mostly bogged down in matter, the dandy's itch for illusion and masquerade persists. Harding is reported to be "delighted to swim through space with the air of a Louis the Eleventh, bearing himself as a King of France hurrying to meet the Emperor Maximilian" (*SC*, 48). Thus one can see a definite continuity in the Lewisian conception of characters as impersonators and of narrative as bombastic rhetoric. By the same token, this conception of illusionism enters into competition with the theory of impersonality, which has the truth of the object for telos.

6

From Realism to Modernism

I︎T HAS LONG BEEN THE PRACTICE TO DEFINE MODERNISM BY SET-
ting it against the tradition of realism. This practice has been encouraged by the modernist aesthetic discourse exemplified by Virginia
Woolf's "Mr. Bennett and Mrs. Brown" (1923), whose target is Ed-
wardian realism and its alleged lack of interest in the particular. From
a critical, contemporary standpoint, one still reads that modernism
made a clean cut with realism. For instance, Levenson argues that by
1914 Hulme, Ford, Pound, and Lewis had reached a point of abstraction without "realistic correspondence and realistic responsibility."[1]
In the first part of my study, I demonstrated the presence of realism
in Lewis's fiction at the generic level. Here I intend to show that a
realist aesthetic played a major role in the formulation of an important
branch of modernism. Realism was not only a means of representation against which to rebel, but also a philosophy of art that, once
transformed, was found useful or even valid. Naturally the aesthetic
of modernism does not simply reproduce that of realism, and it is
interesting to analyze the transformation by focusing on three elements: experience, satire, and language. Out of this analysis, one
should be able to create a genealogy of modernism based on a dialectical relationship with realism.

Realism and modernism share an aesthetic of the present. Realism
evolved out of an historical approach best illustrated by Walter Scott's
historical novels. It has been said that Balzac's works are pivotal in
that they switch from the chronicle of the past to the history of
the present. The continuous relevance of the present in realism and
modernism as well as the avant-garde is manifested by the catchword
"now" used by artists as different as Pound, Lewis, Cravan, Marinetti,
and Apollinaire. Both modernism and realism anchor their practice
of art in time, and this is especially shown by their interest in experimentation that makes change, process, and trial factors of creativity.
From the standpoint of the subject of perception, the emphasis on
the temporal parameters of experience results in a sense of fragmented

reality both in realism and modernism. Already in 1869, the Goncourt brothers created *Madame Gervaisais* in which, in Colette Becker's words, they "analyze reality into a dust of details, juxtapose anecdotes and *tableaux;* the work is based on scattered fragments capriciously assembled according to aesthetic pleasure and memories kept by the two traveling writers."[2] The hinge between this realist aesthetic of perception and modernism is imagism, with Pound's definition of image as "that which presents an intellectual and emotional complex in an instant of time."[3] The aesthetic of the fragment was to be pursued by Pound, for whom, as underlined by Herbert Schneidau,[4] the fragment or "luminous detail" had an aura.

The fragmentation of reality is latent in Zola's 1865 definition of a work of art as *"un coin de la création vu à travers un tempérament."*[5] Both references to a *"coin"* and *"tempérament"* emphasize the particular as opposed to the universal. What prevents Zola's naturalist reality from being shattered into smithereens is his belief in the existence of a single, common reality lending itself to the whim of perceivers but persisting beneath the interpretive shapes of art. The world is "the same for everybody, sending to all one and the same image."[6] By the time modernism is in full swing, the equation has been reversed: "Reality," Lewis wrote in *Blast,* "is in the artist, the image only in life" (135). In his preparatory notes for *Cinders,* T. E. Hulme underlined that *"only in the fact of consciousness is there a unity in the world."*[7]

This shift in emphasis was enough to tip the scales and create a new context for a redefinition of art and the artist. To locate "reality" in the artist amounts to a Nietzschean, perspectivist view on art and reality. However, if one looks again at the first theoretical formulations of realism, one finds that perspectivism is already at the core of the debate. The main proponent for this aesthetic was Champfleury, who in 1850 coined the term "realism." In 1854 he emphasized that the "reproduction of nature by man will be neither *reproduction* nor *imitation,* but always *interpretation.*"[8] Despite the naturalists' attempt to preserve a scientific, objective ethos, the recognition of the interpretive factor persisted and eventually was responsible for the demise of naturalism.

It is in transitional figures like Huysmans and Maupassant that the shift towards perspectivism can be best observed. In a preface to his *Pierre et Jean* (1888) Maupassant heralds a great deal of the aesthetic to dominate the first half of twentieth-century Western literature. "Our different eyes, ears, senses of smell and taste," he writes, "create as many truths as there are men on earth. And our minds which receive instructions from these organs, diversely impressed, understand, analyze and judge as if each one of us belonged to another race." What makes Maupassant's description a modern if not modernist statement is the typical tension between the individuality of perceptual truth and the notion of objective reality. He goes on to elaborate an aesthetic principle that partly remains faithful to the tenet of mimesis and partly opens the door to the most eccentric experiments of the twentieth century. Here is Maupassant: "Thus each one of us merely creates for himself an illusion of the world. . . . And the writer has no other mission than reproduce faithfully this illusion with all the artistic devices that he has learned and which he can use."[9] Such a position leads either to an art of the solipsistic monad, or to an aesthetic of perspectivism and pluralism. In his 1846 Salon, Baudelaire already argued that absolute and eternal beauty was "but skimmed off the surface of sundry beauties,"[10] thereby reinforcing a general movement toward pluralizing a concept traditionally treated monologically if not monotheistically.

In this dialectic between realism and modernism, Baudelaire turns out to play a revealing role. He has the curious privilege of being hailed both as a romantic and as a modern poet of urban culture. The co-presence of "Correspondances" and the Parisian poems not only illustrates the Janus-like character of Baudelaire, but also brings out the complexity of modernism's historical roots. For the twin problem of empirical reality and reality as a construct within the context of artistic creativity is not specific either to modernism or to naturalism. It is in fact the major issue attending the birth of romanticism. Both the search for the object and the self-reflexive interrogation on the creative process are at the core of Wordsworth's poetry. The poem is not only a locus for the self to establish itself through contact with nature, it is also a means of elaborating a poetic.

Naturally my point is not to equate romanticism with modernism. The critical act of discriminating between the two remains necessary and almost obvious simply because "Tintern Abbey" does not read like "The Waste Land." But again, rather than presenting literary theory in terms of breaks, it seems more profitable to stress the sense of dialectical evolution. There is a sea of difference between Wordsworth's search for the sublime and the irony of "The Love Song of J. Alfred Prufrock." But there is no chasm between Wordsworth's demotic and energizing description of St. Bartholomew Fair in *The Prelude* and the early twentieth-century vision of modern urban culture. What eventually prevents the romantic discovery of perspectivism from collapsing into solipsism is the metaphysical and religious beliefs that provide poets such as Blake, Wordsworth, and Coleridge the "one and the same image" of reality that Zola was so keen on retaining.

If one has to identify a point of clear breakaway from realism, it is in the modernist tendency to evolve some kind of dualism in order to transcend material experience. Again, it is not enough to say that modernism is an escapist art, gloating at itself in self-reflexive texts. A great many modernist texts rest on an aesthetic of frustrated dualism. Against the background of realist materialism, dualism is a *pis aller* that makes a special niche for culture and art, but which cannot make the transcendental leap unless, as in Eliot's case, it declares itself spiritual or religious. In *Blast* 2 (1915), Lewis already laid down his dualistic aesthetics: "Art is not active; it cuts away and isolates. It takes men as it finds them, a particular material, and works at it. It gets the best out of it, and it is the best that it isolates. The worst is still there too, to keep the man in touch with the World, and freer because of the separation" (70). Dualism is the only thing left when the philosopher can no longer afford transcendentalism. In fact, it can be argued that the powerful trend of formalism in criticism is an attempt—systematic or not—to let a transcendentalism of some sort slip in by the back door. This can be observed in Worringer's definition of art which, although supposed to unite abstraction and empathy, nevertheless rests on a theory of purism. For Worringer, abstraction as practiced by primitive tribes aims at purifying the object "of all its dependence upon life, i.e., of everything about it that was arbitrary, to render it necessary and irrefragable, to approximate it to its *absolute* value."[11]

What sets Lewis apart in this general modernist transcendental hankering is both his intense aspiration to an ideal of non-materialism and his tragic failure or stubborn refusal to give in to transcendentalism. Like his contemporaries, such as Bell and Fry, he subscribed to the ideal of form from *Blast* 2 (1915), where it is the "added personal logic of Art that gives the grouping significance" (46), to the posthumously published short story "Creativity," where "rightness" is the means of distinguishing between creation and creativity.[12] However, Lewis's formalism does not do away with phenomena. Although the author presents his postwar production as the attempt to flesh out the abstractions of the vorticist years, one has to underline that in his prewar aesthetic statements, he already adhered to a dialectic of abstraction and materialism. In the second number of *Blast* (1915) it is clearly stated: "We must contantly strive to ENRICH abstraction till it is almost plain life, or rather to get deeply enough immersed in material life to experience the shaping power amongst its vibrations, and to accentuate and perpetuate these" (40). Goading the experiments in abstraction is an intense interest in things that Lewis inherited from his training at the Slade, whose philosophy was heavily influenced by realism. W. C. Wees quotes from Forge's history of the art school: "Nothing could replace the precious individuality of the 'thing there'; it was from the artist's study of the natural world that all expression was to devolve."[13]

A perfect continuity exists from *Blast* and "The Foxes' Case" (1925), through *Men without Art* (1934), to *The Writer and the Absolute* (1952) and *The Demon of Progress in the Arts* (1954), which all aim at defending the concrete and the sensuous in art. In the last volume of *The Human Age* (1955) Pullman reflects on Satters's peony, which is about to be stepped on by a giant angel: "It seemed to him miraculously beautiful. It came from the Far-East of the Earth. There physical beauty was understood. The European believed he had evolved spiritual beauty of a high order—but did the spiritual product ever come up to this physical perfection?" (*MF*, 560). The same admiration for natural beauty is revealed in "The Kasbahs of the Atlas," an article written in 1933 on his return from a trip to North Africa. Lewis was struck by the architecture he encountered: "With its tower of mud-concrete [the Kasbah] is a puissant organization, and it owes its organization so much to the earth in which it is set that it has the air almost of some colossal vegetation, sprouting in this element of rock or mud."[14] This fascination for the physical sets Lewis apart from the Hulme of *Speculations*, where he conceives of geometric art as "something absolutely distinct from the messiness, the confusion, and the accidental details of existing things."[15] By contrast, Lewis regards the "act of creation" as an "act of the human will ... the complete existence and exercise of this will entail much human imperfection, which will be incorporated in the book or picture, giving it the nervousness of its contours, and the rich odours, the sanguine or pallid appearance, which recommends it to us" (*LOA*, 209).

The presence of the will in the act of creation reintroduces the empirical and the temporal factors in the definition of art. These two factors are no longer objects of realist, scientific analysis; they constitute art. Among British modernists, D. H. Lawrence is the writer who strove to remain as faithful as possible to the single-mindedly empirical definition of art. For him, beauty is "an *experience*, nothing else. It is not a fixed pattern or an arrangement of features. It is something *felt*, a glow or a communicated sense of fineness."[16]

It seems characteristic of artists and thinkers who sought for a middle position between art as transcending the existential mess (Hulme) and art as pure experience (Lawrence) to follow a Schopenhauerian path. It is curious to see two writers like Lewis and Walter Benjamin, at first sight completely antithetical, develop an aesthetic discourse with an important common point. In his "Essay on the

Objective of Plastic Art in Our Time" (1922), Lewis quotes Schopen-hauer directly: art "pauses at this particular thing: the course of time stops: the relations vanish for it: only the essential, the idea, is its object" (*LOA*, 208). The Schopenhauerian notion of the "essential" or the "idea" cannot be applied wholesale to the modernist context. In particular, Lewis alters and adapts the definition to describe the function of modern abstraction:

> The object, in Schopenhauer's words: 'Plucked out of the stream,' also is plucked so far as will enable it to breathe and live. . . . the 'plucking' consists just in *abstracting* it. When it has been abstracted it is not quite what it was in the stream. It is always a *different* thing . . . when conveyed to us as an object of contemplation. And yet, it is that particular thing, still, that it was in the stream. (*LOA*, 212)

In his *Understanding Brecht,* Benjamin drew on the same philosophical source to define epic theatre:

> The damming of the stream of real life, the moment when its flow comes to a standstill, makes itself felt as reflux: this reflux is astonishment. The dialectic at a standstill is its real object. . . . Epic theatre makes life spurt up high from the bed of time and, for an instant, hover irridescent in empty space. Then it puts it back to bed.[17]

Whether life is plucked out of the stream or spurts up high from the bed of time, the Schopenhauerian trope of the stilling of the flux remains the same.

In both cases, the function of art is to lift the object out of the context of experience without the total annihilation of this context. So what is transcended is the object with which art is concerned; but this does not make transcendence an aim in itself. Instead (and in both cases), a dialectic of some sort is maintained between art as a functional, even teleological, activity and the transcending of the object. The third element of this dialectic is the reader, or viewer, or listener for whom the act of abstraction opens new vistas. Benjamin's and Lewis's formulas represent a fine equilibrium between experience and distance. In Lewis's case this compromise is not lasting, and is actually reached in a text that also proposes an antithetical, pessimisti-cally immanent conception of art whose implications for his works and the still vibrant debate on the relation between art and life will be discussed in the next chapter.

Wyndham Lewis's art of satire is perhaps among the best examples of the dialectical, conflictual relation between realism and modernism.

Like realism, Lewisian satire is an art of the present and the material. It has the body for chief object of attention. The fact that the notion of satire as self-referential art is inconceivable may explain why Lewis remained excluded from "modernism" as long as it was defined as symbolism or pure textuality. Satire is an art of transitivity and always requires or at the very least implies an object of reference. At the same time, Lewis's satire belongs to the twentieth-century context of the bankruptcy of values and beliefs that divests the body of ideological wrappings. As Northrop Frye puts it, satire forces its objects of criticism to join "bodily democracy."[18] Lewis's satire belongs to the age that also witnessed the creation of *The Demoiselles d'Avignon,* the over-inflated puppets of Stanley Spencer, the punched faces of Francis Bacon, the dessicated silhouettes of Giacometti, and the pot-bellied, contorted females of de Kooning—to name just a few. A great part of twentieth-century art is strewn with the bare bones of humanity.

Satire as an art of indecorum and physiological curiosity can already be seen at work in Manet's *Olympia,* which, as has often been pointed out, represents a break with conventional codes for representing the nude. The terminology used by Lewis to define his art of satire almost completely overlaps with the realistic aesthetics of the object. Colette Becker indicates that the realists and naturalists were great readers of works on the physiology and pathology of the mind and the body. She quotes from Claretie who, as critic of *Germinie Lacerteux* in 1865, stated: "The science of the moment . . . is physiology."[19] The same medical trope reappears in *The Mysterious Mr. Bull* (1938), where Lewis uses two revealing metaphors: "The greatest satirists," he writes, "have always been masters of the physical in all its departments: they are mechanics rather than metaphysicians. Where the pills and plasters of the physician cease to be effective, the surgeon steps in with his knife."[20] In addition to the background of realism, Lewis's conception of satire merges with the empirical tradition of satire, which, as shown by Marie Claire Randolph in 1941, from early Celtic civilization to the Renaissance had either the destruction or cure of the body for purpose.[21]

But as an art of immanence, satire as practiced by Lewis leads back to the question of materialistic determinism, from which dualism is the only means of escape. This is the reason why Lewis conceives of satire along the lines of his mind-body dualism while borrowing from realism to buttress his satirical ethos. Thus, in *Satire and Fiction* satire is claimed to be "nothing else but *the truth,* in fact that of Natural science. That objective, non-emotional truth of the scientific intelligence sometimes takes on the exuberant sensuous quality of creative art."[22] This attempt to preserve the scientific ethos of the satirist

constitutes the weakest point of Lewis's theory of satire, as it is an-
chored in the credo of objective, monological reality. This scientific
ethos allows for a division between subject and object that the Lewisian dichotomy of satirist/satirized captures. On the one hand, there
is scientific intelligence, on the other, there are the "*machines, governed
by routine*" (*SF*, 45). Four years later, in *Men without Art,* the same
scientific ethos reappears, although the general context of satire is a
theory of meaning. Said to be "upon the side of the ascetic," it "will,
by illustrating the discoveries of science, demonstrate the futility and
absurdity of human life" (*MWA*, 183).

   It can also be suggested that, paradoxically, Lewis's conception of
satire as a nihilistic enterprise derives from the realist tradition. With
its encyclopedic taste for the accurate detail, realism is underscored
by an aspiration to totality. Lewis's satire aspires to the same sense
of totality when, in *Satire and Fiction,* its object is defined in ontological terms: it is "with man, and not with manners, that what we have
agreed to describe as 'satire' is called upon to deal" (50). What makes
his satire so devastating is not its sting—satire always stings—but its
inclusiveness. Lewisian satire "calls the whole human race to account,"
to borrow Italo Calvino's general comments on the genre.[23] While
realistic comprehensiveness is pursued in order to "mean" reality,
the comprehensiveness of Lewisian satire indicates the exhaustion of
meaning in a world totally folded in matter and flesh: the "'sentient
world' is dross, it is ugly dross, as well; contorted throughout its
length and breadth by the foolish grimaces into which the vulgar
soul within the flesh churns it up, in yahoo laughter, or creases it,
with a sly grin or simper" (*MWA*, 185). At the same time, with the
demise of Zolaesque naturalism, satire has lost the mimetic background of social reality. This implies that the universality of satirical
truth that Lewis invokes is jeopardized at best by perspectivism, at
worst by solipsism. Through the detour of satire we have ended up
in the cul-de-sac of narrative unreliability or indeterminacy. This leads
Peter Petro to state that "modern satire relies almost exclusively on
irony."[24] Lewis's satire is therefore this highly ambiguous construct
oscillating between authoritative comprehensiveness and idiosyncratic
tempérament.

   What prevents his satire from drifting into solipsism is partly his
clinging to the naturalistic ethos of objective reality. In *Men without
Art* he does refer to satire as an "'expressionist' universe" created by
"the intense and even painful sense of the absurd" (232). Grotesque
expressionism is conspicuous in *Tyro Madonna* (1921; Michel, pl. 76),
where the innards of the figures are represented, or in *The Revenge for
Love,* where Margot's perceptual experience of the Spanish dwarf or

the National Guard with his Prussian-blue chin take on oneiric dimensions. However, the overall contexts of the picture or the novel are not expressionistic. A tension develops between the expressionistic subjective experience and the line or the narrative voice, which creates the sense of distorted perception. This tension is responsible for the juxtaposition of two types of terminology that often characterizes Lewis's satirical descriptions of the perceptual field. An example can be taken from *The Apes of God:*

> [The guests'] voices produced a booming volume of sound. Most began by tuning-up the complicated round or sphenoid wind-instrument they had brought with them, that is their respective headpieces—in which the air trumpeted and vibrated in the darkness. But the tumult increased. At length each guest (with the help of his sinuses and with a possible auxiliary trumpet in the laryngeal pouch, and the neatly-ranged teeth) got really started. Soon all were working their bellows forcibly. . . . Eagerly they thrust their heads forward, and launched their verbal symbolizations upon the puffs of deoxydized air, in the direction of their neighbours. These responded—broke across, out-trumpeted their opposites. (*AOG,* 272)

The tension between the scientific ethos and perceptual subjectivity is conveyed by a physiological paradigm on the one hand, and by a vivid, concrete paradigm on the other. Thus "sphenoid," "sinuses," "laryngeal," clash with "headpieces," "bellows," "puffs," or "out-trumpeted."

At the same time, the violence he attributes to the origin of laughter is a clear signal that one has shifted from a scientific, naturalist ethos to a modernist. Although Lewis made the point of presenting his satire as an art of surface and hard outlines, his most important definition of comedy implicitly and quite subtly interprets a psychological mechanism. The definition reads as follows:

> Violence is of the essence of *laughter* (as distinguished of course from smiling wit): it is merely the inversion or failure of *force.* . . . It must be extremely primitive in origin, though of course its function in civilized life is to keep the primitive at bay. But it hoists the primitive with its own explosive. It is a realistic firework, reminiscent of war. (*CWB,* 101)

Laughter as violence or as failure of force is an insightful description of what Ernst Kris later described as the "half-measures characteristic of the comic."[25] Laughter functions as a typical mechanism detonating the destructive drive with its own explosive. Lewis's satire, one has to underline, is an act of self-destruction first and foremost.[26] Characteristically, the insight occurs within the fictional context of "The

Cornac and His Wife" (1927)—and not within the context of an essay on art, which in Lewis always tends to stress the scientific ethos of the satirist.

It is also within the context of the short story "Bestre" (1927) that the scientific ethos is derided. Bestre is the leader of a great carnivalesque mob of grotesques, and his strength as character lies in his function of both satirist and object of satire. Nestled in the flesh, his eye is a satirical weapon that draws its "ammunition . . . from all the most skunk-like provender, the most ugly mucins, fungoid glands, of his physique. Excrement as well as sputum would be shot from this luminous hole, with the same certainty in its unsavoury appulsion" (*CWB*, 83). Each term has been chosen to emphasize the material origin of Bestre's satirical eye. This primitivist definition of satire operates at the expense of the logocentric ethos epitomized by Western Man.

"Bestre" is a very good example of the modernist interruption of realistic aesthetic. While the irrational remains chiefly an object of scientific, rational analysis in naturalism, in modernism it not only becomes a means of disrupting the mimetic illusion, but it also functions as a means of defining the self and art. This shift from the irrational as hereditary disease to the irrational as existential and creative factor was heralded by Baudelaire, who saw in the English pantomime a comedy of violence, as well as by Bergson, who in 1899 (six years before Freud) saw in laughter "something like the logic of dreams."[27] The difference, however, between Bergson and Lewis is their degree of radicalism. For Bergson comedy is defined in contradistinction from life: "The rigid, the ready-made, the mechanical as opposed to the supple, the ever-changing and the living; absent-mindedness as opposed to free activity; this is in short what laughter singles out and wishes to correct."[28] In Lewis laughter is not out to correct anything, it is both the explosive manifestation of the unconscious and an unwitting revealer of the self's material origins. This is most conspicuous in *The Tyros,* which are pictorial representations of grotesque males laying bare the fangs of their aggressive laugh. *A Reading of Ovid* (Compton, pl. 115) is particularly striking, not only on account of its deliberately clashing colors, but also because it enacts an explosive contrast between the animal magnetism of the laughers and the book, emblem of transcending civilization. Against the bourgeois credo of progress, Lewis emphasized the atavism of laughter that "is primitive, hard and unchangeable" (*CWB*, 151).

In addition, the radicalism of the prewar avant-garde provides another context for Lewis's practice of satire. Indeed, the violence at the root of Lewisian laughter draws on the violence of the avant-gardist iconoclastic assault on bourgeois culture, values, and symbols. The confluence of subversive comedy and radicalist avant-gardism is manifest in the lines of *Blast* 1 (1914) where Lewis provides an oxymoronic conception of humour: "It is intelligence electrified by flood of Naivety. / It is Chaos invading Concept and bursting it like nitrogen" (38).

Although Pirandello had an artistic sensibility quite different from Lewis's, his description in 1908 of the humorist's task is a good description of the subversive function of comedy in the developing years of modernism. For Pirandello, the humorist does not attempt to create heroes, legend or history: "he knows what a legend is and how it is created, what history is and how it is made: they are all compositions . . . the humorist amuses himself by disassembling these compositions, although one cannot say that it is a pleasant amusement."[29] In spite of the translation from Italian to English, one can still catch the pun alluding to the stink of "decomposition" with which the humorist is confronted. Pirandello's description of the function of laughter is noteworthy because it resorts to a trope that had a great future. Indeed the act of "disassembling compositions" clearly prepares the ground for Dada and then, later on, deconstruction, for which acts of criticism constitute acts of satire.

In a brief study of Lewis's contribution to the modern spirit of anti-pathos, David Trotter describes the author's satire as a means of (self-) protection against pathos: "Our own predicament, like that of most other people, constantly leaks pathos and the spirit of ferocious banter demands nothing less than cautery: the cautery of the knock-out punch or the shell fired at dummy-men, an extinction of feeling."[30] What Trotter describes so eloquently is not only an aesthetic of impersonality, but above all, a process of defamiliarization or deautomatization. This process is worth underlining for two reasons. First, it extends the field of application of deautomatization too often confined to the linguistic framework associated with Russian formalism. Second, I would argue that, although the aim of deautomatization is detachment, it nevertheless functions within the context of an aesthetics of affect. Vaclav Havel's formula for absurd comedy constitutes a good example of such a function. "The gag," he writes, "awakens the experience of absurdity by defamiliarizing (revealing as absurd) that reality in which the person is in some sense socially ('objectively') alienated from himself without being fully aware of it."[31]

This process of alienation is at the core of the relation between text and reader in Lewis's fiction. When, in "A Soldier of Humour," Lewis refers to the *"the quarrel of humour* [that] divides men forever" (*CWB*,

19), he might as well have described the constant strategy of his modernist narratives. And here one has the widest gap between realism and subversive, noncooperating modernism. Although realism did leave scuffs on bourgeois decorum, a book like Zola's *Nana,* published in 1880, sold fifty-five thousand copies on the first day of publication. Peter Keating also indicates that the best-seller "operated at an extraordinarily high pitch of emotional intensity."[32] By using a rhetoric of aggression, Lewis made sure that he would be left almost unread; however, far from displaying a spirit of anti-pathos, he developed an art of shock and affect. Thus, although sustaining a discourse of rational detachment, Lewis should be differentiated from Brecht. As Andreas Huyssen points out, the shock "achieved by Brecht's *Verfremdungseffekt* does not carry its function in itself but remains instrumentally bound to a rational explanation of social relations which are to be revealed as mystified second nature." Lewis's conception of social relations as governed by a "quarrel of humour" drives him out of the Brechtian pale. Huyssen adds that Benjamin disagreed with the Brechtian theory because he "saw shock as essential to disrupting the frozen patterns of sensory perception, not only those of rational discourse."[33] This in effect amounts to an Aristotelian position with the political level added to the rhetorical power of catharsis. No wonder then that one finds Lewis declare that the "diabolical" role of the artist is that of "providing *catharsis* . . . of getting as near to destruction and terror as that is possible without impairing the organism" (*ABR,* 422).

In fact, if one looks back at one of the founding texts of modernism, it is clear that the target is not so much pathos as empathy. Indeed, in Worringer's essay "Abstraction and Empathy" (1908), abstraction is a means of creating a gap between self and nature and escape from "an immense spiritual dread of space." However, pathos has not been evicted, since for Worringer the "urge" to abstraction does not derive from an intellectual operation but constitutes "a purely instinctive creation."[34] Rhetoricians refer to "bdelygma" as a mimetic figure of antipathy by which aversion for the object of description is aroused.[35] This rhetorical device is interesting because it partly rests on turning topsy-turvy the naturalist account of the relation between mimesis and empathy. One has in the Ratner episode in *The Apes of God* a very good example of this strategy. A description of the physical appearance of Ratner the writer occurs in "The Split-Man." This description has been taken as proof of Lewis's anti-Semitism: that is the chief argument of David Ayers in *Wyndham Lewis and Western Man.* But the same description can be said to rest on an aesthetic of mimetic antipathy with the body as Lewis's chief satirical target and with the reader's shock as end result. An allusion to mimesis is made in the fact that Ratner develops self-disgust while studying himself in the mirror. Such an interpretation does not aim at denying the anti-Semitic streak in Lewis, but at recognizing the complexity of the problem. Mimetic figures of antipathy, which can also be observed at work in the pictorial self-portraits of the early twenties, actually constitute the basis of Lewis's satire.

The analysis of the modernist approach to language has been consistently conducted within the context of the theory of autotelism.[36] This interpretation of modernist linguistic practices has been reinforced by the widespread use of the semiological approach and continental poststructuralism. In a perceptive remark, Andreas Huyssen points out that poststructuralism is not a theory of postmodernism but one of modernism: "There is no doubt that center stage in critical theory is held by the classical modernists. . . . The enemies still are realism and representation, mass culture and standardization, grammar, communication, and the presumably all-powerful homogenizing pressures of the modern State."[37] But the affiliation between poststructuralism and modernism does not go without saying either. The gap between poststructuralism and modernism is nowhere more evident than in connection with language. If it is true that modernist linguistic experiments lend themselves—though not always or necessarily—to a purely textual interpretation, it remains the fact that major modernists simultaneously put forward referential claims concerning creative language. In its subscription to the Saussurean premise that language is a self-contained system, poststructuralism is unable to deal with or even recognize the referential character of the modernist theory of language.

The modernist referential claim for language stems from realism as illustrated by Flaubert's ceaseless search for the *mot juste*. In the British context, Louis Menand points out that it is Pater who supported the elimination of what he called "surplusage" in favor of clarity and the *mot juste*.[38] Common to both realism and modernism is the desire to create and use a language capable of being faithful to a phenomenological conception of the world. Lewis's stated preference for "classical," visual language without fuss or mannerism is therefore not the product of an idiosyncratic stand. A genealogy of modernist referentiality can certainly be recovered from the dust that has accumulated for more than thirty years. In May 1912 Marinetti claimed that "only the asyntactical poet, who make words unbound, will be able to penetrate the essence of matter and destroy the veiled hostility which cuts us from it."[39] When in 1917 Victor Shklovsky claims that art "*is a way of experiencing the artfulness of an object,*" he does not mean that art consists in aesthetizing the object. On the contrary, his notion of deautomatization assumes a relation to the object by means of perception, and aims at increasing "the difficulty and length of perception because the process of perception is an aesthetic in itself and must be prolonged."[40] Stephen Spender's account of "distortion" is fundamentally phenomenological and referential. He regards it as "a way of expressing the felt truth of the relationship of the subjective artist to the objective reality in his time."[41]

These modernist claims support the realist tenet of an existing world of phenomena, while at the same time they reject the theory of mimesis associated with a philosophy of a common, storyless object. The point to underline therefore is that the practice of modernist language seems to have been based on a paradox: the more distorting the medium, the more referential. This paradox is totally alien to the realist conception of language as expressed by Champfleury: art "scorns the vain ornaments of style . . . it is a useful reaction against the makers of . . . gongorism."[42] The modernist anti-mimetic yet referential bias also explains why, in *The Concept of Modernism,* Eysteinsson's argument that *Madame Bovary* can be read as both a modernist and a realist work cannot be applied to *Ulysses* or *A la recherche du temps perdu.* For modernist faithfulness to perceptual reality was conditional on gongorism, verbal impasto, or cubistic prose.

Interestingly enough, the tension between anti-mimesis and referentiality appears in the important transitional writer Huysmans who, through his mouthpiece in *Là-bas* (1891), heralds part of the modernist aesthetic program. While rejecting the account of the irrational in terms of hereditary disease, Huysmans wishes to preserve the "truthfulness of the document, the precise detail, and the rich and nervous language of realism."[43] What catches the eye in the French version is the use of "*étoffe*" to describe realist language. Literally, "*étoffe*" translates into "stuff" in the sense of textile fabric. Whether it accurately describes the realist approach to language is of little importance; more relevant is the fact that the word is used by a recognized dandy for whom garment has symbolic meaning. Huysmans's term is symptomatic of a language to come that lays emphasis on texture. Lewis's practice of allegory with its highly wrought texture indicates a conception of language as artifice and device in line with Huysmans's prediction. The convergence of the conception of the artist as dandy and of art as ornament is already at work in Baudelaire, whose translation of De Quincey's *Confessions of an English Opium-Eater* is, in Feldman's words, combining "translation, paraphrase, plagiarism, quotation, excision, and addition."[44] Today we recognize this process as the hallmark of modernist textuality. What is specific about modernism is the paradox between a textual anti-mimetic practice, which runs out of hand, and a referential theory of language in search of the perceptual object.

Therefore to say with Susan Suleiman that the program of modernism was to "suppress the referential element in writing, and . . . to emphasize its self-referential element"[45] simply ignores the tenets of modernist aesthetics. Similarly, to oust writers in or out of modernism depending on the self-referential degree of their art is both to impose the teleological model of a historical march towards the flat canvas or the autotelic word and to ignore the ambiguity and complexity of most modernist works. This mode of thinking underlies David Lodge's argument that Gertrude Stein is still a traditional writer because her writing rests on an "aesthetic of realization, a pursuit of the thing itself."[46] Today Stein is often regarded as an avant-gardiste, who before the First World War was at the spearhead of experimentation. The latter interpretation should not cancel Lodge's underlining of Stein's aesthetics of realization: the two perspectives on Stein combine to form a typically modernist paradox. Nor is it necessary to see in the claim for referential language what Michael Hollington calls the chimeric "idea of a mystical relationship between words and the things they signify."[47] The relation may have been mystical for some writers, but the referential function of language does not necessarily imply any mystic relation between word and thing.

In *Theory of the Avant-Garde,* part of Peter Bürger's general thesis is that aestheticism reaches a peak when art has become its own topic. This in theory should make *Kunstlerromans* like *A Portrait of the Artist as a Young Man* and *Tarr* works of aestheticism. However, these works do not float in a kind of purely semiotic fluid: they are part of the larger context of novelistic narrative. For instance a fundamental difference exists between Mallarmé's "Prose" and the statements on art by Stephen to Lynch, and by Tarr to Butcher or Anastasya. The difference lies in the fact that, while the statements on art are deliberately hypertextualized and monumentalized in Mallarmé's poem, the aesthetic ideas of the two novels are developed within the context of a dialogue between two characters or more. The function of the dialogue is to temporalize and localize the statements and transform them into "utterances." Of course, the protagonist-artist always tends to lapse into dogmatic monologues, but that is part of a certain radicalism and an itch to lay down decrees and laws of creation. The transformation of aesthetic edicts into localized utterances inspired Thomas Mann who in *Doctor Faust* (1947) has the musicologist

Kretschmar stutter away at his aesthetic lectures. The main point is that the narrative situation of Tarr and Butcher sitting at a café and palavering about art principles in a realistic type of dialogue draws on what Eysteinsson refers to as the "communicative, pragmatic function of language."[48]

7

The Great Divide

In *AFTER THE GREAT DIVIDE*, A COMPARATIVE ANALYSIS OF THE role of mass culture in modernism and postmodernism, Andreas Huyssen temporarily toes Theodor Adorno's line by arguing that "to speak of modernism without mentioning capitalist mass culture is like praising the free market while ignoring the multinationals." Roughly the idea is that modernism developed in reaction to mass culture and commodification. Lewisian novels such as *Snooty Baronet* and *The Revenge for Love* provide valid insights into what Huyssen calls the "repressive desublimation . . . so characteristic of capitalist culture."[1] For instance the commodification and consumerization of exotic culture in a colonial context is at the heart of the cultural critique of *Snooty Baronet*. The fact that a critique of the commodification of the writer—illustrated by Snooty's trip to North Africa organized by his literary agent—develops in parallel can only suggest that both processes have in colonial "capitalist" culture a common enemy. The same critique, in even clearer terms, reappears in *Filibusters in Barbary* (1932), the nonfictional companion to *Snooty Baronet*.

According to Huyssen and, before him, Peter Bürger, the modernist reaction against capitalist mass culture coincides with the modernist divide between elitist art and mass culture. Peter Carey even maintains that modernists produced writings that were so esoteric as to make sure that the masses would not be able to read them. In other words, for these critics, the modernist divide between art and life is chiefly motivated by sociopolitical concerns. Peter Bürger goes on to set up a contrast between, on the one hand, modernism and its conservative withdrawal from life and mass culture and, on the other hand, the avant-garde and its iconoclastic commitment to what Bürger refers to as life praxis or transformation of life via art.

It seems to me that this general theory of the great divide requires critical analysis. This can be done by examining two major aspects of the problem. First we need to examine the political explanation of the modernist divide between art and life. The question that must be asked is as follows: does the modernist critique of capitalism necessarily coincide with an anti-democratic, elitist stance? To provide an answer, I suggest we take the example of Mallarmé, who is usually presented as the priest of high art, withdrawn from the public arena into a private self-referential domain. Mallarmé wrote a mysterious essay, "The Impressionists and Edouard Manet" (1876), which apparently exists only in its English version. In this essay one comes across the statement that the art of the new age was addressed to the *"multitude* [which] *demands to see with its own eyes."*[2] Is it not striking that such an esoteric poet as Mallarmé should conceive of art as something for the multitude? Obviously his art had and still has the effect of alienating the "masses," but the artistic practice is not supported by a conservative or elitist political discourse.

Another example of the complex, far from clear relation between modernism and mass culture is provided by Hugh Kenner when, in *A Sinking Island,* he shows that artists such as Beardsley, Henry James, and James Joyce were awarded prizes for their contributions at an early age to popular newspapers that only modern technology could produce. Kenner's research actually confirms Adorno's claim that "high art is always already permeated by the textures of that mass culture from which it seeks autonomy."[3]

One has also to consider the possibility that the modernist divide between art and life may be motivated by other, extra-political reasons. As Huyssen points out, poststructuralism has presented modernism as an art of "absence"; yet on account of its search for the object, modernism is also an art of the overwhelming, nauseating presence or invasion of the object. The intrusion of the object upon an a priori independent aesthetic field provokes angst. Thus Worringer's theory of autonomous art is not defined in sociopolitical terms but in phenomenological: art is an "autonomous organism . . . devoid of any connection with [nature], in so far as by nature is understood the visible surface of things."[4]

In his early play *The Ideal Giant* (1917), Lewis conveys a preSartrian nausea towards the object. Kemp, the major protagonist, establishes the typical Lewisian distinction between artistic truth or the search for "symmetries and forms" (*CPP,* 127) and biological truth or "the actual biological appearance of Nature" (*CPP,* 128). However, the distinction between art and life collapses entirely when, faced with matter, the artist experiences the "feeling of 'malaise' and disgust. . . . the *physical* uneasiness about this thing said, whether fact or not, the 'hallucination of the Object'" (*CPP,* 128). The hallucination of the object is the factor that caused artists like Lewis to suscribe to the Schopenhauerian elevation of the object out of the stream of life. At the same time, an account of the modernist divide in nonpolitical terms does not necessarily exclude political motivations. It simply broadens the terms of explanation.

A critical analysis of the theory of the great divide has also to reexamine the now well-accepted notion that a sharp distinction has to be made between modernism and the avant-garde. And here the Lewisian case is particularly helpful in demonstrating that, although distinct, modernism and avant-garde are dialectically related concepts. Lewis is an important author because his works conspicuously exemplify this dialectical relationship. It would be tempting to argue that he first was a vorticist, then a modernist, with his shift from abstraction to figurative art reinforcing the interpretation. But the process of interpretation is complicated by the fact that this chronological categorization on the one hand, and Lewis's individual statements and works on the other, do not always coincide.

For instance, Lewis's statement concerning the "Hallucination of the Object" was made just after vorticism reached its apex and at a time when the first radical, avant-gardist version of *Tarr* was published. Yet the statement implies a modernist division between art and life, not avant-gardist integration of art into life. The same type of tension can be brought out by comparing *The Apes of God* (1930) with *The Diabolical Principle* (1931). The novel is almost contemporary with the book of essays that criticizes surrealism for mixing art and life. This criticism fits the profile of the high modernist entrenched in his aestheticism and not budging. Yet with its satire of social conversation in part 12 of the narrative, *The Apes of God* not only refers back to Flaubert's *Dictionnaire des bêtises* but also heralds Ionesco's avant-gardist *La cantatrice chauve*. One has also, in the character of Finnish poet, "this strange painted shamanized northern wanderer" (*AOG*, 356), an example of dadaist performance. The character wanders amongst the various groups of the party, rocking tables "with the detonation of haphazard strophes—fragments of poetry, metrical thunder-claps, bisected couplets, heads, or extremities, of rhymed invective" (*AOG*, 356). The fact that the strophes are from seventeenth-century, French neoclassical Boileau adds to the absurdity of the whole performance. Nothing in the text indicates that the Finnish poet is the object of Lewis's logocentric satire; instead, everything suggests that the character functions as a performing satirist of English bohemia with a dadaist approach.

Lewis is therefore an extremely interesting case because his statements and practice blur the lines Peter Bürger tries to draw between avant-garde and modernism. Again, this blurring occurs not because Lewis was first an avant-gardist then a modernist, but because his conservatism clashes with his avant-gardism. The "Essay on the Objective of Plastic Art in Our Time," published in 1922, is a crucial example of the clash between the two conceptions of art. The first, influenced by Schopenhauer, I have discussed in chapter 6; the second is definitely influenced by the continental development of the historical avant-garde.

The essay was published five years after Marcel Duchamp's display of his famous urinal (1917), and two years after the special number of *The Chapbook* entirely devoted to Dada. Although later in the same essay emphasizing the contemplative function of art, Lewis also makes a comparison that in effect cancels the distinction between art and life. Art, he argues, can be compared to physical games concerned with the attempt to reach perfect equilibrium, speed, power, and so on. The implicit conclusion of such a comparison is art as mechanical perfection. Thus:

> Some adjustment, then, between the approach of a conscious being to that mechanical perfection, and the fact of his mechanical incompetence (since mechanical perfection will not tally with the human thing) is the situation that produces art. The game consists in seeing how near you can get, without the sudden extinction and neutralization that awaits you as matter, or as the machine. (*LOA*, 205)

The claim that art is concerned with mechanizing performance and by extension technology is fundamentally antimodernist (in its traditional definition) and today is interpreted by Huyssen as the "avant-garde's attempt to overcome the art/life dichotomy and make art productive in the transformation of everyday life."[5] Lewis's claim also meets Bürger's argument that what sets the avant-garde apart is not its demand that art should display political content, but that "it directs itself to the way art functions in society, a process that does as much to determine the effect that works have as does the particular content."[6]

Lewis's essay does not constitute a slip of the pen or an isolated, regrettable incident. An even more complex example is provided in *Men without Art*, where he favors the ritual of dressing as the "reflection of a higher culture in man than is the barren metaphysics of the Naked Body" (129). So dressing is a means of distinguishing art from life. However, Lewis's premise is that the dressed body looks like a machine or thing. Therefore, logically enough, he concludes that "art consists . . . in a *mechanizing* of the natural. It bestows its delightful discipline upon our aimless emotions: it puts its gentle order in the place of natural chaos: it substitutes for the direct image a picture" (*MWA*, 129). Lewis's statement is paradoxical to the extent that it combines the avant-gardist mechanical paradigm with the modernist attempt to establish a divide between life as chaos and art as order.

Rather than seeing in Lewis a weird exception confirming the rule laid down by Bürger's theory, I regard the Lewisian case as typical of the interplay between conservativism and avant-gardism that constitutes modernism. It is precisely this interplay that Bürger's theory bypasses yet involuntarily acknowledges. In particular his definition of avant-gardist practices on the basis of "fragmentation" is highly problematic. Here is the definition: "For avant-gardistes . . . material is just that, material. Their activity initially consists in nothing other than in killing the 'life' of the material, that is, in tearing it out of its functional context that gives it meaning. . . . the avant-gardist tears [the material] out of the life totality, isolates it, and turns it into a fragment."[7] It seems to me that Bürger's position on the fragment in the historical avant-garde jeopardizes his general thesis of art as reintegration into life praxis. How can art be life praxis if torn out of "the life totality"?

Furthermore this tearing of the life material out of its functional context sounds curiously like the Schopenhauerian abstraction from the stream of life that both Lewis and Benjamin favored and reinterpreted. In other words, both Lewis and the avant-garde practice isolation from the stream of life or from life totality, but, for some reason, Lewis's practice is downgraded as modernist divide, while the avant-gardist's is hailed as reintegration of art into life.

The dialectical relation between avant-garde and modernism is also exemplified by what Huyssen refers to as "the machine metaphor and the production paradigm."[8] Indeed, one cannot ascribe the technological metaphor or function solely to the historical avant-garde. It is obvious that before surrealism, Dada, vorticism, or futurism the machine had impinged on the definition of art. In his 1846 Salon, Baudelaire already asserted that "a painting is a machine whose systems are all intelligible for an experienced eye."[9] The implicit question is, how should we categorize Baudelaire? The fact that Lewis uses mechanization not only as a metaphor but also as a means of defining the function of art presents the same problem of categorization.

Huyssen's discussion is important because it underlines the facts that modernism and the avant-garde were both involved in the machine paradigm, and that this paradigm is not necessarily and always a positive factor. This is quite obvious in the following statement: "a crucial question for me concerns the extent to which modernism and the avant-garde as forms of an adversary culture were nevertheless conceptually and practically bound up with capitalist modernization and/or with communist vanguardism, that modernization's twin brother."[10] Huyssen's statement is all the more remarkable as the premise of his argument is based on Bürger's notion of the reintegration of art into life.

There are two further twists to the problem. First, Huyssen's questioning of the machine paradigm is not new. Second, there is evidence that the avant-gardists were among the first to develop a critical attitude towards the machine paradigm. In *A Bitter Truth,* Richard Cork's massive research into the relation between art and World War I proves decisively the extent to which the machine paradigm was jolted out of hegemony once painters were confronted with the physical and psychological reality of war. In particular there are telling pages on Léger who as a soldier slowly realized that his prewar mechanicism proved too simplistic. Max Ernst is another artist who parodied the machine paradigm in *Celebes* (1921; Cork, pl. 350) and *The Massacre of the Innocents* (1920; Cork, pl. 349). There is no sense of social triumphalism in these pictures. What Cork's research demonstrates effectively is that under the pressure of the reality of war, a shift in the approach to artistic creation occurred. To use Wallace Stevens's words, "it is not that there is a new imagination but that there is a new reality."[11]

Curiously enough, Richard Cork sees in this phenomenon a shift from modernism to the avant-garde. However, the Léger example alone signals a movement away from the mechanically oriented avant-garde. The question is what is the movement to? I will try to answer the question by analyzing Lewis's war painting *A Battery Shelled* (Michel, pl. 49). This oil painting, produced in 1919, has been the object of debate chiefly because the presence of three soldiers isolated from a busy battery and from the zone of war activity seems to support an elitist comment on mass democracy and its disasters. Cork adds a perceptive analysis at the stylistic level. He points out that the battery and its busy soldiers are represented in vorticist terms, whereas the three isolated soldiers are represented in figurative terms. The words Cork uses are also particularly revealing: he speaks of a clash, paradox, and incongruity between the two styles within the picture. The three isolated soldiers are in part modelled on Lewis and another former vorticist. Cork concludes: "The former Vorticists look as if they might be outside the canvas altogether, removed from a way of seeing which now belongs to a past beyond recovery."[12]

What should be added is that, if the figurative style of this picture indicates a "return" to the object, it cannot be described as conventional realism. Instead, the three figures are quite stylized. *A Battery Shelled* is a key painting because quite extraordinarily it thematizes the dialectical relationship between the modernist paradigm and the avant-gardist by means of its paradoxical combination of a search for the object and a passion for experimentalism—which it owes to avant-gardism. If indeed such is the case, then paintings such as Dix's *Setting Sun* (Cork, pl. 277), Grosz's *Dedicated to O. Panizza* (Cork, pl. 251), and Mark Gertler's *Merry-Go-Round* (Cork, pl. 175) should be categorized not as avant-gardist but as definitely modernist. In the antithetic styles of *A Battery Shelled*, one perceives the avant-gardist fascination for the machine paradigm and the simultaneous modernist attempt to establish a distance from it. The same ambiguity is recorded in the claim Lewis made in 1939 when he said that the "pictures of the Vorticists were a sort of *machines*" (*LOA*, 340). But he added: vorticism "identified itself with [the] brutality [of mechanical life], in a stoical embrace, though of course without propagandist fuss" (*LOA*, 341).

Today the same ambivalence between divide and integration persists in the debate. Although suscribing to Bürger's general thesis of art praxis, Huyssen also states that this "does not mean that all differences between art and daily life should be eliminated. In a liberal human society there would be art *qua* art as well. Today more than ever it is the task of Marxist critics to expose the popular equation of art and life for what it is—nothing but a mystification."[13] Huyssen writes these words after more than thirty years of performance art, which today has reached a state of exhaustion. Attempts to delineate the fields of art and life appear all along the critical spectrum: from Suzi Gablik in *Has Modernism Failed?* to Eysteinsson, who argues that any "gesture, however violent, toward destroying art while working in its context will only carry its meaning because of our preclassification of aesthetic activity."[14]

Has aesthetic distance totally been banned from artistic practice? A work like Joseph Beuys's *Capri Battery* (1985) seems to support the notion of continuity between life and art. Melissa Feldman argues that this artifact belongs to the type of postmodernist works concerned with the "unmediated presentation of forms relating to real life."[15] In its conception and appearance, *Capri Battery* goes right against the theory of avant-gardist fragmentation. It consists in an open, wooden box with at its far end a mirror. The mirror reflects what stands outside the box, just at its edge: a yellow light bulb plugged into a fresh lemon. The obvious desire to establish continuity (contact!) between the natural product and the technical object is poles apart from avant-gardist anti-organic fragmentation.

At the same time, one can see the line between art and non-art reappear surreptitiously. For example, in 1965, Hans Haacke exhibited a blue cloth blown by an artificial source of wind. The work, entitled *Blue Sail,* can be regarded as a pertinent illustration of Arthur Danto's theory that "to see something as art requires something the eye cannot descry—an atmosphere of artistic theory, a knowledge of the history of art: an artworld."[16] This is the role played by the statement accompanying the exhibit: "The wind-driven fabric behaves like a living organism, all parts of which are constantly influencing one another."[17] The burden of aesthetization, authorship and *tempérament* has been transferred from the object to the caption, which conveys the artworld of Danto's description.

Finally, the Lewisian case is also useful for bringing out a striking characteristic of the recent categorization of the avant-garde. In general, avant-gardism has been analyzed as a radical, groundbreaking artistic manifestation. But with analyses by critics such as Bürger or Huyssen, avant-gardism has become an exclusively left-wing phenomenon or one branch or another of Marxism. For Huyssen, avant-garde today is identified as "decentered movements" such as feminism and ecologism. This equation between avant-garde and left-wing politics (to use a broad political term) has a severe drawback. It drives the theory and the identification of the avant-garde into a reductive process of binarism of the following type: avant-garde = life praxis and modernism = autonomy. This equation can be refuted by referring to a single example. I am thinking of the French right-wing group centered around Maurras who, like dadaists and futurists, used disruptive public tactics to protest against certain forms of art. Today one group is referred to as the historical avant-garde, the other as modernists solely on ideological, political grounds.

On a larger scale, some of the high modernists have a significant amount of their corpus devoted to reintegrating art into life praxis, which, however, remains ignored by the theorists of avant-gardism. The part of the corpus I am thinking of is the modernists' political writings. In particular it is possible to argue that Lewis's political writings illustrate Peter Bürger's thesis that the avant-garde wished "to organize a new life *praxis* from a basis in art."[18] In other words, the principle of reintegration of art into life praxis can also be shown to function within the context of modernism. The next step then is to show that Lewis's political writings do present characteristics we associate with art, while aiming at a radical and practical impact on life. This will be the task of part three of my argument.

Part Three
Politics

8
The Genre of Politics

LEWIS DEVOTED AT LEAST TWELVE VOLUMES TO WHAT SHOULD BE called the study of sociopolitics. For a writer who is nowadays perceived essentially as an artist, this phenomenal profusion is very surprising if not arresting. The other noteworthy general observation is that most of Lewis's sociopolitical works were produced between the two occidental wars of this century. These are *The Art of Being Ruled* (1926), *Paleface* (1929), *Hitler* (1931), *The Doom of Youth* (1932), *The Old Gang and the New Gang* (1933), *Left Wings over Europe* (1936), *Count Your Dead: They Are Alive!* (1937), *The Mysterious Mr. Bull* (1938), *The Jews: Are They Human?* (1939), *The Hitler Cult* (1939), and *Anglo-Saxony: A League That Works* (1941). In addition, a postwar book, *America and Cosmic Ma*n, actually worked on in the early forties, was published in 1948. Generally speaking, these books are concerned with the analysis of different components of Western society and of the political thought governing its institutions.

When one looks at what he has to say on the origins of this sociopolitical interest, one finds that Lewis emphasizes his experience of World War I: "On the battlefields of France and Flanders I became curious . . . about how and why these bloodbaths occurred—the political mechanics of war. I acquired a knowledge of some of the intricacies of the power-game, and the usurious economics associated with war-making."[1] That the war was the decisive event that led the author to systematize his political interest is reinforced by another statement occurring in the discussion of Herbert Read's description of the effect of war on the "lost generation." For Lewis, Read's generation had little to lose because, when the war broke out, they were too young to have created anything. He adds:

My career as an artist was not only interrupted, but broken by my War-service, and that was also the case with several of my companions of that time. But at thirty years old the impact of those events is different to what it would be at sixteen, though not necessarily less intense and affecting. . . . there were schoolboys who lost their youth on account of the

163

bursting of the storm, and there were all those men, still young, whose careers, at a critical moment, were stopped dead, and who had to start afresh—not "returning to their old occupations" at all, for the threads had all been broken, and all the "occupations" had been radically transformed.[2]

It is also in *Blasting and Bombardiering* that Lewis explains that he decided to study the mechanics of war and politics after he lost his friends and his mother (who died of the pneumonia which affected both civilians and soldiers after the war). In short, his concern for politics is underpinned by two motives. One is cognitive: his studies can be interpreted as a vast effort to understand the circumstances leading to the war and its aftermath. The other is affective: the war was a catastrophe on the personal level, and he had to cope with it one way or another.

The Art of Being Ruled remains the major political analysis in Lewis's corpus, and a synopsis of its main arguments and concerns provides an apt introduction to the analysis of his political reflexion. The work reflects the then pervasive sense of ideological disorientation, and shares the ambiguous awareness of bygone days and traditions. Yet it is also responsive to revolutionary potentialities. In its defense of what is left of Western man and his civilization, the book is the sociopolitical twin of the more philosophical *Time and Western Man*. In the first part the notion of revolution is tackled. The next two parts are chiefly concerned with the ruler and the ruled. In part two an analysis of industrial thought concludes that primitivism remains at its heart. In part three, it is argued that the main political question is not whether one should have a ruler but, since ruling is necessary, what the best type of ruler is. As opposed to majority rule and Liberalism, Lewis opts for rule by the elite. His rejection of Liberalism is not idiosyncratic but is related to a political process which saw the withering of the Liberal Party as a political force and the simultaneous rise of the Labour party. Fred Reid attributes the downfall of Liberalism not so much to direct Labour competition as to a confluence of colonial, economic, and political problems. The Liberal governments were beset by Unionists, who wanted to keep the British Empire strong and unified regardless of Irish and Indian claims; by supporters of governmental measures in favor of industry as opposed to the traditional policy of laissez-faire; and by social unrest from suffragettes, strikers, and Irish nationalists.[3]

In part four of *The Art of Being Ruled*, Lewis denounces the press, cinema, and radio as means of manipulating the masses. These means of democratic government foster irresponsibility and cause the disappearance of freedom as is argued in part five. As a result, people belong to a vast nursery and rely on the government, which they see as a Big Father. This democracy of Peter-Panism is described in part six. In parts seven, eight, and nine Lewis aims at convincing the reader that feminism and homosexuality are used as weapons by capitalism to destroy the traditional family unit of Western society. Although this destruction has its points, it is predominantly negative because it also affects those values of Western man worth preserving. In parts ten and eleven, Lewis undertakes a study of socialism, which he first presents as a powerful cult with apocalyptic destruction and power as two of its dogmas. Then he assesses Rousseau, Marx, and Proudhon: Rousseau is declared to be the thinker who offers the greatest concern for personal freedom as opposed to Marx's and Proudhon's respective forms of collectivism. In part twelve he deplores the absence of intellectuals supporting the traditional values of Western man. Finally part thirteen is a summary of and conclusion to the main argument of the book.

As Bernard Bergonzi notes,[4] Lewis's fundamental distrust of mass democracy and Liberalism probably contributed to his interest in Hitler's fascism, which took advantage of the difficulties parliamentarian systems were encountering at the time. In its propaganda, fascism laid emphasis on the weakness and inefficiency of democratic governments. It is in *America and Cosmic Man,* his last major political analysis, that Lewis is prepared to consider the notion of democracy in a more tolerant and optimistic manner. The book is divided into two main parts. The first turns towards the past as it studies the political history of the United States of America, with particular attention to figures such as Washington, Jefferson, and Hamilton. In the second part, the argument turns towards the future and utopia. It focuses on the American policies of internationalism and the melting pot as a potential model for the future world society.

A contradiction lies at the core of Lewis's corpus: on the one hand, Lewis defines art not only in opposition to life, but also specifically detached from any political involvement; on the other, Lewis writes a dozen books with a definite sociopolitical commitment. What increases the sense of paradox is that his concern for political detachment appears in his writings of the thirties at a time when he became progressively involved with the politics of the day. In *The Diabolical Principle,* published the same year as *Hitler,* he writes:

> I advance the strange claim (as my private *Bill of Rights*) to act and think non-politically in everything, in complete detachment from all the intolerant watchwords and formulas by which we are beset. I am an artist and

my *mind*, at least, is entirely free: also that is a freedom I hold from no man and have every intention of retaining. (*DP*, 37)

This Bill of Rights constitutes the platform from which Lewis launches his attacks and sallies at writers such as Anderson, Lawrence, and those publishing in *transition*. In *The Writer and the Absolute* the objectivity of the artist's mind is once more asserted, and detachment from politics becomes an evaluative criterion of art. Sartre and Orwell are assessed according to this criterion and naturally fail the test. Although Lewis seems to show more sympathy for Orwell, his verdict is nevertheless negative. As a true *clerc*, Orwell "should have taken up a position of absolute detachment" (*WA*, 188); instead, he remained *engagé*. Indeed, Orwell's theoretical position was diametrically opposite to Lewis's. In "Charles Dickens" (1939) he argues that all art is propaganda.[5]

In practice, the analytical strategies of Lewis's criticism show to what extent he took for granted that a type of relation exists between art and politics. Whenever he analyzes a particular author, he invariably focuses on the relation between the text and the ideologies circulating at the time of writing. Lewis is practicing what today is regarded as the bread and butter of academic criticism, and that is a systematic analysis of "discourse." This is quite obvious in *Time and Western Man*, where the literary study of Joyce, Pound, and Stein is strategically juxtaposed to the analysis of the philosophies of time. The same relation obtains in the case of his political writings. For instance, the chief concern of *Paleface* is presented as follows: "to set in relief the automatic processes by which the artist or the writer . . . obtains his formularies: to show how the formulas for his progress are issued to him, how he gets them by post, and then applies them" (97–98). In D. H. Lawrence's and Sherwood Anderson's cases, Lewis claims that their discourse originates in the social and cultural conditions of the blacks of America. In the case of Alec Waugh and François Mauriac, it is rooted in youth politics. Such a conception of literary discourse has an impact on the generic identity of Lewis's nonfiction, which tends to combine literary and political analyses. This generic hybridization implicitly contradicts the Lewisian theoretical distinction between art and life: if a textual analysis requires both literary and political tools, then the assumption has been made at some point that art and politics converge in the literary text. The most obvious examples of generic hybridizing are *The Lion and the Fox, The Diabolical Principle, Doom of Youth*, or *The Writer and the Absolute*.

At the same time, one can easily select overt statements by Lewis that clearly show a degree of political involvement even though the credo of political detachment is asserted in the same breath. Of course, Lewis was not a political activist, but his pen was not always as free as he claimed it to be. Between the sword and the pen there is room for degrees of engagement. As Sartre put it in 1949, "To speak is to act: whatever is named is already no longer quite the same; it has lost its innocence."[6] Concerning chapters of *Hitler*, which first appeared as a series of articles in *Time and Tide*, Lewis wrote: "I have, of course, stressed the purely Nazi standpoint. It was essential to do that if one is to secure for them a fair hearing in England, where there are far too many Mr. Voigts [pro-Communist] and too few impartial observers."[7] However, in pitting fascism against communism, he prevented himself from weighing the political scales from an impartial viewpoint. He also wrapped his contradictions in paradoxical maxims such as "[My political views] are partly communist and partly fascist, with a distinct streak of monarchism in my marxism, but at bottom anarchist with a healthy passion for order" (*DP*, 126). Yet Lewis's anarchy has definite "masculine" models some of whom displayed an inordinate obsession for "order." In *Left Wings over Europe*, he claims:

> I fly the flag of no party. My shirt is neither red, black, nor purple. Jefferson and Hitler, Burke and Bismarck—there are many names certainly I could mention which I should select for my political pantheon. And I may at once mention the fact that the name of our old friend Karl Marx would not be among them. I am, indeed, so remarkably *unred* that you may think me black.[8]

Here is contradiction in a nutshell. How can one stand for Hitler and against Marx, and still claim political detachment? By promoting Hitler, Lewis was definitely swimming against the ideological mainstream of the thirties, but he was certainly not nonpolitical. In the same pamphlet he actually assesses Hitler and Nazi Germany as an example of how true democracy can work.

This contradiction has a historical and cultural background that is apparent in Lewis's own texts. The numerous quotations from *Culture and Anarchy* in *The Art of Being Ruled* indicate that he considered himself heir to Arnold's thought on the role of the artist in society. Arnold's own position is ambiguous. On the one hand, and to use Bradbury's analysis, Arnold suggests that the "literary mind can meaningfully act *in* modern society, and that to do otherwise is a loss for society and for the arts." On the other, he supported the principle of disinterestedness. By it, Arnold "meant to say that the writer was independent of particular class or sectarian interests in society, particular social needs and urgencies, and committed to the ideal realm of art and the wish to make it prevail in society."[9] In 1967, Stephen Spender underlined the continuity between the Victorians and the modernists: "ever since the nineteenth century (Shelley, Arnold, Clough, Ruskin, Morris) it has been the case that the English poet mixed up in politics may spend a lifetime divided between two voices: that of the social, and that of esthetic, conscience."[10]

However, confining oneself to this British tradition prevents one from seeing the complexity and modernity of the problem. It also traps the reader into succumbing to the rhetoric of Lewis's pamphlets. In the midst of statements and counterstatements, one finds one that cancels Lewis's Arnoldian artistic detachment and establishes an Orwellian type of link between art and political life. In *The Diabolical Principle* art is said to to be able to "effect more, even politically, in the most fundamental sense, than any pure propaganda or popular sociological moralist religion" (151). Whether Lewis always adhered to this belief is beside the point. The fact that he made this statement at least once destabilizes the general argument that modernism stuck to the Arnoldian principle of detachment from (political) life.

One can never insist enough on the radicalism of Lewis's analyses and conclusions. Above all, the texts had in their day the rhetorical capability to affect readers. The best way of supporting this assertion is to quote one of Lewis's readers. Thus in 1937 Mallalieu perceived in Lewis the critic "the social force."[11] Even today some of Lewis's statements have retained rhetorical freshness and ideological insight. This freshness will come as a surprise to the readers who had previously been persuaded that the author was politically retarded. For instance, Lewis observes that, although the Western democracies keep harping proudly on their freedom, they are at the beck and call of industrial capitalism, which is "*dictator-minded*. It belongs to the same epoch as Lenin, Hitler, and Mussolini."[12] Parliamentary politics has little power whereas Big Business has cinema, the press, and the radio to subject people to a "technique of suggestion" (*DY*, 39). He points out that there "are far more politics . . . in Donald Duck or Colonel Blimp than is popularly recognized. Low and Disney govern us as truly as Mr. Baldwin."[13] Such insights anticipate Orwell's analyses in "Boys' Weeklies" (1939) or "Raffles and Miss Blandish" (1944), but also their continental counterpart, the Roland Barthes of *Mythologies* (1957). Of course, for power to have its grip on the ruled, the education of youth remains essential: "Force is a passing and precarious thing, whereas to get inside a person's mind and change his very personality is the effective way of reducing him and making him yours" (*ABR*, 98). Hence the capitalist state is an educationalist state.

Lewis also successfully argues that such movements as feminism and youth have the effect of weakening the father figure, which for industrial power is a godsend since the father-worker can be manipulated like plasticine. By the same token, by promoting financial independence, Big Business attracts a lot of women and young people in search of a job that, however, is not necessarily better renumerated. This allows the general level of wages to remain low since there is no shortage of "manpower."

The fact that Lewis's political writings display unambiguous rhetorical power implies that they were conceived of as a means of affecting readers and of exerting some kind of impact on social reality. Therefore social and political pragmatism characterize his political writings. But that is not all. The texts do not read as pure political argumentation—if such purity ever existed. The striking generic characteristic of Lewis's political texts is that they read not only as political pamphlets, but also as allegories. This is particularly well illustrated by a passage from *Left Wings over Europe* (171–73). Lewis imagines an observer situated in a plane flying over a plain with, at each extremity, ranges of rugged hills. The people living in the plain are in the main unpolitical and governed by parliamentary democracy. Their land is coveted by the inhabitants of the two ranges of hills. Both types of hillmen are characterized by what is called "personal government." However, those on the left hill want to abolish the plain government whereas those on the right propose to purify and improve the plain government. As everybody has guessed, the left highlanders represent the red principle of communism, while the right highlanders stand for the black principle of fascism.

At the same time the antagonistic relation between fascism and communism in the Lewisian narrative goes beyond political and historical circumstances. Or, rather, the historical frame of reference functions like the first level of a typically polysemic, allegorical narrative. Indeed, one has only to consider the definitions of and associations with the two ideological terms. In *Left Wings over Europe,* it is stated that the right-wing extremist's "impulses . . . [derive] from a higher centre than the impersonal automatisms of reptile life, exemplified by [Marxian] retrograde 'dialectic'—impulses which were productive of all the great arts and sciences of the West" (*LWOE,* 36). Or in *The Writer the Absolute,* Thomas Paine is said to have "overlooked the fact that it is the violence, not the social justice, which attracts, calling into being the wolfish multitude, which is the *body* of the revolution. The thinking animals who are the *brain* cannot make the revolutions alone" (*WA,* 69). Before and after the Second World War, Lewis's political discourse deals at one level with historical reality, and at another develops an allegory of the mind-body dualism. Like marine life growing on sea rocks, Lewisian associations have fastened on "fascism" and "communism." In fact, his political writings constitute the only narratives of his corpus that present a full, allegorical treatment of the mind-body dualism: while the essays of *Time and Western Man* privilege the intellectual principle, and the fiction the Wild Body, the political pamphlets offer a powerful Manichean psychomachia between mind and body. From a pictorial viewpoint, this is vividly rendered by the design on the front cover of *Count Your Dead: They Are Alive!* where two ideological demonic agents whirl in a vorticist physical clash (Michel, pl.123).

In *A War Imagined*, Samuel Hynes conveys the sense of belligerence infecting the years preceding the war:

> Irish men, women and workers . . . were all exerting pressures against society and its mores. . . . A civil war, a sex war, and a class war: in the spring of 1914 these were all foreseen in England's immediate future, and with a kind of relish. Rhetorically speaking, they were already being fought; the language of war had become, by then, the language of public discourse.[14]

Hynes's conception of the First World War as the outcome of a process of escalation is very perceptive and useful to suggest a continuity between the prewar language of public discourse and the postwar rise of fascism and Stalinism. I believe that a similar kind of continuity can be argued for in the case of Lewis's writing career. Although his progress as an artist was fractured by the world conflict, a link exists between the avant-gardist radicalism of the *Blast* manifestos and the political radicalism of his post-war pamphlets. To this extent, *Hitler* is the child of *Blast*.

In particular the convergence of avant-gardist radicalism and political extremism is manifested by the utopian character of Lewis's political allegory. There is a caliph's design to his politics. This aspect has to be underlined because it stands in sharp contrast to the chiefly dystopian character of his fiction. It is as if the utopian streak had been denied expression in the fiction, the better to be resurrected in the political nonfiction. In *The Mysterious Mr. Bull* Lewis exclaims: "I was born, if ever a man was, for utopias, built upon a dazzlingly white and abstract ground. I was cut out to erect visionary residences, for the 'free spirit'" (229). In a letter to Julian Symons, published in 1937, Lewis maintains the same notion: "Almost by nature, I am the pure revolutionary: like Godwin, say. In me you see *a man of the tabula rasa*, if ever there was one."[15] Or in *America and Cosmic Man*, his most utopian work, the advent of cosmic man or the universal melting pot is predicted to occur in America described in paratactic terms: a "vast place, so recently a kind of *tabula rasa* physically, this world that is still new, being the cradle of a new type of man."[16]

The generic mixture of political essay and allegorical narrative is extremely important, and this for two reasons. First, it prevents the reader from regarding Lewis's political analysis as a purely objective report on a historical situation. What is questioned here is not the empirical character of his analyses, which has been demonstrated in by D. G. Bridson.[17] Instead I am looking at what happened to this empirical background when seen through a *tempérament*. Second, this generic mixture breaks down binary oppositions between modernism and the avant-garde, as Lewis's political writings present themselves with recognizable artistic, literary characteristics while functioning as basis for the organization of the polis. This convergence of artistic status and ideological praxis defines his political texts as avant-gardist texts. However, far from being progressive, some of the significant ideological tenets governing the praxis of these texts are regressive and ultra-conservative. It is precisely this explosive combination of radical avant-gardism and regressive ideology that constitutes Lewis's exacerbated version of modernism. The next chapter is devoted to bringing out the simultaneously pragmatic and poeitic character of Lewis's political discourse.

9

The Politics of Chiron

THE AIM OF THE FOLLOWING CHAPTER IS TO DEMONSTRATE THAT Lewis's political discourse presents all the signs of an artifact that functions as the basis for the pragmatic organization of political life. Therefore, even though they have an empirical orientation, his political essays should not be regarded as purely objective analyses of a historical context. What puts a creative spin on his political analyses is the presence of allegory, which remains a consistent generic aspect of his writings. At the same time, this allegorical and creative characteristic allows exchanges to occur between the nonfiction and the fiction.

Lewis's reading of history is partly based on an application of his mind-body dualism to historical events. For instance, the 1789 French revolution is regarded as a manifestation of the Wild Body. Darwin turns out to be a major landmark because he is the thinker who exposed the animal nature of the self. "Ever since Darwin," Lewis writes, "men have doubted the christian premises and tended to regard themselves as animals rather than 'humanists'" (*DP,* 113). In *The Hitler Cult,* the function of the mind-body dualism as premise to political analysis is quite conspicuous: on the one hand man consists in a "muddled, emotional, semi-animal nature" and, on the other, in a "perpetual *half understanding*" (*HC,* 178). By the same token, Christianity is pronounced an inadequate philosophy: "To be half kind, half humane, half charitable, half self-sacrificing; such is the handicap. The Sermon on the Mount . . . was a denial of this betwixt-and-between character of human beings" (*HC,* 178).

George Watson has argued that the point common to writers such as Eliot, Pound, and Lewis, who were all attracted to different modes of authoritarianism, is that each was influenced by T. E. Hulme's doctrine of Original Sin.[1] As far as Lewis is concerned, the point is certainly valid—he does refer to Hulme's doctrine in *Blasting and Bombardiering*—and one might add that more than influence, one has a convergence of views. For Lewis's conception of man already underlies his earliest short stories published from 1908 to 1911. It is this conception of man as an imperfect and limited creature, which, Watson argues, constitutes a predisposition to authoritarian forms of regime: "if any common and consistent factor is to be sought, then it can only be the doctrine that the individual should acknowledge his limits and humble himself to a master."[2] Although not exhaustive, Watson's explanation provides one piece of the puzzle.

For Lewis, politics harks back to the primitive competition between the conflicting wills of individuals seeking to assert their superiority. This makes politics stand three removes from Thanatos, sport and war being closer to it. *Monstre Gai* is particularly concerned with bringing out the brutish, vulgar streak of politics. The title itself initiates the process of allegorization of the concept of power that the Bailiff personifies. The political confrontation between the Bailiff and Hyperides leads to the physical destruction of Hyperides in what reads like the Senecan conclusion to a revenge tragedy:

> The Gay Monster, in his dark-curtained puppet-stage, danced like a lunatic, shooting out his arms and tearing off his beard. The followers of Hyperides with a roar rushed towards the black pall of smoke within which their Master was now invisible. Then suddenly the black smoke parted, exactly like two long black curtains being pulled aside. Within, and now visible to all, was the figure of Hyperides, his beard sheared off below the chin, an enormous nail driven through his throat, behind entering the thick board against which he had stood; on his head was stuck a white pointed hat tied beneath his chin. FOOL was painted on it. (*MG,* 284–85)

This conception of politics as the expression of will to power is not a conclusion Lewis would have reached after his 1939 recantation of Hitler and what he represented. It in fact lies at the heart of his political vision, and the thesis is already put forward in *The Art of Being Ruled.* The thirst for violence is described as a *savoir mourir:* "the white races seem almost incurably brutal, and always ready, after the regulation press provocation, to slaughter themselves" (*ABR,* 50). What other kind of vision of humanity should one have expected from a writer who had served on the front of World War I?

It is within the context of the denunciation of power that Lewis's reference to Machiavelli should be understood. His major analysis of the Renaissance thinker occurs in *The Lion and the Fox,* which, oddly enough, Lewis called his "first political book" (*RA,* 174). Machiavelli is endowed with the same function as Darwin: he "forces civilization to face about and confront the grinning shadow of its Past, and acknowledge the terrible nature of its true destiny."[3] Man running with his atavistic Past at his heels, yet forced to face about—this powerful metaphor reveals the *poeisis* of Lewis's political writing. The title itself derives from an allegory concerned with the description of government in *The Prince* (1513). The prince, Machiavelli argues, must rule according to man's brutish nature:

> "So, as a prince is forced to know how to act like a beast, he should learn from the fox and the lion; because the lion is defenceless against traps and a fox is defenceless against wolves. Therefore one must be a fox in order to recognize traps, and a lion to frighten off wolves. Those who simply act like lions are stupid."[4]

In addition Lewis cites another passage concerned with the allegory of the centaur, which exemplifies the dual nature of the self as half intellect, half animal. Only half of the passage is quoted in *The Lion and the Fox,* but here it is in full:

> ". . . there are two ways of fighting: by law or by force. The first way is natural to men, and the second to beasts. But as the first way often proves inadequate one must needs have recourse to the second. So a prince must understand how to make a nice use of the beast and the man. The ancient writers taught princes about this by an allegory, when they described how Achilles . . . [was] sent to be brought up by Chiron, the centaur, so that he might train [him] this way. All the allegory means, in making the teacher half beast and half man, is that a prince must know how to act according to the nature of both, and that he cannot survive otherwise."[5]

From *The Lion and the Fox* through *The Childermass* to *The Revenge for Love,* the tropes Lewis uses to express power struggle between individuals draw on this Renaissance piece. The hold of this allegory on his political imagination can be gauged by its persistence.

Indeed, the conception of history in his last novel, *Self Condemned,* can be read as the logical extension of the centaur allegory. Rotter reports that for Harding, history should be concerned with the "story of ideas, theory of the state, evolution of law, scientific discoveries, literature, art, philosophy, the theatre and so on" (*SC*, 83). Although this is not stated in the text, such a conception is basically Hegelian. From a purely Lewisian viewpoint, history is concerned with Western Man, or consciousness, or the rational, creative semi-nature of man. However, Rotter reports that Harding also recognizes that history may be written as "an Alicean chaos," or as a "violent burlesque" (*SC*, 87). History then becomes the chronicle of the Schopenhauerian Will.

The chief difference between this dual interpretation of history and Machiavelli's allegory of the centaur is that the Renaissance thinker uses the allegory as a firm principle for defining government whereas Rotter's report is characterized by denial: "we should reject entirely anything (not withstanding the fact that it undoubtedly happened) which is unworthy of any man's attention, or some action which is so revolting that it *should not* have happened. . . . it is time that men ceased proudly unrolling the blood-stained and idiotic record of their past" (*SC*, 93). What the recognition of politics as power brings about is not a political approach taking account of such a premise. Instead, one ends up with the interpretation of history based on the selection of the better half of human nature. In other words, and from a generic standpoint, one has shifted from a pessimistic allegory of human nature to a poeitic history of the not-self as pure consciousness. By the end of the novel, this *poeisis* of history is defeated first by Harding's decision to write the dark side of events and, eventually, by the absence of meaning or value in Harding's life, which deprives the writing of history of any ethos and utopia. Nothing can redeem the violence of Hester's death, and nothing can redeem the violence of war and destruction.

In his theoretical discussion of power, the demonic agent of his political allegory is the Machiavellian hero who personifies mechanical force:

> a completely equipped one, clothed from head to foot in defensive armour of the latest possible pattern, and hedged round with stratagems. Every resource of the intellect was supposed to be his, which was assumed to be entirely docile to this mechanical destiny of waiting, hand and foot . . . on physical force, and such intellectual satisfaction as can be derived from its exercise, at other people's expense. (*LF*, 96)

Lewis gave pictorial embodiment to the Machiavellian man-machine in his 1936 *The Surrender of Barcelona* (Michel, pl. IV). The armored figures standing in the foreground of the picture have lost their humanity, or rather, this humanity is solely defined by the armor and the helmet that identify them as political men-machines. Politics in Lewis should therefore be read as another case of inferior religion governing the self. This explains why he was attracted to Fouillée's concept of *idée force*. For Fouillée, an idea is "the conscious form taken by our feelings and impulses; every idea covers not only an intellectual act, but also a certain direction of the sensibility and of the will" (*ABR*, 7). The rhetorical trope of prosopopoeia is common to this definition of *idée force* and Lewis's ontological definition of the self as thing. To go back to the picture mentioned above: nothing indicates that the armors are filled with bodies. This is particularly true of the three center figures at the forefront of the picture. They could actually be interpreted in prosopopoeial terms; that is, as metallic things shaped like human bodies and behaving like persons ruled by the idea of politics as will to power.

The concept of will to power underlies both the narrative and thematics of the trilogy of *The Human Age*. Here I will concentrate on the first volume, *The Childermass*. The second half of the volume is concerned with the destruction of independent, critical consciousness. Barney, the defiant young Cockney, opposes the Bailiff and is one allegorical agent of critical consciousness. Their confrontation is based on the contrast between the lion and the fox. As he defies the Bailiff and his crowd, Barney grows into the "youthful slum-lion" (*CM*, 191), but he is bound to be defeated by the vulpine Bailiff. Barney's head is eventually chopped off in a display of gory exhibitionism to satisfy the senses of the dithyrambic crowd. The Bailiff's ruling encourages the expression of obscurantism and tribal, collective drives.

Lewis's conception of politics as pathos has a direct impact on the genre of *The Childermass*. The second half of the narrative is actually a hybrid of dramatic genres that aims at stressing both the rhetorical and illusionistic character of politics. This is suggested by the explicit reference to four types of drama. First, the Bailiff is said to speak in a *peribolos* containing "a large auditorium on the model of the antique theatre" (*CM*, 124); then his arrival is said to take place "at the centre of the stage of the Miracle heralded by the sudden detonation of a solitary furious trumpet" (*CM*, 123–24); third, and as underlined earlier, the execution of the Bailiff's political opponents takes the form of violent Senecan scenes characteristic of Renaissance revenge tragedies; finally the Bailiff's political black mass is described as farce performed in a Punch-and-Judy theater. This accumulation of references to the genre of drama is directly linked with the main implied thesis of the narrative: politics is rhetorically successful whenever it has turned its audience into dithyrambic spectators.

As underlined by Vincent Sherry,[6] Lewis's critique of mass democracy relies on the visual for its tropes and conceptualization. In *The Childermass* cinema is used as a trope to express the shortsightedness of masses glued to the screen on which the Bailiff has an "image" projected. This image comes straight from the traditional dream-vision of allegory:

Two ponderous sounds enter the atmosphere along with the image. They are Bab and Lun, of the continuous Babber'ln. The tumultuous name of the first giant metropolis echoes in the brains of the lookers-on.

Heavily and remotely its syllables thud in the crowd-mind, out of its arcanum—the *Lon* as the lumbering segment of the name of another nebulous city, and the mysterious pap of *Bab* that is the infant-food of Babel. A stolid breath of magic, they are manufactured, as they are uttered, as a spell: nothing but an almost assonantal tumbling upon the tongue and lips, preserving the dead thunder and spectacle of a fabric of gigantic walls. (*CM*, 136–37)

Lewis's critique of the ear-ideology takes the form of a characteristically allegorical, onomastic wordplay: Babylon is split into "Bab," which alludes to baby and the democracy of Peter Pans; and into "Lon," which alludes to London as the urban model for modern dystopia.

The frequently mentioned satire of James Joyce's "poliglottony" and of Gertrude Stein's "stuttering" is part of the novel's larger anatomy of language as a means of ideological enslavement. Characteristically it is the villain of the story who exposes the mechanics of political power:

"The logos we do not regard as an artistic trifle by any means. We're very serious about the word. With us the verb is The Verb and no nonsense, *Heavens admits no jest*. As a concession the creature is allowed to speak. But there is speaking and speaking. . . . We regard *words* from long experience of them and some small competence in their uses ourselves as extremely powerful engines and in consequence highly dangerous. . . . articutelateness is not a recommendation to us. . . . Certain forms of prayer—exclamations of astonishment or of rapture at the mechanical marvels of creation . . . the sounds indispensable for conducting the operation of hunting eating evacuating and love-making: that is one thing. . . . But the sort of engine that words may easily develop into when extended beyond those simple operations of stimulus-and-response, attending the fixed phases of the animal-life, is quite another matter." (*CM*, 200–201)

Lewis's modernity lies in his full grasp of the ideological and political power of means of communication. This insight comes through not only in *The Childermass* but also in *The Art of Being Ruled* and, above all, *The Revenge for Love*, with its comprehensive analysis of ideological discourse from the extreme right to the extreme left. In this respect, all these books are landmarks in the history of rhetoric and ideology, and preceded Orwell's *1984*.

Lewis's critique of mass democracy can therefore be read as an immense critique of politics as pathos: either the ruler is a manifestation of will to power or the ruled are the victims of a politics of empathy. The political ideal of *The Childermass* is personified by Hyperides, whose function is to stay outside the rhetoric of the Bailiff's politics. When Barney meets his death, he remains detached, "now stretched out in the relaxed repose of the sistine Adam. One finger points inertly forward as though awaiting the touch of the hurrying Jehovah. Twisted backwards, his hollow melancholy face surveys the scene on which his back is turned, without interest" (*CM,* 192–93). Hyperides' description is actually based on an ekphrastic rendering of Michelangelo's *The Creation of Adam* from the frescoes of the Sistine Chapel (1508–12), here extraordinarily endowed with a political ideal of detachment. One has to go back to *The Art of Being Ruled* to find the origin of this political ethos: "Utopia is not necessarily an *active* Utopia. Quiescence, obedience, and receptivity are required for action, as well as the active factors. . . . to be *receptive* rather than active (to just lie down and *couver* rather than execute) is by no means a humiliating role. And the *spectator's* godlike role is not a contemptible one at all" (*ABR,* 178). By contrast the crowd of *The Childermass* symbolically consists of automata caught in a chaotic vortex that has the Bailiff for its central point of fascination. In order to escape from the diabolics of the political Wild Body, one has to reverse the situation and, from the dithyrambic spectator spinning in the vortex of action, one should become the spectator at the still centre of the vortex.

One has here a signal example of the paradoxical character of Lewis's thought: while he depoliticizes the modern process of alienation by seeing in it the ontological problem of the self as thing, he politicizes his aesthetic of intellectual contemplation by using it as a political principle and criterion. The vorticist still point of contemplation is superimposed on fascism, in which Lewis sees an "intense, conscious, more highly evolved, and sharply defined centre of life" (*ABR,* 367). We have in this superimposition the avant-gardist project of organizing life praxis from the basis of art—to use Bürger's own terms.

Critics such as Bridson, Pritchard, and Bürger argue that in Kreisler one sees the premonitory representation of the Hitler type.[7] It is worth underlining that, in its totalitarian paroxysm, *The Art of Being Ruled* is also in part a manifestation of "archaic regression" that Jameson sees in Kreisler.[8] The truly totalitarian implication of Lewis's political discourse is revealed when his utopian imagination runs riot:

[The eradication of mass-democracy] will have been the creation of a tyrant or dictator, with virtual powers of life and death: for with his highly disciplined, implicitly obedient, fascist bands, no person anywhere will be able to escape assassination if he causes trouble to the central government, or holds, too loudly, opinions that displease it. As the press will be—is already—under the direct control of the central government, and its editors and responsible staffs appointed by it, death, imprisonment, or banishment can be inflicted on anybody, anywhere, without ruffling the surface of opinion—indeed, can occur, if required, without its being reported. In such a state it is difficult to see how 'politics' could exist. (*ABR*, 370–71)

The political utopia turns into the fait accompli of a totalitarian dystopia characterized by a regime of terror, censorship, and political anonymity observed from a hypothetical yet prophetic, retrospective viewpoint. The following could have inspired some of the scenes of Orwell's *1984*:

the time will soon come when a copy of Tolstoy's *War and Peace* will be read by the person possessing it, if at all, *en cachette*. . . . [The book] should only be placed in the hands of those who are in a position to understand it. The people who read such books, after all, should be the rulers. (*ABR*, 118–19)

We have in these passages the reason why in *Rude Assignment* Lewis is so keen on referring to *The Lion and the Fox* as his first "political book." This book was published in 1927, one year later than *The Art of Being Ruled*, and is unequivocal in its condemnation of violence and coercion. By contrast, the very discourse of Lewis's first political book is impure and betrays the politics of the intellect. Sisson's observation that words "have their lower as well as their higher magic and [that] they are inextricably bound to action, which aspires to thought, and uses rhetoric"[9] applies very well to the character and undertaking of *The Art of Being Ruled*.

Lewis's second major faux pas is to have advocated political expediency. The justification of the means by the end is first adhered to in *The Art of Being Ruled*, where it is argued that

in the ultimate interest of all of us we should sacrifice anything to the end that this most priceless power of any (the intellectual power by which, as a kind, we express and illustrate ourselves . . .) be put in a position finally to be effective. Instead of the vast organisation to exploit the weaknesses of the Many, should we not possess one for the exploitation of the intelligence of the Few? (*ABR*, 89)

It is this philosophy of expediency that lures his thought towards zones of totalitarian politics. The same argument reemerges in *Hitler*, where the Nazi leader is presented as an "armed socialist prophet"[10] whose use of force is interpreted as an "argument for *an emergency*"

(*H*, 128). The rhetoric of *Hitler* is of prime importance because it resorts to allegorical personification to support the ideological and pragmatic discourse of the pamphlet. Thus: "Gentleness, beauty, sweet reason must veil their heads, they must give way to arguments of *power*" (*H*, 130).

In other words, within this political context, Lewis's use of allegorical rhetoric does not function as a means of seeing through ideologies or inferior religions, but as a means of political persuasion. The ideological function of allegory goes even further: while the sublime character of allegorical personification is stymied by the satirical devices of Lewis's fiction, it is given full expression in the political pamphlets in order to create a political hero in contrast to the demonic agents of mass democracy. Thus a person is defined in terms of "organization" (*PF*, 78) as opposed to the amorphic: "It is only when a mob of things is organized, and has become possessed of *persons* (interpreting and administering its laws and its tradition) that it can be said to have a 'common good'" (*PF*, 89). Since Lewis has previously argued that only a few can be "persons," it follows that the "good" is common to only a few. What such definition implies is that the ruler is a "person," while the ruled are the mob of things. The difference between the statements of "The Meaning of the Wild Body" and those just quoted lies in the utopian transcendence from mob to person, and the cancellation or at least modification of the prosopopoeial definition of the self in term of a thing behaving like a person. One has here a good indication of the *poeisis* of Lewis's political imagination, which, in contrast to his fictional pieces, succeeds in inventing a positive destiny for a positive hero. In *Blasting and Bombardiering* Lewis argues that Joyce, Eliot, Pound, and himself "*are the first men of a Future that has not materialized*" (256). Nor did this renascence materialize in Lewis's fiction, which repeatedly signifies the abortion of man, the ideologic phantom. But it reaches a peak in *The Art of Being Ruled* and later on in *Hitler,* in which the artist turns into a social architect determined to build a new Baghdad.

The elitist aspect of his political allegory is indicated by his attraction to the figure of the aristocrat, which derives from a typically modernist anti-bourgeois stance. In *The Art of Being Ruled* aristocracy is not favored: "There is nothing 'aristocratic' about the intellect" (*ABR*, 431). This argument is valid insofar as it implies that the politics of the intellect cannot be applied to the declining aristocracy of Great Britain. However, it is misleading insofar as it does not acknowledge the author's belief in the innate gift of the intellect, the function of which is to introduce a supposedly natural distinction between man and man. In political terms, two distinct classes are thus introduced: the haves, who rule, and the have-nots, who are ruled.

Commenting on Verrall, the aristocratic figure of *Burmese Days* (1934), Lewis remarks: "yes, I suppose Orwell *is* a little too much impressed with his young aristocrat. But what member of the middle-class, born before 1914, could be otherwise?" (*WA,* 159). Should one see in these comments a veiled self-analysis? According to Meyers, Lewis's mother did try to keep up appearances guided by a melan-choly for gentility. Lewis himself spent a good deal of his twenties as a penniless aristocrat financially dependent on his parents and doing the grand tour of continental Europe (albeit an unorthodox one). In one statement of *Blasting and Bombardiering,* it is clear that he regards himself as the product of an aristocratic education. Among the differ-ences he notes between himself as a bombardier during World War I and his fellow-soldiers is his willingness to go to war, which he attri-butes to his "aristocratic" training, his "period as a student in Ger-many, [and] the influence of a peculiarly martial father" (*BB,* 31).[11] Although without any economic basis, the ideological function of the gentleman remains predominant in Lewis's political views. In a naïve and politically inadequate depiction of the ruler, political leadership is defined in anti-bourgeois terms. The life of the ruler will be

> full of the shock of the forces of outer vastness from which the masses are sheltered. . . . The ruler must be completely disillusioned—a suspicion of belief and he would be lost; the cares of his numerous duties will prevent him from sleeping very much; he will not be able to regard life as agreeable in any way . . . hearty laughter or anything that we associate with *bourgeois* relaxation would never visit him. (*ABR,* 96)

It is in fiction that, on the whole, Lewis succeeds in maintaining an ironic distance between himself and the image of the aristocrat. But at the political level, this image remains mesmerizing.

The definition of the political ruler occurs in the context of a dis-course on purity. Like the ideal Tarr-like artist, the ruler is the ancho-rite of politics: in *Hitler,* a puritanical ideal is maintained and contrasted with the description of corruption in Berlin. Lewis advo-cates the "ascetic of Politics—an asceticism not without its nobility, one that is little understood" (*H,* 28). Thus the political allegory implicitly rests on the mind-body agon and creates a gap between ruler-intellect and ruled-body. A Platonic tradition can be invoked as philosophical context for the tropes of Lewis's political discourse. In the ninth book of *The Republic,* only the man who has control over his body is entitled to rule and govern.[12]

However, the Platonic tradition offers only a partial explanation that does not take account of the modern phenomenon of *mass* democracy. In *The Politics of Modernism,* Raymond Williams refers to "*conservative* forms of order, seen as offering at least some framework of control for the unruly impulses both of the dynamic psyche and of the pre-rational 'mass' or 'crowd'."[13] Williams does not mention Lewis, but it seems to me his analysis offers a very convincing description of the psychopolitical process underlying the politics of the intellect. Indeed, the metaphorical equation between mass and unconscious on the one hand, and individual and intellect on the other is manifest in Lewis's texts. For instance, in *The Art of Being Ruled,* the social crowd is equated with the "mob of the unconscious." The equation between intellect and individual or "person" appears, ironically enough, in a passage where Lewis counters accusations of political elitism concerning "The Crowd-Master" first published in *Blast* (1915):

> what was meant by "Crowdmaster" was that I was master of myself. Not of anybody else—that I have never wanted to be. I was master *in* the crowd, not master *of* the crowd. I moved freely and with satisfaction up and down its bloodstream, in strict, even arrogant, insulation from its demonic impulses.
> This I regarded as, in some sort, a triumph of mind over matter. It was a triumph (as I saw it then) of the individualist principle. (*BB,* 89–90)

Lewis's emphasis on an ethical interpretation as opposed to a political is justified but it yields only half of the truth. The emergence of the tropes of crowd-as-unconscious and ruler-as-intellect in his political discourse confirms the fact that the ethical, psychological, and political levels are all connected.

The presence of "The Crowd-Master" with its mind-body dualism in the avant-gardist 1915 *Blast* also shows the continuity between the radicalism of the review and Lewis's postwar political extremism. Whether the dualism is interpreted from a purely psychological viewpoint that would have developed in political terms, or from an ideological viewpoint as already carrying psychological overtones, the continuity is there. Furthermore the short story in *Blast* establishes a continuity of an even greater scope by alluding to Baudelaire's "*Les Foules.*" The name of the mysterious Lewisian protagonist is Multum, whose allegorical emblematism is deciphered as follows: "An opposition and welding of the two heaviest words that stand for the multitude on the one hand, the Ego on the other" (*Blast* 1915, 99). The intertextual reference is to this passage in Baudelaire's prose poem: "*Multitude, solitude: termes égaux et convertibles pour le poète actif et fécond*."[14] Lewis's political radicalism operates at the expense of Baude-laire's equation by opposing instead of converting multitude and ego. Thus the same newspapers that lent their subversive typography to *Blast* become twenty years later in *Doom of Youth* indicting evidence in "dossiers" compiled by Lewis to conduct his ideological critique of mass democracy.

Lewis's campaign against the mobs of the unconscious led him to make racial analyses, which, despite critical efforts to the contrary, have to be acknowledged as racist in character. The tenacious belief in Western Man's intellectual prerogative still underlies the argument of *The Jews: Are They Human?* For instance, the "extremely jewish Jews . . . have a number of habits—of which they are inordinately proud—which they will lose in a short while, in all likelihood, as a result of observing our vastly superior way of deporting ourselves."[15] In the same book Lewis occasionally remembers that Einstein and Proust were Jewish and that some of the best art comes from the Orient. The blacks are a cursed model for white culture. In *Paleface*, conditions are laid down: "We ask nothing better than to go over into the reformed world-order, am I not right? but we will not be *pushed* over, no, nor barked at as we go by the Big Borzois and other mongrels, or in short, march out to a chorus of Dark Laughter" (85). The Borzoi merges with the Lewisian motif of the dog, this symbol of animal nature and lower origins in the self: Paleface runs away with at his heels the traumatic bark of Dark Laughter. Too close to lower nature and, like the mongrel, unbearably ill-defined, the black is unconsciously perceived as a threat. The fact that Lewis's racism, as it comes to that, is governed by the allegory of the mind-body dualism is reinforced by his portrait of the American Indian, who, "with his legendary calm aloofness, his faultless self-discipline and self-reliance, so that a solitary Brave was as much to be feared as a troop" (*PF*, 233) is superior to the white American when the latter lapses into hysteria as well as to the "jigging, laughing and crying, yapping and baaing, average Negro" (*PF*, 233). This Noble Red Man comes straight from James Fenimore Cooper, whose larger-than-life characterization is a perfect fit for Lewis's archetypal unconscious torn between the desire for intellectual mastery and disgust for the body. In *Left Wings over Europe*, the same unconscious agon opposes the "industrious and ingenious Italian" to the "lazy, stupid, and predatory Ethiopian" (164–65). Hence the fascist invasion of Abyssinia is a godsend for the poor Ethiopian.

Lewis's racism is not an offshoot of his political extremism, as he constantly held his position until *The Hitler Cult* in 1939. So the roots of his racism are not solely historical but also feed on personal mythology. Although he is right in pointing out the black self-identification with the white middle class, he never takes the time to ponder the psycho-sociological dimension of such a phenomenon. Instead, the values of the intellect are pitted against those of what he perceives as essentially a race of the inferior Wild Body. Thus, jazz is described as "the aesthetic medium of a sort of frantic proletarian sub-conscious, which is the very negation of those far greater arts . . . of other more celebrated 'Coloured' races, such as the Chinese or the Hindu" (*PF*, 65). The associative aspect of Lewis's political unconscious is patent here: jazz—black—subconscious—body—proletariat. The fact that he adds that blacks have their philosophers and scientists does not impair the above argument. The problem is not that some blacks are intellectual and others are not, but rather, that jazz should necessarily be a "sort of *inferior* Black art" (*PF*, 65). In *The Hitler Cult*, Lewis goes as far as supporting the notion of a natural interdict against miscegenation: it is a fact, he argues, that "a 'colour-bar,' not only social, but also biological, does exist; and it is quite sufficiently effective to prevent any really unsuitable cross-breeding. It certainly is powerful enough to discourage the magnificent Nordic Aryans of New York City from intermarrying with the Negro to any great extent" (*HC*, 68). One has to wait until *America and Cosmic Man* to see black art treated without reference to a criterion of inferiority. In America, the "coloured people are the artistic leaven; out of their outcast state they have made a splendid cultural instrument. The almost solar power of their warm-heartedness has been a precious influence" (*ACM*, 208).

America and Cosmic Man represents something of a temporary U-turn in Lewis's political vision. Moving up and down the multiracial crowds of North America, he reports experiencing and enjoying a "kind of disembodied feeling" (*ACM*, 184). Freedom as liberation from the body and matter is a recurrent motif of the work. The dominant imagery is that of movement in space, not stasis: "all moved outside, out of the area of great pressure, into an area where the pressure was lifted from them and they could breath freely. They would suddenly have the sensation of walking on air, of having been delivered of an incubus" (*ACM*, 188). The symbolic movement of outwardness, the Bachelardian poetics of ascension, and the shaking-off of a nightmarish, sexual creature, all these symbolic elements powerfully combine to convey an apocalyptic sense of freedom from matter and a sudden release from as well as relief of tension. The ultimate feeling is paradisiacal, the political utopia has become a heaven "*where the spirit is released from all the too-close contacts with other people*" (*ACM*,

187). This newly-found *patria mia* is the heaven Arghol was in search of and denied.

The book is also interesting because it is part of those works in which Lewis was struggling with his political past. First in this series is *Count Your Dead: They Are Alive!* (1937) the conclusion of which does not bring support to fascism but condemns all political ideologies as expressions of will to power; second is *The Hitler Cult* (1939), Lewis's public recantation; fourth is the autobiographical *Rude Assignment* (1950), in which he acknowledges his fascination for power between the two wars. *America and Cosmic Man* comes third in 1948, and in part represents an attempt to backtrack on the recantation process.

Indeed, in this final political work Lewis argues that in 1926 he already supported the notion of freedom as opposed to that of "Duty," which is always held at the expense of "epicurean values" (*ACM*, 188). In fact the author tries to reverse his former interpretation of the phenomenon of "emancipation" that, in 1926, was certainly not praised as an expression of epicurean values but satirized as an "intoxicated dance of puppets" (*ABR*, 142). That the author's argument is disingenuous is shown by his attempt to tamper with the 1926 formula that reads: "*Emancipation and irresponsibility are commutative terms*" (*ABR*, 146). Alleging to quote from *The Art of Being Ruled*, Lewis writes that "freedom and irresponsibility are commutative terms" (*ACM*, 187). The substitution of "freedom" for "emancipation" is extremely important because, in Lewis, they do not have the same connotation. Indeed "emancipation" is dependent on the demands of the Wild Body. In 1926, it is asserted that "not 'freedom,' or the eccentric play of the 'personality,' but submission to a group-rhythm, is what men desire" (*ABR*, 166). By contrast, "freedom," as sought by the ruler, is a spiritual ideal; the more conscious, the less subservient to the body. By means of his substitution Lewis tries to ignore the distinction between consciousness and body on which a great part of his political discourse rests. The likeliest reason for such revisionism is that, by 1948, he had fully realized that the seeds of his authoritarian and totalitarian vision were already in *The Art of Being Ruled*.

Having cancelled the distinction between mind and body, Lewis finds himself on the side of epicurean values; or does he? What should be understood by "epicurean"? If the term is used in its popular way to refer to sensual pleasure, then he is definitely attributing a positive role to the body. If the term refers to the philosophy that taught that the body is the source of all pains, then his discourse has remained fundamentally unchanged. Indeed, in *America and Cosmic Man*, the yearning for intellectual purity is stronger than ever. Unhampered by historical tradition and attachment to the soil, the emigrant to America has only one attachment that is "to a slightly happy-go-lucky vacuum, in which the ego feels itself free." Lewis goes on:

> It is . . . something like the refreshing anonymity of a great city, compared with the oppressive opposite of that, invariably to be found in the village. Everything that is obnoxious in the Family is encountered in the latter: all that man gains by escape from the Family is offered by the former. The United States is full of people who have escaped from their families, figuratively. (*ACM*, 186)

His reflexion on his journey to North America during World War II presents itself as an allegorical search for a figurative type of freedom: the escape from material origin is accomplished through the emigration of the soul, or nonphysical self, into an area free of physical pressure.

So Lewis has revised his political positions and assumptions, but the tropes of his writing persist. The theme of freedom reappears in the social context of the short story "The Rot" in *Rotting Hill*. The story is set against the background of a newly socialized United Kingdom, and can be regarded as an allegorical interpretation of Marxist materialism. At a literal level, workers are called in to renovate a flat threatened by rot. However, ideological clashes are expressed by means of the polysemic function of "rot." The term does not refer to organic matter in decay only, it is also the vehicle for ideological messages. The meaning of "rot" varies according to which class one belongs to. For the worker, the bourgeois—including the idle artist— is the rot. For the writer, the new society is in a state of decay: "The English had a public conscience as big as a house. But its fibre is devoured. It is completely rotted."[16] So the whole kingdom is rotting and falling down, falling down.

In typically allegorical fashion, the plot develops on the basis of a pun on the Soviet political insignia of the hammer to which the blows of the carpenter and his workers allude. Hammer in hand, the workers destroy the bourgeois flat, symbol of wealth and of exploitation of mankind. This "token class-war" starts as follows:

> Then—preceded by a brief silence, upstairs and downstairs, and as it seemed outside as well—the first blow fell. . . . We were glad the rot had found out so palpable a fake as the archaic rafters, of which we were ashamed if anything: but the carpenter thought his blows fell upon our hearts. The plaster boxes, beneath repeated blows from his axe, and the

hammers of his men, came crashing down. We recognized immediately that we, and not the plaster, were the true target of the assault. (*RH,* 102)

The ominous, apocalyptic blows of invisible hammers and the willess, absentminded creatures whose reactions are at "coolie levels" (*RH,* 97) establish a definite link between the vision of "The Rot" and that underlying *The Childermass,* where the coolies are "peons" and where the same ominous blows are suggested. Indeed, in a surrealistic scene Pullman and Satters walk across a time-picture dating from the eighteenth century. What lies at the horizon of this picture is the French Revolution, which is alluded to by a "great outbreak of hollow hammering, accompanied by an oscillation of the earth of the panorama. . . . Pulley, legs apart, his weather-eye pedantically open, hands stuck deep and fast in jacket-pockets, sways easily upon his quarterdeck of the good ship Time, and surveys his abject lieutenant zigzagging and next falling into an oak-bush" (*CM,* 98). The hollow hammering also alludes to the 1917 Soviet revolution, which, in *The Art of Being Ruled,* Lewis relates to the events of 1789. So from 1926 to 1951 the same allegorical tropes persist. It is also striking to see the resurgence of an ambivalent discourse on freedom. On the one hand, multitude and ego are convertible as the narrator shows understanding for the workers' elation at being free: "these men were intoxicated with what I still regard as sacred beverage—liberty" (*RH,* 109). (Here "liberty" has the advantage of relative neutrality over "freedom" and "emancipation.") On the other, distaste for the "mass" is expressed in Lewis's typically allegorical style, combining hyphenation and dash to lock his ideological personifications in paratactic compartments: "Sun-dazzled earth-worms—slaves in the Senate. Might for the Midget—Madness—MILLENNIUM" (*RH,* 105). The narrator, who withdraws from life into his office, sees in these workers Wild Bodies at the mercy of an inferior religion none other than Marxism with its time-machine of redeeming apocalyptism.

For, ultimately, the rot of the story is *time* as the manifestation of matter. The workers are chiefly idlers, squandering "immense mouthfuls of time" (*RH,* 101). As worshippers of millenarianism and as professional idlers, they remain enslaved by time. In *Malign Fiesta* it is said: "If you do not master time, time will master you" (471). In "The Rot," the mastery of time is not attributed to the conventional vorticist still point of observation, even though the latter is associated with the narrator's viewpoint. Instead, Lewis presents the allegory of the utopian workingman:

Road-workers were remaking sections of the road. They worked under the direction of foremen, who never left the road, and the men never stopped: they seldom spoke to one another, except about what they were doing. . . . [They] were trained to work quickly, they were the same men who had made the airfields during the war, and remade them at top speed. . . . though there was no rushing but concentrated deliberation—of progressive unmaking, layer by layer, and then of remaking, from earth-line to the street-level—the tension of the time-table was felt. (*RH*, 110–11)

This passage is based on the vision of man's masterful utilization of time and shaping of matter, which, for Lewis, constitute the surest means of freedom. From a sheer artistic viewpoint, the short story is a successful generic hybrid of social realism, which roots the plot in historical reality, and of allegory, which lets its fundamentally poeitic character coincide with a social utopia drawing on the values of *Time and Western Man*. For is not this ideal road-worker an expert of the concrete Great Without as well as a spatializer?

10

Self-Exegesis

WHAT REMAINS PUZZLING IS THE FACT THAT LEWIS SHOULD HAVE seen in Hitler a political savior. Bernard Bergonzi points at the author's fighting in World War I as one of the factors making for the author's "protofascism": the war is seen as the "matrix of Fascism."[1] Although in *The Old Gang and the New Gang* Lewis argues that any feeling of resentment against the generals of 1914–18 is politically naïve, *The Apes of God* contains a curious episode that clearly establishes a link between fascism and World War I. Chapter 10 of part 12 consists of a satire of old colonels invited to Lord Osmund's Lenten party. The satire includes a scene in which Blackshirt, whose name says it all, yells at Colonel Ponto and kicks him in the buttocks.

However, not all who fought became fascists and, even more significant, not all who were "protofascists" and lovers of order and authority fought during the war. In addition, the argument according to which the author was not the only person to be deluded by Hitler proves not only unhelpful but also incomplete. For other people were also able to see through Hitler and fascism well before 1939. L.C.B. Seaman reports that as "early as April 1933, Chamberlain's own half-brother, Austen, joint architect of [the treaty of] Locarno when foreign secretary in 1925, had made it plainly: 'Germany is afflicted by this narrow, exclusive, aggressive spirit, by which it is a crime to be in favour of peace and a crime to be a Jew. This is not a Germany to which we can afford to make concessions'."[2] In his diary, Harold Nicolson, on a visit to Rome with Mosley in 1932, wrote that Hitler's movement aimed at destroying individuality and freedom, and that his political program was a "dogma about the young, by the young and for the young." And in an article published anonymously in *New Oxford Outlook* (1934), Richard Crossman wrote that Hitler's final values "are not principles, are not indeed intellectual at all: they are emotional attitudes, metaphysical reactions."[3] As the champion of individuality and personality, as the satirist of youth cult, and as the supporter of the politics of the intellect, Lewis let himself be hoodwinked by Hitler's image.

189

It could be argued that *Hitler* was written at a time when little was known of the Nazis' actual intentions. "What we really need to criticize Lewis for," Reed Way Dasenbrock writes, "is not his preference for Fascism but his failure to inform himself about either Fascism or Leninism."[4] But then Lewis went on to write in favor of Hitler's action in 1936 when *Left Wings over Europe* was published. Some would counter that this was a political potboiler. In answer to this, it should be remarked that Lewis's position is ambiguous in other works too. But above all, the author would have shown an implausible degree of recklessness by exposing himself to the risk of a bad reputation and possible censorship. Why should he have written political potboilers to damage himself? Again, why is it that in *Time and Western Man* Lewis saw though Mussolini and then was taken in by Hitler? Why did Lewis remain "disengaged" in 1926 only to commit himself in 1931?

In an analysis of the relation between literature and propaganda, A. P. Foulkes describes the mechanism of propaganda in the following terms: it "does not often come marching towards us waving swastikas and chanting '*Sieg Heil*'; its real power lies in its capacity to conceal itself, to appear natural, to coalesce completely and indivisibly with the values and accepted power symbols of a given society."[5] Rather than using this definition mechanically, I will modify it slightly to understand how ideology functions in Lewis's writings.

The fundamental process of ideological self-delusion applies to Lewis, except that the coalescence between the political power and the author's values was not the product of a political strategy but one of Lewis investing his own values into the political system. This process can be observed in the first pages of *Hitler* where the author relates how he witnessed the mass meeting of Nazi supporters in Berlin with Goebbels and Goering as main orators:

> In this gigantic assembly of twenty thousand people there was something like the physical pressure of one immense, indignant thought—it was impossible to be present and not to be amazed at the passion engendered in all these men and women, and the millions of others of whom these were only a fraction, by the message of these stormy platform voices, calling upon them to pursue relentlessly the path marked out, and to recapture their freedom at whatever cost. (*H*, 10–11)

The fascination with the crowd and its latent power is indicated by Lewis's transformation of the crowd, which was so far described as a Wild Body, into the allegorical personification of an "indignant thought." In other words, a process of rationalization takes place to justify empathy with the "physical pressure" of the crowd. In *The*

Hitler Cult, eight years later, the author has awakened from his forgetful trance, and the intellect is once more claiming its rights over the crowd-body. Here is another version of what happened that night at the mass meeting:

> Goering was in his shirt-sleeves; soon he was deluged with sweat. . . . From the sea of people underneath (I was in the gallery) rose a surge of hoarse applause, sinking to a sultry murmur while it strained its ears for fresh incitments to riot, then suddenly ascending to a scream of hate. I shall always remember the giant rustling and breathing of this mastodon, in the intervals of pandemonium—of this Berlin mob, the New Proletariat in its first months of epileptic life. (*HC,* 5)

By 1939 the protagonists of Lewis's politics have fallen back into their assigned positions, and the allegory has been revamped. On the one hand, a crowd conducted by a sweaty German Bailiff revels and grovels on the lower floor, while on the other, the detached observer prominently located at a god-like, superior level, watches the ominous displays of a Leviathan proletariat. In this new version Lewis seeks to assert the precedence of the intellect over the temptation of the Wild Body.

The first version remains invaluable because it reveals that no propaganda or ideology can be effective unless based on an emotional appeal to the audience, reader, or viewer. In other words, for ideology to "appear natural," it has to take the path of the unconscious or pathos. The recantation of *The Hitler Cult* constitutes an in-extremis official gesture that does not really deal with the experience of the "physical pressure" of the crowd. Lewis's attempt to grasp the role of pathos in ideological self-delusion is actually apparent in the twin publications of *Count Your Dead: They Are Alive!* and *The Revenge for Love.* It is pursued in *The Vulgar Streak, Self Condemned,* and it culminates in *The Human Age.*

In addition, a perceptible change in the fictional treatment of characters can be observed, and this has been underlined by various critics. The emotional dimension of the later novels has been ascribed to an aging, more humane personality. But it can be argued that the pathos of these narratives—which translate into expressionism, references to psychoanalysis, love stories, and tears of self-pity—has finally reintegrated Lewis's writing because its relation to ideology has become the crucial question. Thus *The Revenge for Love* has Ruskin for major intertextual reference, not just as author of *Lilies and Sesame,* but also as theoretician of the pathetic fallacy. The revenge for love is not that love itself produces its own mawkish ideologies; rather it is that love (Freud would have said libido) is a major factor in ideological adherence. This is the reason why each major political issue of the novel always combines with an apparently parallel discourse on love. The scene between Hardcaster and Gillian in part 3 and that between Hardcaster and Malaheu in part 7 are only two prominent examples.

In this context, with its polysemic levels of meaning, allegory can function like a modern means of analysis of the unconscious. The obliquity of this analytical process of creation is very well expressed by Whitman's description of modern allegory as it finally emerged in Bernard Silvestris's *Cosmographia* by the end of the twelfth century: "he *acts out* his *exegesis* by the *composition* of *allegorical agents*."[6] Here is the clue to the last two volumes of the *The Human Age*, which combine poeitic energies with the interpretive character of allegory to analyze the mechanism of ideological self-identification.

Before tackling this final major allegory, I will first resume the psychoanalytical interpretation I initiated in chapter 4. The author is often singled out for his antagonistic stance towards important intellectual figures whom he satirizes and rejects. It is worth noticing that the Enemy's aggressivity considerably abates when it comes to certain political figures who constitute his political pantheon. Although he condemns his Machiavellian politics, Lewis admires Frederick the Great, who is portrayed as a "*condottiere,* of an extremely *raffiné* variety" (*LF,* 99). Bismarck, Hitler, Napoleon—the latter as a "cosmopolitan, a Great European" (*JATH,* 47), Alexander Hamilton (who met his death in a duel), and Franklin Roosevelt; all of these obviously exert a certain fascination on the author. The particularities of these figures are that most of them are military figures, and that all of them are invested with a role of authority. So, on the one hand, the Enemy endeavors to remain free from any idolatry yet, on the other, his dealing with some political figures indicates a total assimilation of a tradition of patriarchal politics. The figure who exerted the highest degree of fascination on Lewis is Hitler, of course. Looking back courageously at his political blindness, the author remarks: "I confess that in one respect I was badly taken in, in 1930. What more than anything else caused my judgement to trip was that unusual trinity of celibacy, teetotalism, and anti-nicotine" (*HC,* 37). It is worth underlining that in his own self-analysis, Lewis does not attribute his mistake to a misreading of historical or political facts. Rather, emphasis is laid on a misapprehension of personality.

Within Lewis's psychopolitics this self-analysis cannot be more accurate. Hitler is the perfect ruler because, being a celibate, a teetotaller, and a non-smoker, he is *a fortiori* a pure intellect. This is the logic of the mind-body agon. Lewis was never taken in by Hitler, he was always fascinated by an image of Hitler, and more accurately, by self-projection. In Hitler he saw the perfect mirror-image of an imaginary self to which the ego always aspires. When Lewis says that Hitler "is nothing if not irrational" (*HC,* 49), he not only comments on the historical figure but also on the role of this figure in his own unconscious.

I suggest that Lewis's father, Charles Lewis, stands as the origin of this ideal self that the author believed he could detect in Hitler. The father's essential characteristic is that he is absent. Leaving his wife when Lewis was eleven, he created a painful vacuum that nothing ever replenished. In this respect, it can be argued that one reason for Lewis's insightful analysis of the father figure in Western society is that he had been sensitized to the question from an early age. Peter Keating provides a general background concerning the decline of the Victorian family, which is helpful in understanding Lewis's particular case. He points out that what he calls "the urgent need for release from parental ties"[7] is apparent in symbolic parricides in *The Way of All Flesh* or *Sons and Lovers,* as well as in symbolic matricides as in *The Portrait of the Artist as a Young Man.* The irony concerning Lewis's background is that the loosening of the paternal ties coincides with a tightening of maternal ties. Neither proved satisfactory; both proved destabilizing.[8] From a larger historical viewpoint, this crisis was compounded with the aftermath of World War I. The end of the war was perceived as the end of despotic, patriarchal governments. With the dismantling of powers such as imperial Russia, Austria-Hungary, and the Ottoman Empire, a whole tradition based on powerful symbols of authority vanished. Lewis's fascination with authoritarian politicians can be interpreted as an attempt to brace an already shaky edifice both from a personal and a collective viewpoint.

A good deal of Lewis's analysis of society can be subsumed under the study of the family cell and its disintegration. For the decreasing authority of the father figure takes on its full meaning within the context of the whole family. The destruction of this figure also jeopardizes the identity of the other two members of the basic family. In *The Art of Being Ruled,* it is argued that the "trinity of God, Subject, and Object is at an end. The collapse of this trinity is the history also of the evolution of the subject into the object or of the child back into the womb from which it came" (*ABR,* 17). It is quite clear that the evolution of the subject into the object is caused by the absence of an apex, which is the God of the trinity referred to in the first place. But if the subject is the child, and the object the womb, then the "god" is probably the phallus. Inexorably the oedipal complex emerges again.

Lewis's reading of Western society and culture verges on a psycho-analytical interpretation. The feminine crowd is the product of the evolution of the subject or child into the object or womb. By contrast, the Lewisian subject attempts to counter this evolution by means of a self-identification with a God that corresponds to an ideal father-principle or the God of the not-self. A great part of Lewis's sociopolitics derives from a twist of fate: the coincidence between the absence of the father in his personal development and the increasing decline of Western society as a markedly patriarchal organization. Lewis's modernist fascination with strong public personalities is shared by other writers. As early as 1914, in an article entitled "The Renaissance," Pound argued that democracies "have always fallen, because humanity craves the outstanding personality."[9] In *Etruscan Places* (1932), Lawrence's mythopoeisis is stigmatized by a fascination with the figure of authority referred to as the "*Lucumo*":

> A *Lucumo* . . . sitting very noble in his chariot driven by an erect charioteer, might be driving in at sundown, halting before the temple to perform the brief ritual of entry into the city. . . . glowing ruddy in flesh, his head stiffly trimmed in the Oriental style, the torque of gold round his neck, and the mantle or wrap bordered with scarlet falling in full folds, leaving the breast bare, he was divine, sitting on the chair in his chariot in the stillness of power.[10]

Is it a coincidence that when Lawrence evokes his Etruscan divinity he should switch to an allegorical mode? The *Lucumo* is made the personification of some mysterious authority; the style is characteristically paratactic and proceeds by mosaic cumulation; and, by emphasizing the ornamental and the sartorial, the description of this hierarchical figure creates a *kosmos*. Both Lawrence's *Lucumo* and Lewis's historical models indicate the presence of what, in *The Tradition of Return*, Jeffrey Perl refers to as the tradition of return or *nostos*. It is quite probable that the more intense *nostos* is in the modernist work, the more authoritarian its political discourse tends to be. In Lewis the rereading of history according to a preconceived idea combines a "politics of return" with a return to the father figure.

What are the characteristics of the father figure in Lewis? It is essential to establish that the father figure is fundamentally ambivalent. On the one hand, Charles Lewis was the military hero,[11] the fine rider, and the accomplished sailor. He was also a writer. For all this, he was admired and secretly emulated, though not always with success. On the other hand, he was the father who broke up the family cell by eloping with the maid. Sexuality and fatherhood are indelibly associated for the young Lewis. For this destructive, irrepressible sexual appetite the father was loathed. Lewis's sociopolitical ambiguity on the question of the father could be profitably traced back to the ambivalence of the father figure in his own worldview. The father figure is asserted when Lewis supports the conception of the ruler as a figure of unquestionable authority. But the father figure is neutralized when Lewis momentarily sides with the feminist against a patriarchal society. However, the ruler-philosopher of Lewis's political utopia does not duplicate the father figure perceived in Charles Lewis. The ruler actually stands as a compromise by combining the authority and the heroic stature of Lewis's father with the intellect of the not-self. The emphasis on the values of the mind cannot be said to derive from Charles Lewis who, despite his literary production, seems to be perceived mostly as a man of action or Wild Body. Lewis's attachment to the values of the intellect seems to have been elaborated in response to the father figure's chief defect. Charles Lewis betrayed an appetite for the sexual body, hence his idealized image will project him as pure intellect, a truncated God. Lewis's Hitler is therefore the perfect personification of the idealized father, as he combines military authority and decisive action with the apparent asceticism of the intellect.

The components of the father figure I have just grossly sketched constitute the basis for the self-exegesis acted out by Lewis through the allegorical agents and narrative framework of the last two volumes of *The Human Age* (1955), the two sequels to *The Childermass* published in 1928. As in the case of *The Apes of God,* the ideology of the trilogy is not monolithic but in fact subject to an evolution from the first volume to the third. The ideological tenor of *The Human Age* depends not only on the roles of the political ruler and the protagonist-citizen, but also on the role of the voice that conducts the narrative throughout the trilogy. In the case of the first two volumes, the ruler is the Bailiff. In the last, he has been superseded by Sammael. In all three volumes, the protagonist-citizen is Pullman.

The relation between Pullman and the ruler differs in the three volumes, and indicates a fluctuation in Lewis's vision worth studying. In *The Childermass* the Bailiff is a master of political opportunism and sensationalism. He is one of "those great engineers in the human-plastic" (*CM*, 287). A buffoon, he is a dangerous adept in duplicity. Although his behavior is reported to be "cool and masculine" (*CM*, 18), Pullman is vulnerable and under the sway of the Bailiff's power. His fascination is recurrently described in the novel. When he hears the word "Bailiff," he "withdraws into a hypnotic fixity of expression, as if something precise for him alone had been mentioned under an unexpected enigma" (*CM*, 5). During the exchanges between the

Bailiff and Hyperides, he sides with the Bailiff and thus becomes part of the crowd of Not-Selves. In *The Childermass* Pullman is a typically allegorical *eiron*. This also implies that the Bailiff's political sensationalism and Pullman's political naïveté are implicitly contrasted with the values associated with the narrative voice. These values make up what Lewis referred to as the politics of the intellect, which allows one to unmask and defeat ideological imposture. From a rhetorical viewpoint, the politics of the intellect constitutes the ethos of the narrative in *The Childermass*.

What is striking, however, is that this ethos does not rest only with the narrative voice. Indeed, Lewis splits his narrative ethos among various characters such as Hyperides and Macrob, who become temporary mouthpieces. What is more, the Lewisian ethos is occasionally associated with the Bailiff's statements, and this accounts for the diabolical fascination exerted by the character. Thus the Bailiff's description to Hyperides of his inferno is both Shakespearean and vorticist:

> "What is brewing here is a dust-storm you understand or an event of no more importance—this is a very arid place, I try to make it a little juicy as you have often observed with displeasure, it is the Plain of Death and is full of an empty whirling underneath—its movements signify nothing: these myrmidons will whirl about and my particles there will agitate and collide, vortex within vortex, mine and thine, with a buzzing of *meum* and *tuum*, a fine angry senseless music, it will be an unintelligible beating of the air if we go on just as it will be if we do not." (*CM*, 291)

The splitting of the novel's ethos among minor characters or antagonists such as the Bailiff is systematic in Lewis's narrative. It indicates that, in the transfer from *The Art of Being Ruled* and *Time and Western Man* to *The Childermass*, logocentrism has lost some of its momentum. It is only in the last two volumes of *The Human Age* that this potential for dialogism and dynamic critique of a single coherent narrative voice and viewpoint is fully tapped.

The major difference between *The Childermass* and *Monstre Gai* is that Pullman is not depicted as a political *eiron*. At the beginning of part 6 he shares his views with Mannock, and sees through the Bailiff, who, he argues, took advantage of the Padishah's boredom and contempt for men to gain control over Third City. Pullman displays a degree of awareness not to be found in *The Childermass*. The Bailiff of *Monstre Gai* remains a political, ruthless manipulator and a student of human nature as when he claims that "all men are much the same. An amoralist . . . such is the modern man" (*MG*, 131). So in this second volume, the gap between the protagonist and the ruler has been considerably widened.

The sense of discontinuity between *The Childermass* and *Monstre Gai* experienced by the reader is therefore not just temporal. The break between the first volume and the second is also reinforced by a major stylistic contrast. Pyrotechnics is certainly an appropriate description for texts such as *The Childermass* or *The Apes of God*. But it is completely irrelevant to the style of the two sequels of *The Human Age*, which are narrated by means of a colorless, matter-of-fact, prosaic voice. Something occurred that compelled Lewis to redefine what constituted the signet of his style. At the same time, the transition from the first volume of the trilogy to the second is marked by an evolution of the narrative ethos. With the redefinition of Pullman as a perceptive protagonist, the ethos of the intellect that justifies and enables the unmasking of ideological imposture is chipped at.

Indeed, for all his faith in "critical objective intelligence" (*MG*, 165), Pullman is inexorably dragged into the political vortex of the Bailiff. The narrative carries Faustian overtones as Pullman has a compact with the Devil in order to preserve the intellectual values most precious to him. The Bailiff invites him to stay in the Phanuel Hotel, described as a secluded, luxurious place filled with books and isolated from the moronic majority. Another narrative "pretext" to this allegory of ideological temptation is *The Odyssey*, which Pullman reads in the silence of his posh apartment. He is not totally blind to the nature of the Bailiff's paradise, but he does not take the logical step which would be to remain out of the Devil's orbit. A nocturnal psychomachia is dramatized in which Pullman must choose a political ally. On behalf of the intellect, he selects the Bailiff: "Odious and monstrous as the Bailiff was, he was the supernatural element, paradoxical as that might seem, most favourable to man" (*MG*, 267). Written with hindsight, *Monstre Gai* is partly the tale of a great political temptation for the sake of the spiritual ideal of "Western Man." The conclusion to this second volume is based on the Lewisian archetype of flight that can be traced back to *Mrs. Dukes' Million*, where by the end of the story Royal becomes an aviator. In *Monstre Gai* Pullman and Satters take off to escape from the chaos of Third City. He finally rises out of matter, but his supernatural ascension is pathetic since he flies in the arms of the Gay Monster.

So the new characterization concerning Pullman is not used to second a logocentric narrative ethos. Quite the contrary, the new characterization directly undermines the logocentric discourse that, from the vantage point of his political essays, governed the ideological satire of *The Childermass*. Hence the narrative voice has lost its authority and is now used to state blandly the political impotence of the intellect. It seems to me that this change is indirectly linked to Lewis's reflexion on his more or less overt support of fascism. In this context, one can plausibly argue that the purpose of *Monstre Gai* for Lewis was to examine his own self-delusion with regard to Hitler. Naturally a simplistic equation between the Bailiff and Hitler or between Pullman and Lewis is not implied here. Instead, what is explored is the mechanism of ideological self-delusion. While *The Childermass* partly shows Pullman's naïve admiration for the ruler, *Monstre Gai* endeavours to show how, despite his intellectual awareness, Pullman makes the fatal mistake of associating himself with a political expression of terror.

The last two sequels of *The Human Age* constitute a powerful example of the implicit but crucial link between the artist's sociopolitical thinking and his/her choice of creative terms. In chapter 3 of my study I showed to what extent Lewis's style draws on the typically ornamental aspect of allegory without, however, sustaining its traditional sense of hierarchy and sublimity. Strikingly enough, Lewis's reflexion on ideological self-identification with figures of power occurs within a text totally devoid of allegorical sublimity. With the downfall of the traditional authority of the masculine intellect the sublimity of ornamental pyrotechnics fizzles out.

In *Malign Fiesta* the Bailiff is ousted by Sammael who, with his asceticism, stands even closer to Lewis's former conception of the ruler. Like Hitler, Sammael is a celibate, and he neither smokes nor drinks. As an extremist, he is more dangerous than the Bailiff, who is the Bestre of Lewis's politics. Sammael is a soldier without humor, whose violence breaks out in the most diabolical manner. As in *Monstre Gai*, Pullman is presented as an intellect and examiner of human nature. Of him it is said that he "was a highly analytical historian of men and women, and a critic of human action. He had been a great student of Freud and Jung" (*MF*, 443). This reference to psychological study is far from gratuitous. The last volume of the trilogy is a courageous self-analysis and rests on the same allegorical subplot as that of *Monstre Gai*: despite prescience and knowledge, Pullman lets himself be tempted, and realizes his mistake only too late.[12]

One should pause on the repetitive aspect of this plot: it is surprising that simultaneously Lewis should have published two volumes that tell the same story. Repetition is actually thematized in *Malign Fiesta* in the description of Pullman's thoughts after observing Sammael the Devil throw the female Sinner to the demons:

The same situation began to develop as the conflict in Third City when the time came when he ought to have severed his connection with that *monstre gai*. Here it was a new kind of monster—and there was no alternative in a shorter or longer term, except death.—He felt, if he played along with this monster until the end, that then a third and last monster ought to make his appearance; and with him there would be no choice. . . . His heart would be blacker than Satan, his magic more deadly than Medusa. (*MF,* 373)

This sense of sameness has both a fatalistic and rhapsodic character. From a psychological standpoint, it functions like a haunting obsession. It is as though *Malign Fiesta* was yet another massive attempt at elucidating the mechanism of ideological self-delusion. The difference between the two attempts lies in the scope of interpretation proposed by Lewis. *Malign Fiesta* goes further than ideological self-delusion: it suggests an equation between political authority and patriarchal authority. Twice this combination has led Lewis into the temptation of power. And ironically, each occurence coincides with a world war: hypnotized and searching for identity, the autobiographical Cantleman joins in with the Great War; in search of a political savior, the author of *Hitler* gets caught in one of the major ideological snares of twentieth-century history.

This is the reason why characterization undergoes yet another alteration in *Malign Fiesta.* Sammael the ruler is as ambiguous as the Bailiff, and the Miltonic theme of deceit is pursued. His project of genesis is the creation of the moronic majority decried in *The Childermass.* Pullman himself interprets Sammael's creation of the "Human Age" as a sacrifice of "individuality for the mass mind of man, a thousand minds, each possessing the freshness and creativeness of a momentary existence—accumulating in itself the knowledge of millions" (*MF,* 480). Yet, at the same time and contrary to the Bailiff of *Monstre Gai,* the Devil is endowed with logocentric authority. For instance, he is said to favor Iranian thought because it is conceptual. The hierarchic nature of the character is signalled by an allegorically sartorial description:

A very becoming headdress, reminiscent of Highland caps and bonnets, was the first innovation, fixed gallantly among the lord Sammael's flowing black hair; there was the mauve-blue smock, most wonderfully tailored, and there was a short stick in his hand, with which he tapped his leg as he walked, from below the handle of which hung a tasselled cord of hunter green. (*MF,* 435)

At his most fascinating this figure of authority displays all the features of the typical *kosmos* with its attention to the ornamental and the hierarchic talisman.

With the Freudian emphasis on the Highland cap, the stick, and the leg, the description is also intent on making Sammael a personification of the masculine principle but, above all, of the father figure. In this parodic genesis, Sammael is the progenitor or procreator of the Human Age. The equation between the devilish ruler and the father figure is momentous because it introduces the emotional and psychological factor in ideological self-identification that Lewis began to grope with in the different context of *The Revenge for Love*. An emblematic scene occurs twice in the narrative, showing Sammael with a small blond-haired girl lying in a basket by the fireplace. Pullman notices the child when he pays his first visit to the Devil, and then before he goes with him to Angeltown. In these two episodes, Sammael's attitude is ambiguous: like the Lewisian father figure, he is both a source of love and a potential threat.

This fatherly image is further reinforced in a scene where Sammael talks to Gatiel, one of his angels: "Gatiel stood there, like an enormous child, bathing the other's face from his large eyes with an undescribable radiation of love. It was not veneration but love, though more than veneration was there as well. . . . Such golden innocence, never contaminated by the smallest fraction of criticism, Pullman had never seen" (*MF*, 451). In the relation between Pullman and Sammael, filial love is also alluded to especially when Pullman, reflecting on his attraction to the Devil's luxurious car, refers to the "dream of a very snobbish little boy" (*MF*, 435). Like Gatiel, and "closing his eyes (perforce) to what reason taught him to see," Pullman is hypnotized by the Devil. *Malign Fiesta* is therefore the story of temptation and love between the child in Pullman and the father in Sammael.

To put it simply, this feeling of love between father and son, never expressed before, may be interpreted as a secret longing in Lewis, although the father was officially an enemy. It is the same fascination that led Lewis to see in Hitler a ruler corresponding to the political ideal of *The Art of Being Ruled*. According to Timothy Materer, in a rejected chapter of *Rude Assignment* Lewis wrote: "As a portraitist I feel I should have detected the awful symptoms" of a power obsession in Hitler. Materer finds Lewis's explanation "particularly significant and revealing because it comes from a satirist and portrait painter who held that the artist's eye could always discern the truth about a person or situation from the surfaces of reality."[13] What Lewis's political delusion corresponds to is a superimposition of an unconscious reality onto a historical reality. The eye of "objective truth" is betrayed by the inner eye fascinated by the aggrandized, idealized father-image of a personal mythology. Hence Lewis is inconsistent concerning youth politics: as Wagner notes, in *The Doom of Youth* and *The Old*

Gang and the New Gang he denounces youth politics, including Hitler's youth politics.[14] This incoherence can be plausibly traced back to a psychological struggle between love and hate, rejection of and allegiance to the father. For, naturally, the father-son relationship lies at the bottom of Lewis's reflexion on "youth."

The last volume of *The Human Age* can therefore be seen as the work where the problems of narrative ethos, political authority and father figure are explored in an allegorical context that allows a process of self-exegesis to take place. After the scene concerning the execution of the female sinner by Sammael and just before Pullman's decision to side with the Devil, the following is inserted:

> "I read Dante rather late," Pullman [said]. . . . He had developed this personal mariolatry. Substituting Beatrice for Mary. Then he had a mother-fixation, as it would be called. He summons Virgil from the dead in order to act on his journey into Hell as his big maternal Nanny. . . . I do not suggest he should have moved among the shades with cranerie or lack of courteous pity for their misfortune, but he need not have come shrinking among them, never far from his mother's apron-strings. . . . A contemporary Italian explains these things as a result of Dante's never having a father. But what a fatherless child misses in such a case is not the protection of the maternal nurse, but the authority of the hero belonging to the extrovert masculine side of life. (*MF,* 429)

Although not located at the outset of the narrative, this crucial passage with its reference to *Inferno* functions like the allegorical "threshold" of Quilligan's description. The meaning of the narrative is suggested through the interpretation of a contemporary interpretation of Dante's allegory. The reference is layered and oblique because its real object is neither the contemporary interpretation nor Dante, but the elucidation of a psychological problem. Its strategic position in the narrative allows it to function both as clue to the allegory and as psychological motivation: the Lewisian fascination for the father figure is an attempt to escape from the mother's influence, or to resist the evolution of the subject-child back into the womb. Lewis's political discourse with its emphasis on the masculine, intellectual ruler is therefore motivated by the quest for the dead Father.

If one examines the first few pages of the argument of *Hitler,* the superimposition of the political and psychological levels that this self-exegesis suggests is confirmed. Indeed, Hitler and the Nazis are introduced against the backcloth of sexual inversion: *Berlin im Licht* is the "*quartier-general*" of dogmatic Perversity—the Perverts' Paradise, the Mecca of both Lesb and So" (*H,* 21). What is important is not that historically Berlin *was* the site of sexual promiscuity, but rather Lewis's narrative treatment of this historical reality: against the background of the city, the Nazis are presented as allegorical personifications of the intellectual, cold, detached self. In other words, they personify the masculine principle, which makes them rulers. In *The Old Gang and the New Gang*, Hitlerism is again presented as masculine model for Nazi youth groups, whereas Bolshevism is identified as a "mothersome old party" (*OGNG*, 24). In Trotsky, Lewis sees a "half man and half matron" (*OGNG*, 24). Such terminology should alert the reader to the surrealistic aspect of Lewis's political reflexion, which in its mixture of pamphletism and allegory goes far beyond an "objective" report on the political and historical scene of the 1930s. Wyndham Lewis's achievement in the last two sequels of *The Human Age* is to have grasped and acted out this fundamental truth.

Abbreviations

ACM	*America and Cosmic Man*
AIP	*America, I Presume*
ABR	*The Art of Being Ruled*
AOG	*The Apes of God*
BB	*Blasting and Bombardiering*
CM	*The Childermass*
CPP	*Collected Poems and Plays*
CWB	*The Complete Wild Body*
CYD	*Count Your Dead: They Are Alive!*
DP	*The Diabolical Principle and the Dithyrambic Spectator*
DY	*The Doom of Youth*
HC	*The Hitler Cult*
JATH	*The Jews: Are They Human?*
LF	*The Lion and the Fox*
LOA	*Lewis on Art*
LWOE	*Left Wings over Europe*
MDM	*Mrs. Dukes' Million*
MF	*Malign Fiesta*
MG	*Monstre Gai*
MMB	*The Mysterious Mr. Bull*
MWA	*Men without Art*
OGNG	*The Old Gang and the New Gang*
PF	*Paleface*
RA	*Rude Assignment*
RFL	*The Revenge for Love*
RH	*Rotting Hill*
SF	*Satire and Fiction*
SB	*Snooty Baronet*

SC	*Self Condemned*
UFP	*Unlucky for Pringle*
TWM	*Time and Western Man*
VS	*The Vulgar Streak*
WA	*The Writer and the Absolute*

Notes

INTRODUCTION: RECLAIMING MODERNISM

1. Fredric Jameson, *Fables of Aggression: Wyndham Lewis, the Modernist as Fascist* (Berkeley and Los Angeles: University of California Press, 1978), 8.

2. T. S. Eliot, *"Tarr," Egoist* 5 (September 1918): 106.

3. W. H. Auden and Louis MacNeice, *Letters from Iceland* (London: Faber, 1937), 247.

4. Ernest Hemingway, *A Moveable Feast* (New York: Scribner's Sons, 1964), 109.

5. Hugh Kenner, "Pursued in Public," review of *Kenneth Burke in Greenwich Village: Conversing with the Moderns, 1915–1931* by Jack Selzer, *Times Literary Supplement,* 7 March 1997, 25.

6. Bradford Morrow and Bernard Lafourcade, *A Bibliography of the Writings of Wyndham Lewis,* (Santa Barbara, CA: Black Sparrow Press, 1978).

7. Authors and works referred to in the context of the present discussion are the following: Reed Way Dasenbrock, *The Literary Vorticism of Ezra Pound and Wyndham Lewis* (Baltimore: Johns Hopkins University Press, 1984); Vincent Sherry, *Ezra Pound, Wyndham Lewis and Radical Modernism* (New York: Oxford University Press, 1993); Julian Symons, *Makers of the New* (London: André Deutsch, 1987); Peter Bürger, "Modernity and the Avant-Garde in Wyndham Lewis's *Tarr*," *News from Nowhere: The Politics of Modernism* 7 (1989): 9–18; Bernard Lafourcade, "A Cock-and Bull Story," afterword to *Snooty Baronet* (Santa Barbara, CA: Black Sparrow Press, 1983); Sue-Ellen Campbell, *The Enemy Opposite* (Athens: Ohio University Press, 1988); and Jameson, *Fables of Aggression.*

8. Astradur Eysteinsson, *The Concept of Modernism* (Ithaca: Cornell University Press, 1990).

9. Carol Vanderveer Hamilton, "Anarchy as Modernist Aesthetic," in *The Turn of the Century: Modernism and Modernity in Literature and the Arts,* eds. C. Berg, F. Durieux, and G. Lermont (Berlin: Walter de Gruyter, 1995), 79; and H. Porter Abbott, "Late Modernism: Samuel Beckett and the Art of the *Oeuvre*," in *Around the Absurd: Essays on Modern and Postmodern Drama,* eds. Enoch Brater and Ruby Cohn (Ann Arbor: The University of Michigan Press, 1990), 73–96.

10. James L. Kinneavy, John Q. Cope, and J. W. Campbell, *Writing Basic Modes of Organization* (Dubuque, IA: Kendall/Hunt Publishing, 1976), Chapter 3, 54–86.

11. Fredric Jameson, "Postmodernism and Consumer Society," in *The Anti-Aesthetic: Essays on Postmodern Culture,* ed. Hal Foster (Port Townsend, WA: Bay Press, 1983), 57.

12. Peter Nicholls, *Modernisms: A Literary Guide* (Berkeley and Los Angeles: University of California Press, 1995), 196.

13. Lyn Pykett, *Engendering Fictions: The English Novel in the Early Twentieth Century* (London: Edward Arnold, 1995), 10.

14. Thierry de Duve, *Pictorial Nominalism* (Minneapolis: University of Minnesota Press, 1991), 101.

15. Philippe Dagen and Michel Décaudin, "Les peintres, le poète et le critique," in *Apollinaire: Critique d'art,* eds. B. R. El-Habib and V. Gille (Paris: Gallimard, 1993), 243–48.

16. Peter Bürger, *Theory of the Avant-Garde,* trans. M. Shaw (Minneapolis: University of Minnesota Press, 1984).

17. *Nostos* is used by Jeffrey Perl in *The Tradition of the Return: The Implicit History of Modern Literature* (Princeton: Princeton University Press, 1984); nostalgia is a term used by Ellen G. Friedman in "Where are the Missing Contents? (Post)Modernism, Gender, and the Canon," *PMLA* 108, no. 2 (March 1993): 240–52; repression of the transgressive unconscious is a concept used by Shari Benstock in "Expatriate Sapphic Modernism: Entering Literary History," in *Rereading Modernism: New Directions in Feminist Criticism,* ed. Lisa Rado (New York: Garland Publishing, 1994), 3–19; and regressive protofascism is a concept used by Jameson in *Fables of Aggression.*

18. Wladimir Krysinski, "Les Avant-gardes d'ostentation et les avant-gardes du faire cognitif: vers une description des langages transgressifs," in *The Turn of the Century,* 30.

19. Richard Sieburth, "Pound's *Dial* Letters: Between Modernism and the Avant-Garde," *American Poetry* 6, no. 2 (Winter 1989): 3–10.

20. The dissertation was eventually published as *Knowledge and Experience in the Philosophy of F. H. Bradley* (London: Faber and Faber, 1964).

21. Quoted by Louis Menand in *Discovering Modernism: T. S. Eliot and His Context* (New York: Oxford University Press, 1987), 47.

22. Michael McKeon, *The Origins of the English Novel 1600–1740,* (Baltimore: Johns Hopkins University Press, 1987), 12–13.

23. In Lawrence S. Lockridge, "Coleridge and the Perils of 'Self-Realization,'" in *Coleridge's Theory of Imagination Today,* ed. C. Gallant (New York: AMS, 1989), 257–75.

24. Robert Langbaum, *The Word from Below: Essays on Modern Literature and Culture* (Madison: University of Wisconsin Press, 1987), 42–43.

25. Percy Bysshe Shelley, "A Defence of Poetry," in *English Critical Essays: Nineteenth Century,* ed. Edmund D. Jones (Oxford: Oxford University Press, 1932), 159.

26. Marshall Brown, "Romanticism and Enlightenment," in *The Cambridge Companion to British Romanticism,* ed. S. Curran (Cambridge: Cambridge University Press, 1993), 31.

27. George Dekker, "James and Stevenson: The Mixed Current of Realism and Romance," in *Critical reconstructions: The Relationship of Fiction and Life,* eds. R. M. Polhemus and R. B. Henkle (Stanford, CA: Stanford University Press, 1994), 127–49.

28. Timothy Materer, "Lewis and the Patriarchs: Augustus John, W. B. Yeats, T. Sturge Moore," in *Wyndham Lewis: A Revaluation,* ed. J. Meyers (London: Athlone Press, 1980), 47–63.

29. T. Sturge Moore, *Art and Life* (London: Methuen, 1910).

30. See for instance Bonnie Kime Scott, ed., *The Gender of Modernism: A Critical Anthology* (Bloomington and Indianapolis: Indiana University Press, 1990); Ann L. Ardis, *New Women, New Novels: Feminism and Early Modernism* (New Brunswick, NJ: Rutgers University Press, 1990); and Bruce Clarke, *Dora Marsden and Early Modernism: Gender, Individualism, Science* (Ann Arbor: University of Michigan Press, 1996).

31. Jeffrey Perl, *Skepticism and Modern Enmity: Before and After Eliot* (Baltimore: Johns Hopkins University Press, 1989), 33.

32. Michael Levenson, "The Private Life of a Public Form: Freud, Fantasy and the Novel," in *Critical Reconstructions,* eds. R.M. Polhemus and R.B. Henkle (Stanford: Stanford University Press, 1994), 52–70.

33. Terry Eagleton, "Capitalism, Modernism and Postmodernism," *New Left Review* 152 (July/August 1985): 70.

34. Wyndham Lewis, ed., *Blast* (Santa Barbara, CA: Black Sparrow Press, 1981), 91. Subsequent quotations from this work are cited parenthetically in the text using the reference *Blast.*

35. John Milton, book 3, line 47–53 of *Paradise Regained,* in *The Complete Poems,* ed. B. A. Wright, intro. Gordon Campbell (London: Dent, 1986), 414.

36. William Wordsworth, "Preface to the Second Edition of *The Lyrical Ballads,*" in *Selected Poems and Prefaces,* ed. Jack Stillinger (Boston: Houghton Mifflin, 1965), 449.

37. Wordsworth, book 7, lines 671–721 of *Poems and Prefaces,* 287–88.

38. Sanford Schwartz, *The Matrix of Modernism* (Princeton: Princeton University Press, 1985) and Judith Ryan, *The Vanishing Subject: Early Psychology and Literary Modernism* (Chicago: University of Chicago Press, 1991).

39. Helmut Lethen, "Modernism Cut in Half: The Exclusion of the Avant-Garde and the Debate on Postmodernism," in *Approaching Postmodernism,* eds. Douwe Fokkema and Hans Bertens (Amsterdam and Philadelphia: John Benjamins Publishing, 1986), 236.

40. Richard Pearce, *The Politics of Narration* (New Brunswick, NJ: Rutgers University Press, 1991), 14–15.

41. Marianne DeKoven, "The Politics of Modernist Form," *New Literary History* 23, no. 3 (1992): 685.

42. Eagleton, "Capitalism, Modernism, and Postmodernism," 69–70.

43. The statement from Dada is quoted by Alan Young in *Dada and After: Extremist Modernism and English Literature* (Manchester: Manchester University Press, 1981), 23. Conrad's statement is quoted by Richard Quinones in *Mapping Literary Modernism: Time and Development* (Princeton: Princeton University Press, 1985), 88–89.

44. Michael Levenson, *A Genealogy of Modernism* (Cambridge: Cambridge University Press, 1984).

45. Menand, *Discovering Modernism,* 74.

46. Michael Kaufmann, "T. S. Eliot's New Critical Footnotes to Modernism," in *Rereading the New: A Backward Glance at Modernism,* ed. K.J.H. Dettmar (Ann Arbor: University of Michigan Press, 1992), 79.

47. D. H. Lawrence, *Selected Essays* (Harmondsworth: Penguin, 1950), 64.

48. Herbert Schneidau, *Waking Giants: The Presence of the Past in Modernism* (Oxford: Oxford University Press, 1991), 228–29.

49. Fragmentation in modernism is discussed in critics as varied as Irving Howe in *The Idea of the Modern in Literature and the Arts* (New York: Horizon Press, 1967), 29 and 34; Pearce in *Politics of Narration,* 13; Schneidau in *Waking Giants,* 224–25 and 228–29; Randall Stevenson in *Modernist Fiction: An Introduction* (London: Harvester-Wheatsheaf, 1992), 136; and Claude Leroy in "Modernity and Pseudonymity," in *Modernism: Challenges and Perspectives* eds. M. Chefdor, R. Quinones, and A. Wachtel (Urbana: University of Illinois Press), 266–67.

50. Wyndham Lewis, *Collected Prose and Poems,* ed. Alan Munton (Manchester: Carcanet New Press, 197), 145. Subsequent quotations from this work are cited parenthetically in the text using the abbreviation *CPP.*

51. Tom Normand, *Wyndham Lewis the Artist: Holding the Mirror up to Politics* (Cambridge: Cambridge University Press, 1992).

52. Marc Angenot, *La parole pamphlétaire* (Paris: Payot, 1982), 75.

CHAPTER 1. THE AGON

1. From Hugh Kenner in *Wyndham Lewis* (London: Methuen, 1954) through Bernard Bergonzi in *The Turn of a Century* (London: Macmillan, 1973) to Campbell in *Enemy Opposite*, Lewis 's dualism of mind and body has been variously formulated.

2. Gillian Beer, "Speaking for Others: Relativism and Authority in Victorian Anthropological Literature," in *Sir James Frazer and the Literary Imagination*, ed. Robert Fraser (London: Macmillan, 1990).

3. All quotations are from John Dewey's *The Influence of Darwin on Philosophy* (New York: Peter Smith, 1951), 1, 6, and 8–9.

4. See "Butler vs. Darwin" in Peter Raby's *Samuel Butler* (London: Hogarth Press, 1991), 161–77.

5. David Parker argues that the primitivism of vorticism derives from "Nietzschean and Darwinian thought," in "*Tarr* and Wyndham Lewis's War-Time Stories," *Southern Review* 8 (1975): 15–16; Ian Duncan mentions the "post-Victorian, post-Darwinian frame of reference" of *Mrs. Dukes's Million* in "Towards a Modernist Poetic: Wyndham Lewis's Early Fiction," in *Letteratura/Pittura*, ed. Giovanni Cianci (Pallermo: Sellerio, 1982), 70.

6. Wyndham Lewis, *Tarr* (Harmondsworth: Penguin, 1982), 23. Subsequent quotations from this work are cited parenthetically in the text using the reference *Tarr*.

7. Wyndham Lewis, *Creatures of Habit and Creatures of Change*, ed. Paul Edwards (Santa Barbara, CA: Black Sparrow Press, 1989), 149. Subsequent quotations from this work are cited parenthetically in the text using the abbreviation *CHCC*.

8. T. S. Eliot, *Selected Essays* (New York: Harcourt Brace and World, 1950), 433.

9. T. E. Hulme, *Speculations* (London: Routledge and Kegan Paul, 1965), 4.

10. Wordsworth, *Poems and Prefaces*, 110.

11. Matei Calinescu, *Faces of Modernity* (Bloomington: Indiana University Press, 1977).

12. Wyndham Lewis, *Time and Western Man* (London: Chatto and Windus, 1927), 435. Subsequent quotations from this work are cited parenthetically in the text using the abbreviation *TWM*.

13. Ryan, *Vanishing Subject*, 28 and 141.

14. Quoted in ibid., 205.

15. Wyndham Lewis, *The Childermass* (London: Chatto and Windus, 1928), 69–70. Subsequent quotations from this work are cited parenthetically in the text using the abbreviation *CM*.

16. Wyndham Lewis, *The Complete Wild Body*, ed. Bernard Lafourcade (Santa Barbara, CA: Black Sparrow Press, 1982), 359. Subsequent quotations from this work are cited parenthetically in the text using the abbreviation *CWB*.

17. Wyndham Lewis, *Blasting and Bombardiering* (London: Eyre and Spottiswoode, 1937), 22. Subsequent quotations from this work are cited parenthetically in the text using the abbreviation *BB*.

18. Pierre Brunel, *Le mythe de la métamorphose* (Paris: Armand Colin, 1974), 149–50 (my translation).

19. Wyndham Lewis, *Mrs. Dukes' Million,* ed. Frank Davey (Toronto: The Coach House Press, 1977), 295. Subsequent quotations from this work are cited parenthetically in the text using the abbreviation *MDM.*

20. Wyndham Lewis, *Snooty Baronet,* ed. Bernard Lafourcade (Santa Barbara, CA: Black Sparrow Press, 1983), 28. Subsequent quotations from this work are cited parenthetically in the text using the abbreviation *SB.*

21. Raby, *Butler,* 141–42.

22. Karl Miller, *Doubles: Studies in Literary History* (Oxford: Oxford University Press, 1985).

23. For comparisons between Beckett and Lewis, see Michel Beatty in *"Enemy of the Stars:* Vorticist Experimental Play," in *Theoria* 46 (1976): 42; Lafourcade in *The Complete Wild Body,* 405; and Dennis Brown in *Intertextual Dynamics within the Literary Group: Joyce. Pound, Lewis and Eliot* (London: Macmillan, 1990), 117–18.

24. Wyndham Lewis, *Self Condemned,* ed. Roland Smith (Manchester: Carcanet Press, 1983), 170. Subsequent quotations from this work are cited parenthetically in the text using the abbreviation *SC.*

25. Wyndham Lewis, *Monstre Gai* (London: Methuen, 1955), 20. Subsequent quotations from this work are cited parenthetically in the text using the abbreviation *MG.*

26. *The Letters of Ezra Pound and Wyndham Lewis,* ed. Timothy Materer (London: Faber and Faber, 1985), 78.

27. Wyndham Lewis, *Malign Fiesta* (London: Methuen, 1955), 536. Subsequent quotations from this work are cited parenthetically in the text using the abbreviation *MF.*

Chapter 2. Genre and Meaning: The Nonfiction

1. Margot Norris, "The Postmodernization of *Finnegans Wake* Reconsidered," in *Rereading the New,* ed. K.J.H. Dettmar, 343.

2. Wyndham Lewis, *The Vulgar Streak,* ed. Paul Edwards (Santa Barbara, CA: Black Sparrow Press), 74 and 31. Subsequent quotations from this work are cited parenthetically in the text using the abbreviation *VS.*

3. As argued by Geoffrey Wagner in *Wyndham Lewis: A Portrait of the Artist as the Enemy* (London: Routledge and Kegan Paul, 1957), 217.

4. Tzvetan Todorov, *Les genres du discours* (Paris: Seuil, 1978).

5. See note 3 in introductory chapter.

6. Angenot, *La parole pamphlétaire,* 38. All quotations from Angenot are my translation.

7. Hugh Kenner, *"Mrs Dukes' Million:* The Stunt of an Illusionist," in *Wyndham Lewis: A Revaluation* (London: Athlone Press, 1980), 85–91.

8. Angenot, *Parole pamphlétaire,* 103.

9. Theodor Adorno, "The Essay as Form," in *New German Critique* 32 (1984): 166.

10. Richard Chadbourne, "A Puzzling Literary Genre: Comparative Views of the Essay," in *Comparative Literary Studies* 20, no. 2 (1983): 138.

11. William H. Gass, "Emerson and the Essay," in *Habitations of the Word: Essays* (New York: Simon and Schuster, 1985), 23.

12. Adorno, "Essay as Form," 158.

13. In "The Classification of Genres," Thomas Kent goes as far as stating that "when a text changes generic categories it also changes meaning"; in *Genre* 16 (1983): 9.

14. Angenot, *Parole pamphlétaire,* 39.

15. Ibid., 351 and 43.

16. Richard Cork, *A Bitter Truth: Avant-Garde and the Great War* (New Haven: Yale University Press, 1994).

17. Peter Keating, *The Haunted Study: A Social History of the English Novel 1875–1914* (London: Secker and Warburg, 1989), 309.

18. K. K. Ruthven, *Ezra Pound as Literary Critic* (London: Routledge, 1990), 138.

19. Ford Madox Ford, *The Critical Attitude* (London: Duckworth, 1911). See in particular "On the Functions of the Arts in the Republic" and "The Passing of the Great Figure."

CHAPTER 3. GENRE AND MEANING: THE FICTION

1. Edwin Honig, *Dark Conceit: The Making of Allegory* (New York: Oxford University Press, 1966), 6.

2. Jon Whitman, *Allegory: The Dynamics of an Ancient and Medieval Technique* (Oxford: Clarendon Press, 1987), 218–19.

3. Wyndham Lewis, *The Apes of God,* ed. Paul Edwards (Santa Barbara, CA: Black Sparrow Press, 1981), 376. Subsequent quotations from this work are cited parenthetically in the text using the abbreviation *AOG.*

4. Angenot, *Parole pamphlétaire,* 99.

5. Maureen Quilligan, *The Language of Allegory: Defining the Genre* (Ithaca: Cornell University Press, 1979).

6. Concerning the 1914 version of the play, Brown perceptively notes that "the future that is born here (most prescient in a year pregnant with the Great War) is a male twinning whose antagonisms result in a desperate double-death"; in *The Modernist Self in Twentieth-Century English Literature: A Study in Fragmentation* (London: Macmillan, 1989), 61.

7. Whitman, *Allegory,* 2.

8. Ibid., 269.

9. Bernard Dupriez, *A Dictionary of Literary Devices: Gradus A–Z,* trans. A. Halsall (Toronto: University of Toronto Press, 1991), 340 and 357.

10. Quoted by Keating, *The Haunted Study,* 394.

11. Wyndham Lewis, *The Revenge for Love* (Harmondsworth: Penguin, 1983), 80. Subsequent quotations from this work are cited parenthetically in the text using the abbreviation *RFL.*

12. Eysteinsson, *Concept of Modernism,* 182.

13. In *Ezra Pound, Wyndham Lewis and Radical Modernism,* Sherry asserts the following: "No less cynical in motive than sinister in practice, Lewis's left-handed play with language moves to a purpose as rightist and single-minded, moreover, as the political animus that generates the experiment" (135–36).

14. Gérard Genette, *Palimpsestes: La littérature au second degré* (Paris: Seuil, 1982).

15. Edward Said, "The Text, the World, the Critic," in *Textual Strategies: Perspectives in Poststructuralist Criticism,* ed. Josué V. Harari (Ithaca: Cornell University Press, 1979), 165.

16. John Holloway, "Machine and Puppet: A Comparative View," in *Wyndham Lewis: A Revaluation,* ed. Meyers, 3–14.

17. Wyndham Lewis, *Unlucky for Pringle*, eds. C. J. Fox and Robert T. Chapman (London: Vision Press, 1973), 47. Subsequent quotations from this work are cited parenthetically in the text using the abbreviation *UFP*.

18. Dupriez, *Dictionary of Literary Devices* ,359.

19. Ibid., 358.

20. Henri Mitterand, *Le discours du roman* (Paris: Presses universitaires de France, 1980) 8–9 (my translation).

21. Lawrence, *Selected Essays,* 91.

22. Angus Fletcher, *Allegory: The Theory of a Symbolic Mode* (Ithaca: Cornell University Press, 1964), 40.

23. See end of chapter 1 where this passage is quoted.

24. Quilligan, *Language of Allegory,* 42.

25. Fletcher, *Allegory,* 109.

26. Kenner in *Wyndham Lewis;* John Russell, *Style in Modern British Fiction* (Baltimore: Johns Hopkins University Press, 1978); Jameson in *Fables of Aggression;* Lafourcade in "Metaphor-Metonymy-Collage," in *Enemy News* 25 (1987): 6–11; and Paul Edwards in "Wyndham Lewis's Narrative of Origins: 'The Death of the Ankou'," *The Modern Language Review* 92 (January 1997): 22.

27. Fletcher, *Allegory,* 94 and 108.

28. Ibid., 171.

29. Eugeni Zamyatin, "On Literature, Revolution and Entropy," *The Idea of the Modern in Literature and the Arts,* ed. I. Howe (New York: Horizon Press, 1967), 178.

30. Quoted by Alan Young in *Dada and After,* 10.

31. Filippo Marinetti, *Les mots en liberté futuristes* (N.p.: Le Arti, 1986), 70.

32. Sanford Schwartz, *The Matrix of Modernism,* 90.

33. Eysteinsson, *Concept of Modernism,* 194–96.

34. George Orwell, *Collected Essays* (London: Secker and Warburg, 1961), 75 and 80.

35. Mary Ann Caws, "Gestures toward the Self: Representing the Body in Modernism," in *Modernism: Challenges and Perspectives,* 253.

36. Russell, *Style in Modern British Fiction,* 123–57.

CHAPTER 4. MAN AND WOMAN

1. Sigmund Freud, *Leonardo da Vinci and a Memory of His Childhood* (Harmondsworth: Penguin, 1963) and "Dostoevsky and Parricide," in vol. 21 of *The Complete Psychological Works of Sigmund Freud,* ed. J. Strachey (London: Hogarth Press and the Institute of Psychoanalysis, 1957), 177–94; Jacques Lacan, "Le séminaire sur 'La lettre volée'" in *Ecrits I* (Paris:Seuil, 1966), 19–75 and "Hamlet," *Ornicar?* 24 (Automne 1981), 7–31; Julia Kristeva, *Desire in Language: A Semiotic Approach to Literature and Art* (New York: Columbia University Press, 1980) and *Pouvoirs de l'horreur: essai sur l'abjection* (Paris: Seuil, 1980); and Wayne Koestenbaum, *Double Talk: The Erotics of Male Literary Collaboration* (London: Routledge, 1989).

2. Jacques Lacan, *Ecrits,* trans. Alan Sheridan (London: Tavistock, 1985), 65.

3. Peter Brooks, "The Idea of a Psychoanalytic Literary Criticism," *Critical Inquiry* 13, no. 2 (Winter 1987), 337; Koestenbaum, *Double Talk,* 9; Colin MacCabe "The Revenge of the Author," in *Subject to History: Ideology, Class, Gender,* ed. D. Simpson (Ithaca: Cornell University Press, 1991), 34–46; Shari Benstock, "Expatriate Sapphic Modernism: Entering Literary History," in *Rereading Modernism: New*

Directions in Feminist Criticism, ed. Lisa Rado (New York, Garland Publishing, 1994), 3–19.

4. Alan Durant, "Pound, Modernism and Literary Criticism," *Critical Quarterly* 28, no. 1 (1986): 154–66.

5. Jacques Derrida, "Freud and the Scene of Writing," in *Writing and Difference,* trans. Alan Bass (Chicago: University of Chicago Press), 196–231.

6. MacCabe, "Revenge of the Author," 39.

7. Nicholls, *Modernisms,* 187.

8. Brooks, "Psychoanalytic Literary Criticism," 342–43.

9. Ibid., 347.

10. Lacan, *Ecrits,* 58.

11. Brooks, "Psychoanalytic Literary Criticism," 346.

12. Elaine Showalter, *Sexual Anarchy: Gender and Culture at the fin de siècle* (New York: Viking, 1990).

13. Pykett, *Engendering Fictions,* 15.

14. Ibid., 24.

15. Wyndham Lewis, *The Art of Being Ruled* (London: Chatto and Windus, 1926), 192. Subsequent quotations from this work are cited parenthetically in the text using the abbreviation *ABR.*

16. In a letter to John Quinn, written on June 14, 1920 Lewis stated: "I have been put out of action for several months by my mother's death." This letter can be found in *The Letters of Wyndham Lewis,* ed. W. K. Rose (London: Methuen, 1963), 119. Lewis's mother died in February 1920.

17. Yet another version of the story exists, published in a reedition by Anne Lewis of *Blasting and Bombardiering* (London: Calder and Boyars, 1967), 66–68. The section entitled "London" includes additional material (descriptions and dialogue) that was absent from the 1937 version. Lewis's own version tends to temper Cantleman's enjoyment of and fascination for the crowd. Obviously Mrs. Lewis inserted passages which had been discarded or rejected by the author.

18. Nicholls, *Modernisms,* 270. Lacan's quotation is from *Ecrits,* 104.

19. These ideas are expressed by Lacan in *Ecrits,* 199.

20. Ann L. Ardis, "Reading 'as a Modernist'/Denaturalizing Modernist Reading Protocols: Wyndham Lewis's *Tarr,*" in *Rereading Modernism,* 373–90.

21. Freud, *Leonardo da Vinci,* 124.

22. Kenneth Lewes, *The Psychoanalytic Theory of Male Homosexuality* (New York: Simon and Schuster, 1988).

23. Freud, *Leonardo da Vinci,* 141.

24. G. H. Wiedeman, "Survey of Psychoanalytic Literature on Overt Male Homosexuality," *Journal of the American Psychoanalytic Association* 10, no. 2 (1962): 394.

25. Wiedeman, "Some Remarks on the Aetiology of Homosexuality," *International Journal of Psychoanalysis* 45, no. 1 (1964): 215.

26. Leon Saul and Aaron Beck, "Psychodynamics of Male Homosexuality," *International Journal of Psychoanalysis* 42 (1961): 43–48.

27. Lacan, *Ecrits,* 290.

28. Jeffrey Meyers, *The Enemy: A Biography of Wyndham Lewis* (London: Routledge and Kegan Paul, 1980).

29. For an interpretation emphasizing the role of the father, see Saul and Beck, "Psychodynamics of Male Homosexuality," as well as Francis Pasche, "Symposium on Homosexuality," 210–13.

30. Freud, *Leonardo da Vinci,* 138.

31. Ibid., 140.

32. Charles Socarides, "A Theory of Aetiology in Male Homosexuality," *International Journal of Psychoanalysis* 49 (1968): 33.

33. As reported by Frank Davey in his note to *Mrs. Dukes's Million,* 367.

34. In "Quel mauvais roman que ma vie! *Twentieth Century Palette,*" Lafourcade summarizes and analyzes Lewis's unfinished and unpublished last novel. My reference is to this synopsis published in *Wyndham Lewis: Letteratura/Pittura* (Palermo: Sellerio, 1982), 218–45.

35. Lafourcade, *Twentieth-Century Palette,* 228.

36. Parker, "Wyndham Lewis's War-Time Stories," 170.

37. Jameson, *Fables of Aggression,* 169–77.

38. Pasche, "Symposium on Homosexuality," 212.

39. See for instance letters nos. 13 and 15 in *The Letters of Wyndham Lewis,* 13 and 16.

40. Lafourcade, "Off to Budapest—with Freud," *Enemy News* 15 (1982): 6–10.

41. Lafourcade, "Du purgatoire au panorama," *Etudes anglaises* 26, no. 2 (1973): 201.

42. Kenner, *The Pound Era* (London: Faber and Faber, 1972), 502.

43. Signalled by Jameson, *Fables of Aggression,* 142.

44. Holloway, "Machine and Puppet," 14.

45. Meyers, *The Enemy,* 7.

46. As noted by Lafourcade in "A Cock-and-Bull Story," 264.

47. Wyndham Lewis, *The Diabolical Principle and the Dithyrambic Spectator* (New York: Haskell House, 1971), 50. Subsequent quotations from this work are cited parenthetically in the text using the abbreviation *DP.*

48. Freud, "Psychoanalytic Notes on an Autobiographical Account of a Case of Paranoia (Dementia Paranoides)," in vol. 12 of *The Complete Psychological Works of Sigmund Freud,* ed. James Strachey (London: Hogarth Press and the Institute of Psychoanalysis, 1957), 63.

49. Freud, "Psychoanalytic Notes," 71.

50. Both statements by Kate Lechmere are from "Wyndham Lewis from 1912," *Journal of Modern Literature* 10, no. 1 (1983): 164 and 165.

51. Meyers, *The Enemy,* 53.

52. Ibid., 110–11.

53. Ibid., 26, 18, 109–10, and 87.

54. Levenson, "Form's Body: Wyndham Lewis's *Tarr,*" *Modern Language Quarterly* 45, no. 3 (1984): 251.

55. For the symbolic importance of money in Lewis, see Lafourcade, "Off to Budapest."

56. Jameson, *Fables of Aggression,* 100.

57. Paul O'Keeffe, afterword to *Tarr the 1918 Version* (Santa Rosa, CA: Black Sparrow Press, 1990), 381.

58. O'Keeffe, afterword to *Tarr,* 377.

59. Ibid., 377.

60. Otto Rank, *The Don Juan Legend,* trans. G. G. Winler (Princeton: Princeton University Press, 1975), 95.

61. Wyndham Lewis, *America, I Presume* (New York: Howell and Soskin, 1940), 229. Subsequent quotations from this work are cited parenthetically in the text using the abbreviation *AIP.*

62. Meyers, *The Enemy,* 261.

63. Walt Whitman, *Leaves of Grass,* eds. S. Bradley, H. W. Blodgett, A. Golden, and W. White (New York: New York University Press, 1980), 110–11 and 106–7.

64. Wyndham Lewis, *Paleface* (London: Chatto and Windus, 1929), 141. Subsequent quotations from this work are cited parenthetically in the text using the abbreviation *PF*.

65. John Milton, book 1, lines 254–55 of *Paradise Lost* in *The Complete Poems*, 164.

CHAPTER 5. A GENEALOGY OF IMPERSONALITY

1. Statements referred to in the context of this discussion are the following: Malcolm Bradbury and James McFarlane, "The Name and Nature of Modernism," in *Modernism, 1890–1930,* 25 and 50; Howe, *The Idea of the Modern,* 18 and Eagleton, "Capitalism, Modernism and Postmodernism," 67.

2. Wyndham Lewis, *The Writer and the Absolute* (Westport, CT: Greenwood Press, 1975), 3. Subsequent quotations from this work are cited parenthetically in the text using the abbreviation *WA*.

3. Jessica Feldman, *Gender on the Divide: The Dandy in Modernist Literature* (Ithaca: Cornell University Press, 1993).

4. Eliot, "Tradition and the Individual Talent," in *The Sacred Wood* (London: Methuen, 1920), 140.

5. Wyndham Lewis, *Men without Art,* ed. Seamus Cooney (Santa Rosa, CA: Black Sparrow Press, 1987), 225. Subsequent quotations from this work are cited parenthetically in the text using the abbreviation *MWA*.

6. Wyndham Lewis, *The Lion and the Fox* (London: Methuen, 1951), 285–86. Subsequent quotations from this work are cited parenthetically in the text using the following abbreviation: *LF*.

7. Eliot, Review of *The Lion and the Fox,* by Wyndham Lewis. *Twentieth Century Verse* 6–7 (1937): 111–12.

8. Ezra Pound, *ABC of Reading* (Norfolk, Connecticut: New Directions, 1934), 26.

9. Henri Bergson, *Comedy,* trans. W. Sypher (New York: Doubleday Anchor Books, 1956), 160.

10. Hulme, *Speculations,* 134.

11. Eliot, *For Lancelot Andrewes* (Garden City, NY: Doubleday, 1929), 21.

12. T. S. Moore, *Art and Life* (London: Methuen, 1910), 248.

13. Pound, *Literary Essays,* ed. T. S. Eliot (London: Faber and Faber, 1954), 42.

14. I. A. Richards, *Principles of Literary Criticism* (London: Kegan Paul, Trench, Trubner, 1934), 16.

15. Richards, *Principles,* 2.

16. Richards, *Science and Poetry* (New York: Norton, 1934), 30.

17. Richards, *Principles,* 105.

18. All quotations are from Roland Barthes, "The Death of the Author," in *Literature in the Modern World,* ed. D. Walder (Oxford University Press, 1990), 229, 232, and 231.

19. Derrida, *Writing and Difference,* 37.

20. All quotations are from Ortega y Gasset, *The Dehumanization of Art* (Princeton: Princeton University Press, 1968), 32.

21. Michel Foucault, "What is an Author?" in *The Foucault Reader,* ed. Paul Rabinow (New York: Pantheon Books, 1984), 119.

22. Foucault, "What is an Author?" 102–3.

23. Maurice Blanchot, *The Space of Literature,* trans. A. Smock (Lincoln: University of Nebraska Press, 1982), 93.

24. James Joyce, *A Portrait of the Artist as a Young Man* (St Albans: Triad/Panther Books, 1977), 94.

25. In *The Foucault Reader*, 381–90.

26. Aristotle, *The Poetics*, in *On Poetry and Style*, ed. and trans. G.M.A. Grube (New York: Bobbs-Merrill, 1958), 1447b, p.4.

27. Hulme, *Speculations*, 242.

28. Derrida, "Structure, Sign, and Play," in *Writing and Difference*, 288.

29. Derrida, "*Cogito* and the History of Madness," in *Writing and Difference*, 54.

30. Marcia Ian, *Remembering the Phallic Mother: Psychoanalysis, Modernism, and the Fetish* (Ithaca: Cornell University Press, 1993), 200.

31. Feldman, *Gender on the Divide*, 13.

32. Ibid., 17 and 3.

33. Ibid., 56.

34. Wyndham Lewis, *The Code of a Herdsman*, ed. Alan Munton (Glasgow: Wyndham Lewis Society, 1977), 7.

35. Wyndham Lewis, *The Hitler Cult* (London: Dent, 1939), 78. Subsequent quotations from this work are cited parenthetically in the text using the abbreviation *HC*.

36. Wyndham Lewis, "The Vita of Wyndham Lewis," ed. Bernard Lafourcade, *Enemy News* 20 (1984): 10–15.

37. Feldman, *Gender on the Divide*, 33.

38. Stéphane Mallarmé, "Prose." In *Oeuvres complètes* (Paris: Gallimard, 1945), 55–57. Translated by Keith Bosley as "[She] says the word: *Anastase!* / Born for eternal vellum" in *Mallarmé: The Poems* (Harmondsworth: Penguin, 1977), 137.

39. Feldman, *Gender on the Divide*, 34.

40. Lewis's use of the mask has been discussed by several critics: in *Wyndham Lewis*, Wagner argues that characters such as Cantleman, Blenner, William Bland Burn, and the Enemy are Lewisian personae. See also Kenner's *"Mrs Dukes' Million:* The Stunt of an Illusionist"; Julian Symons's "Wyndham Lewis's First Novel," in *Critical Observations* (London: Faber and Faber, 1981), 58–64; and Marshall McLuhan, "The Lewis Vortex: Art and Politics as Masks of Power," in *Letteratura/Pittura*, 167–70.

Chapter 6. From Realism to Modernism

1. Levenson, *A Genealogy of Modernism*, 125.

2. Colette Becker, *Lire le réalisme et le naturalisme* (Paris: Dunod, 1992), 120. All quotations from Becker are my translation.

3. From "A Few Don'ts by an Imagiste," in *Imagist Poetry*, ed. Peter Jones (Harmondsworth: Penguin, 1972), 130.

4. Schneidau, *Waking Giants*, 228–29.

5. Emile Zola proposed this definition of art in a newspaper article entitled "Proudhon and Courbet." An edition of this article can be found in *Emile Zola: Ecrits sur l'art*, ed. Jean-Pierre Leduc-Adine (Paris: Gallimard, 1991). Alison Hilton translates this famous definition in the following terms: "A work of art is a corner of nature seen through a temperament," in *Emile Zola and the Arts*, ed. Jean-Max Guieu and Alison Hilton (Washington, DC: Georgetown University Press, 1988), xii.

6. Becker, *Lire le réalisme* 139.

7. Hulme, *Speculations*, 222–23.

8. Becker, *Lire le réalisme*, 137.

9. Both statements by Maupassant are quoted by Becker, *Lire le réalisme*, 123.

10. Charles Baudelaire, *Oeuvres complètes 2* (Paris: Gallimard, 1975), 493 (my translation).

11. Wilhelm Worringer, "Abstraction and Empathy," in *Modern Art and Modernism*, ed. F. Frascina, C. Harrison, and D. Paul (London: Harper and Row), 161.

12. Wyndham Lewis, "Creativity," in *Blast*, ed. Hugh Kenner (Santa Barbara, CA: Black Sparrow Press, 1984), 208–9.

13. W. C. Wees, *Vorticism and the English Avant-Garde* (Manchester: Manchester University Press, 1972), 28.

14. Wyndham Lewis, *Wyndham Lewis on Art*, eds. Walter Michel and C. J. Fox (New York: Funk and Wagnalls, 1929), 262. Subsequent quotations from this work are cited parenthetically in the text using the abbreviation *LOA*.

15. Hulme, *Speculations*, 87.

16. Lawrence, *Selected Essays*, 15.

17. Walter Benjamin, *Understanding Brecht*, trans. A. Bostock (London: NBL, 1973), 13.

18. Northrop Frye, *Anatomy of Criticism: Four Essays* (Princeton: Princeton University Press, 1957), 235.

19. Becker, *Lire le réalisme*, 45.

20. Wyndham Lewis, *The Mysterious Mr. Bull* (London: Robert Hale, 1938), 145. Subsequent quotations from this work are cited parenthetically in the text using the abbreviation *MMB*.

21. Marie Claire Randolph, "The Medical Concept in English Renaissance Satiric Theory," in *Satire: Modern Essays in Criticism*, ed. R. Paulson (Englewood Cliffs, NJ: Prentice-Hall, 1971), 135–89.

22. Wyndham Lewis, *Satire and Fiction* (Folcroft, Pennsylvania: Folcroft Press, 1967), 48. Subsequent quotations from this work are cited parenthetically in the text using the abbreviation *SF*.

23. Italo Calvino, *The Uses of Literature*, trans. P. Creagh (New York: Harcourt Brace Jovanovich), 64.

24. Peter Petro, *Modern Satire: Four Studies* (New York and Amsterdam: Mouton Publishers, 1982), 21.

25. Ernst Kris, *Psychoanalytic Explorations in Art* (New York: Schocken Books, 1964), 183.

26. Hugh Kenner, "The Satirist as Barbarian," in *English Satire and the Satiric Tradition*, eds. Rawson and Mezciems (Oxford: Basil Blackwell, 1984), 264–75 and Jameson in *Fables of Aggression*. Both note the boomerang effect of satire. The satiric impulse, Jameson writes, is "a dangerous force, that threatens . . . to return destructively upon the artist himself, searing everything it finds there" (139–40).

27. Baudelaire in *Oeuvres complètes 2*, 538 and Bergson in *Comedy*, 87.

28. Bergson, *Comedy*, 145 (translation modified).

29. Luigi Pirandello, *On Humor*, eds. and trans. A. Illiano and D. P. Testa (Chapel Hill: The University of North Carolina Press, 1974), 143.

30. David Trotter, *The Making of the Reader* (London: Macmillan, 1984), 77.

31. Vaclav Havel, "Anatomy of the Gag," trans. M. Schonberg, *Modern Drama* 23, no. 1 (1980): 23.

32. Keating, *The Haunted Study*, 444.

33. Both statements by Andreas Huyssen are from *After the Great Divide: Modernism. Mass Culture, Postmodernism* (Bloomington: Indiana University Press, 1986), 14.

34. Both statements by Worringer are from "Abstraction and Empathy," 161 and 162.

35. See Albert Halsall, *L'Art de convaincre* (Toronto: Paratexte, 1988), 230–31.

36. See note 1 of chapter 5.

37. Huyssen, *After the Great Divide*, 208–9.

38. Menand, *Discovering Modernism*, 59.

39. Marinetti, *Les mots en liberté futuristes*, 22 (my translation).

40. Victor Shklovsky, "Art as Technique," in *Contemporary Literary Criticism: Literary and Cultural Studies*, ed. R. C. Davies and R. Schleifer (New York: Longman, 1989), 58.

41. Stephen Spender, *The Struggle of the Modern* (London: Hamish Hamilton, 1963), 89.

42. Becker, *Lire le réalisme*, 50.

43. Ibid., 166–67.

44. Feldman, *Gender on the Divide*, 97.

45. Susan Suleiman, *Authoritarian Fictions* (New York: Columbia University Press, 1983), 22.

46. David Lodge, "The Language of Modernist Fiction," in *Modernism 1890–1930*, 489.

47. Michael Hollington, "Svevo, Joyce and Modernist Time," in *Modernism 1890–1930*, 441.

48. Eysteinsson, *Concept of Modernism*, 186.

CHAPTER 7. THE GREAT DIVIDE

1. Both quotations are from Huyssen *After the Great Divide*, 25 and 15.

2. Mallarmé, "The Impressionists and Edouard Manet," in *Modern Art and Modernism*, 43.

3. Hugh Kenner, *A Sinking Island* (New York: Alfred A. Knopf, 1988). Adorno's statement is quoted by Huyssen in *After the Great Divide*, 35.

4. Worringer, "Abstraction and Empathy," 159.

5. Huyssen, *After the Great Divide*, 9.

6. Bürger, *Theory of the Avant-Garde*, 49.

7. Ibid., 70.

8. Huyssen, *After the Great Divide*, 187.

9. Baudelaire, *Oeuvres complètes II*, 432.

10. Huyssen, *After the Great Divide*, 183.

11. Wallace Stevens, *The Necessary Angel* (New York: Vintage Books, 1951), 22.

12. Cork, *A Bitter Truth*, 226–27.

13. Huyssen, *After the Great Divide*, 158.

14. Eysteinsson, *Concept of Modernism*, 172; Suzi Gablick, *Has Modernism Failed?* (London: Thames and Hudson, 1984).

15. Melissa Feldman, *Signs of Life: Processes and Materials 1960–90* (Philadelphia: Institute of Contemporary Art, 1990), 10–11.

16. Arthur Danto, "The Artworld," in *Twentieth-Century Theories of Art*, ed. James M. Thompson (Ottawa: Carleton University Press, 1990), 540.

17. Quoted by Melissa Feldman in *Signs of Life*, 25.

18. Bürger, *Theory of the Avant-Garde*, 49.

CHAPTER 8. THE GENRE OF POLITICS

1. Wyndham Lewis, *Rude Assignment*, ed. Toby Foshay (Santa Barbara, CA: Black Sparrow Press, 1984), 149. Subsequent quotations from this work are cited parenthetically in the text using the abbreviation *RA*.

2. Wyndham Lewis, *The Old Gang and the New Gang* (London: Desmond Harmsworth, 1933), 58–59. Subsequent quotations from this work are cited parenthetically in the text using the abbreviation *OGNG*.

3. Fred Reid, "The Disintegration of Liberalism, 1895–1931," in *The Context of English Literature 1900–1930*, ed. M. Bell (London: Methuen, 1980), 94–125.

4. Bernard Bergonzi, "An Artist and His Armour," *The Times Literary Supplement* (31 October 1980): 1215.

5. Orwell, *Collected Essays*, 73. As Campbell points out in *The Enemy Opposite*, Lewis's claim to ideological freedom brings about the "problem of perspective: from what position does the critic analyze his culture without being shaped by it?" (187).

6. Jean-Paul Sartre, *What Is Literature?*, trans. B. Frechtman (Gloucester: Peter Smith, 1978), 16.

7. In *The Letters of Wyndham Lewis*, 201.

8. Wyndham Lewis, *Left Wings over Europe* (London: Jonathan Cape, 1936), 17. Subsequent quotations from this work are cited parenthetically in the text using the abbreviation *LWOE*.

9. Both statements by Malcolm Bradbury are from *The Social Context of Modern English Literature* (Oxford: Basil Blackwell, 1971), 40–41 and 119.

10. Stephen Spender, "Writers and Politics," *The Partisan Review* 34, no. 3 (1967): 368.

11. H. B. Mallalieu, "Social Force," *Twentieth Century Verse* 1–18 (New York: Krauss Reprint, 1966): 148.

12. Wyndham Lewis, *The Doom of Youth* (New York: Robert M. McBride, 1932), 34. Subsequent quotations from this work are cited parenthetically in the text using the abbreviation *DY*.

13. Wyndham Lewis, *Count Your Dead: They Are Alive!* (London: Lovat Dickson, 1937), 27. Subsequent quotations from this work are cited parenthetically in the text using the abbreviation *CYD*.

14. Samuel Hynes, *A War Imagined: The First World War and English Culture* (London: The Bodley Head, 1990), 5–7.

15. *The Letters of Wyndham Lewis*, 246.

16. Wyndham Lewis, *America and Cosmic Man* (Port Washington, NY: Kennikat, 1969), 170. Subsequent quotations from this work are cited parenthetically in the text using the abbreviation *ACM*.

17. D. G. Bridson, *The Filibuster: A Study of the Political Ideas of Wyndham Lewis* (London: Cassell, 1972).

CHAPTER 9. THE POLITICS OF CHIRON

1. George Watson, *Politics and Literature in Modern Britain* (London: Macmillan, 1977).

2. Watson, *Politics and Literature*, 83.

3. Wyndham Lewis, *The Lion and the Fox* (London: Methuen, 1951), 76. Subsequent quotations from this work are cited parenthetically in the text using the abbreviation *LF*.

4. Quoted by J. R. Hale in "Machiavelli and the Self-Sufficient State," In *Political Ideas*, ed. D. Thomson (Harmondsworth: Penguin, 1986), 29–30.

5. Hale, "Machiavelli," 29.

6. Sherry, *Radical Modernism*, 102.

7. Bridson in *The Filibuster;* William Pritchard in *Wyndham Lewis* (New York: Twayne, 1968); Bürger in "Modernity and the Avant-Garde in Wyndham Lewis."

8. Jameson, *Fables of Aggression,* 103.

9. C. H. Sisson, "The Politics of Wyndham Lewis," *Agenda* 7, no. 3 and 8, no. 1 (1969): 110.

10. Wyndham Lewis, *Hitler* (London: Chatto and Windus, 1931), 49. Subsequent quotations from this work are cited parenthetically in the text using the abbreviation *H*.

11. From a biographical viewpoint, the war seems to have had the effect of social estrangement. In letters to Pound, Lewis wrote: "A horrible phonograph played by my horrible brothers-in-arms renders intelligible writing difficult. The unspeakable, vulgar brutes have introduced *The End of a Perfect Day* and a score more obnoxious pieces into a dugout 12 feet by 8," *The Letters of Ezra Pound and Wyndham Lewis,* 95. In another letter he wrote: "Nature & my training have made me curiously sensitive to ugly & stupid influences. The whole point of *Me* is that (& *not* that I don't happen to be over physically nervous.) This causes me to suffer a great deal more than most people by my surroundings," *The Letters of Ezra Pound and Wyndham Lewis,* 109–10.

12. Plato, *The Republic,* trans. F. M. Cornford (New York: Oxford University Press, 1956), 78–79, 83, and 90.

13. Raymond Williams, *The Politics of Modernism: Against the New Conformists,* ed. T. Pinkney (London: Verso, 1989), 59.

14. Baudelaire, *Oeuvres complètes 1,* 291. Francis Scarfe translated the passage in the following terms: "Multitude and solitude are equal and interchangeable terms for the active and productive poet," in *The Poems in Prose with La Fanfarlo* (London: Anvil Press Poetry, 1989), 59.

15. Wyndham Lewis, *The Jews: Are They Human?* (London: George Allen and Unwin, 1939), 23. Subsequent quotations from this work are cited parenthetically in the text using the abbreviation *JATH*.

16. Wyndham Lewis, *Rotting Hill,* ed. Paul Edwards (Santa Barbara, CA: Black Sparrow Press), 97. Subsequent quotations from this work are cited parenthetically in the text using the abbreviation *RH*.

Chapter 10. Self-Exegesis

1. Bergonzi, "An Artist and His Armour," 1215.

2. Quoted by L.C.B. Seaman in *A New History of England 410–1975* (Brighton: The Harvester Press, 1981), 453.

3. Nicolson's and Crossman's statements are quoted by Watson in *Politics and Literature,* 73 and 75.

4. Reed Way Dasenbrock, afterword to *The Art of Being Ruled* by Wyndham Lewis (Santa Rosa, CA: Black Sparrow Press, 1989), 443.

5. A. P. Foulkes, *Literature and Propaganda* (London: Methuen, 1983), 3.

6. Whitman, *Allegory,* 220–21.

7. Keating, *The Haunted Study,* 237.

8. Materer argues in favor of a search for father figures in Lewis's friendships with T. S. Moore, Yeats, and Augustus John ("Lewis and the Patriarchs," 47–63).

9. Pound, *Literary Essays,* 224.

10. Lawrence, *Etruscan Places* (London: Martin Secker, 1932), 106–7.

11. Lewis's stock of military images and themes does not derive from his military experience only. The latter reinforced a usage with an archetypal origin in his father who fought in the Secession War and was a military hero; see Meyers, *The Enemy*, 2. In *Rude Assignment*, Lewis draws a self-portrait as a child: "Born into a military aristocracy life begins full of excited little bangs and falsetto war-cries" (18). Holloway observes that Lewis's "experience of the war was a focus rather than a true genesis," in "Wyndham Lewis: The Massacre and the Innocents," in *The Chartered Mirror* (London: Routledge and Kegan Paul, 1960), 123.

12. In a letter to Hugh Kenner written in 1955, Lewis analyzes this similarity:

> You will notice that *Malign Fiesta* significantly ends by two White Angels carrying off Pullman. He finds himself, in the final book, in the Celestial Camp . . . . *Monstre Gai* shows him entrapped by the Bailiff, in whose power he reluctantly remains . . . . The Bailiff is, of course, not Divine. *Then the same situation is repeated in Malign Fiesta, only even more tragically,* and the figure in that case is Divine, though Diabolic. In the last book of all the hero, Pullman, is at last in Divine Society. (*The Letters of Wyndham Lewis*, 562 [my emphasis])

13. Both quotations are from *The Letters of Ezra Pound and Wyndham Lewis*, 123.
14. Wagner, *Wyndham Lewis*, 50–51.

Selected Bibliography

Abbott, H. Porter. "Late Modernism: Samuel Beckett and the Art of the *Oeuvre*." In *Around the Absurd: Essays on Modern and Postmodern Drama,* edited by Enoch Brater and Ruby Cohn, 73–96. Ann Arbor: University of Michigan Press, 1990.

Adorno, Theodor. "The Essay as Form." *New German Critique* 32 (1984): 151–71.

Angenot, Marc. *La parole pamphlétaire*. Paris: Payot, 1982.

Ardis, Ann L. *New Women, New Novels: Feminism and Early Modernism*. New Brunswick, NJ: Rutgers University Press, 1990.

———. "Reading 'as a Modernist'/Denaturalizing Modernist Reading Protocols: Wyndham Lewis's *Tarr*." In *Rereading Modernism: New Directions in Feminist Criticism,* edited by Lisa Rado, 373–90. New York: Garland Publishing, 1994.

Aristotle. *On Poetry and Style*. Translated and edited by G.M.A. Grube. The Library of Liberal Arts. New York: Bobbs-Merrill, 1958.

Ayers, David. *Wyndham Lewis and Western Man*. London: Macmillan, 1992.

Barthes, Roland. "The Death of the Author." In *Literature in the Modern World,* edited by D. Walder, 228–32. Oxford: Oxford University Press, 1990.

Baudelaire, Charles. *Oeuvres complètes*. 4 vols. Paris: Gallimard, 1975.

———. *The Poems in Prose, with La Fanfarlo*. Edited and translated by Francis Scarfe. London: Anvil Press Poetry, 1989.

Beatty, Michel. "Enemy of the Stars: Vorticist Experimental Play." *Theoria* 46 (1976): 41–60.

Becker, Carole. *Lire le réalisme et le naturalisme*. Paris: Dunod, 1992.

Beer, Gillian. "Speaking for Others: Relativism and Authority in Victorian Anthropological Literature." In *Sir James Frazer and the Literary Imagination,* edited by Robert Fraser, 38–60. London: Macmillan, 1990.

Benjamin, Walter. *Understanding Brecht*. Translated by A. Bostock. London: NBL, 1973.

Benstock, Shari. "Expatriate Sapphic Modernism: Entering Literary History." In *Rereading Modernism: New Directions in Feminist Criticism,* edited by Lisa Rado, 97–121. New York: Garland Publishing, 1994.

Bergonzi, Bernard. "An Artist and His Armour." *Times Literary Supplement,* 31 October 1980, 1215–1217.

———. *The Turn of a Century*. London: Macmillan, 1973.

Bergson, Henri. *Comedy*. Translated by W. Sypher. New York: Doubleday Anchor Books, 1956.

Blanchot, Maurice. *The Space of Literature*. Translated by A. Smock. Lincoln: University of Nebraska Press, 1982.

Bradbury, Malcolm. *The Social Context of Modern English Literature*. Oxford: Basil Blackwell, 1971.

———. "The Name and Nature of Modernism." In *Modernism, 1890–1930,* edited by M. Bradbury and J. McFarlane, 19–55. Harmondsworth: Penguin, 1976.

Bradbury, Malcolm, and James McFarlane, eds. *Modernism, 1890–1930.* Harmondsworth: Penguin, 1976.

Bridson, D. G. *The Filibuster: A Study of the Political Ideas of Wyndham Lewis.* London: Cassell, 1972.

Brooks, Peter. "The Idea of a Psychoanalytic Literary Criticism." *Critical Inquiry* 13, no. 2 (Winter 1987): 334–48.

Brown, Dennis. *Intertextual Dynamics within the Literary Group—Joyce, Pound, Lewis and Eliot.* London: Macmillan, 1990.

———. *The Modernist Self in Twentieth-Century English Literature: A Study in Self-Fragmentation.* London: Macmillan, 1989.

Brown, Marshall. "Romanticism and Enlightenment." In *The Cambridge Companion to British Romanticism,* edited by S. Curran, 25–47. Cambridge: Cambridge University Press, 1993.

Brunel, Pierre. *Le mythe de la métamorphose.* Paris: A. Colin, 1974.

Bürger, Peter. "Modernity and the Avant-Garde in Wyndham Lewis's *Tarr*." *News from Nowhere: The Politics of Modernism* 7 (1989): 9–18.

———. *Theory of the Avant-Garde.* Translated by M. Shaw. Minneapolis: University of Minnesota Press, 1984.

Calinescu, Matei. *Faces of Modernity.* Bloomington: Indiana University Press, 1977.

Calvino, Italo. *The Uses of Literature.* Translated by P. Creagh. San Diego and New York: Harcourt Brace Jovanovich, 1986.

Campbell, Sue-Ellen. *The Enemy Opposite.* Athens: Ohio University Press, 1988.

Carey, Peter. *The Intellectuals and the Masses.* London: Faber and Faber, 1992.

Caws, Mary Ann. "Gestures toward the Self: Representing the Body in Modernism." In *Modernism: Challenges and Perspectives,* edited by M. Chefdor, R. Quinones, and A. Wachtel. Urbana: University of Illinois Press, 1986.

Chadbourne, Richard. "A Puzzling Literary Genre: Comparative Views of the Essay." *Comparative Literary Studies* 20, no. 2 (1983): 133–53.

Clarke, Bruce. *Dora Marsden and Early Modernism: Gender, Individualism, Science.* Ann Arbor: University of Michigan Press, 1996.

Compton, Susan, ed. *British Art in the Twentieth Century.* Munich: Prestel, 1987.

Cork, Richard. *A Bitter Truth: Avant-Garde and the Great War.* New Haven: Yale University Press, 1994.

Dagen, Philippe, and Michel Décaudin. "Les peintres, le poète et le critique." In *Apollinaire: Critique d'art,* edited by B. R. El-Habib and V. Gille, 243–48. Paris: Gallimard, 1993.

Danto, Arthur. "The Artworld." In *Twentieth Century Theories of Art,* edited by James M. Thompson, 531–45. Ottawa: Carleton University Press, 1990.

Dasenbrock, Reed Way. Afterword to *The Art of Being Ruled* by Wyndham Lewis. Santa Rosa, CA: Black Sparrow Press, 1989.

———. *The Literary Vorticism of Ezra Pound and Wyndham Lewis: Towards the Condition of Painting.* Baltimore: Johns Hopkins University Press, 1985.

Davey, Frank. Editor's note on *Mrs. Dukes' Million* by Wyndham Lewis. Toronto: Coach House, 1977.

Décaudin, Michel. "Being Modern in 1885 or Variations on 'Modern,' 'Modernism,' 'Modernité'." In *Modernism: Challenges and Perspectives,* edited by M. Chefdor, R. Quinones, and A. Wachtel, 25–32. Urbana: University of Illinois Press, 1986.

De Duve, Thierry. *Pictorial Nominalism.* Minneapolis: University of Minnesota Press, 1991.

Dekker, George. "James and Stevenson: The Mixed Current of Realism and Romance." In *Critical Reconstructions: The Relationship of Fiction and Life,* edited by R. Polhemus and R. B. Henkle, 127–49. Stanford, CA: Stanford University Press, 1994.

DeKoven, Marianne. "The Politics of Modernist Form." *New Literary History* 23, no. 3 (1992): 675–90.

———. *Rich and Strange: Gender, History, Modernism.* Princeton: Princeton University Press, 1991.

Derrida, Jacques. *Writing and Difference.* Translated by Alan Bass. Chicago: University of Chicago Press, 1978.

Dewey, John. *The Influence of Darwin on Philosophy.* New York: Peter Smith, 1951.

Duncan, Ian. "Towards a Modernist Poetic: Wyndham Lewis's Early Fiction." In *Letteratura/Pittura,* edited by Giovanni Cianci, 67–85. Palermo: Sellerio, 1982.

Dupriez, Bernard. *A Dictionary of Literary Devices: Gradus A–Z.* Translated by A. Halsall. Toronto: University of Toronto Press, 1991.

Eagleton, Terry. "Capitalism, Modernism and Postmodernism." *New Left Review* 152 (July/August 1985): 60–73.

Edwards, Paul. Afterword to *The Caliph's Design* by Wyndham Lewis. Santa Barbara, CA: Black Sparrow Press, 1986.

———, ed. *Wyndham Lewis: Art and War.* London: Wyndham Lewis Memorial Trust and Lund Humphries, 1992.

———. "Wyndham Lewis's Narrative of Origins: 'The Death of the Ankou.'" *Modern Language Review* 92 (January 1997): 22–35.

Eliot, T. S. *For Lancelot Andrewes.* Garden City, NY: Doubleday, 1929.

———. Review of *The Lion and the Fox. Twentieth Century Verse* 6–7 (1937): 109–12. Reprint. New York: Krauss Reprint, 1966.

———. *Selected Essays.* New York: Harcourt Brace and World, 1950.

———. "*Tarr.*" *Egoist* 5 (September 1918): 106.

———. "Tradition and the Individual Talent." In *The Sacred Wood.* London: Methuen, 1920.

Eysteinsson, Astradur. *The Concept of Modernism.* Ithaca: Cornell University Press, 1990.

Feldman, Jessica. *Gender on the Divide: The Dandy in Modernist Literature.* Ithaca: Cornell University Press, 1993.

Feldman, Melissa. *Signs of Life: Process and Materials, 1960–90.* Philadelphia: Institute of Contemporary Art, 1990.

Fletcher, Angus. *Allegory: The Theory of a Symbolic Mode.* Ithaca: Cornell University Press, 1964.

Ford, Madox Ford. *The Critical Attitude.* London: Duckworth, 1911.

Foshay, Toby. *Wyndham Lewis and the Avant-Garde: The Politics of the Intellect.* Montreal: McGill-Queen's University Press, 1992.

Foucault, Michel. *The Foucault Reader*. Edited by Paul Rabinow. New York: Pantheon Books, 1984.

Foulkes, A. P. *Literature and Propaganda*. London: Methuen, 1983.

Freud, Sigmund. "Dostoevsky and Parricide." In *The Complete Psychological Works of Sigmund Freud*, edited by James Strachey, vol. 21. London: Hogarth Press and the Institute of Psychoanalysis, 1957.

———. "Hysterical Phantasies and their Relation to Bisexuality." In *The Complete Psychological Works of Sigmund Freud*, edited by James Strachey, vol. 9. London: Hogarth Press and the Institute of Psychoanalysis, 1957.

———. *Leonardo da Vinci*. Translated by A. Tyson. Harmondsworth: Penguin, 1963.

———. "Psychoanalytic Notes on an Autobiographical Account of a Case of Paranoia (Dementia Paranoides)." In *The Complete Psychological Works of Sigmund Freud*, edited by J. Strachey, vol. 12. London: Hogarth Press and the Institute of Psychoanalysis, 1957.

———. "Some Neurotic Mechanisms in Jealousy, Paranoia and Homosexuality." In *The Complete Psychological Works of Sigmund Freud*, edited by J. Strachey, vol. 18. London: Hogarth Press and the Institute of Psychoanalysis, 1957.

Friedman, Ellen G. "Where Are the Missing Contents? (Post)Modernism, Gender, and the Canon." *PMLA* 108, no. 2 (March 1993): 240–52.

Frye, Northrop. *Anatomy of Criticism: Four Essays*. Princeton: Princeton University Press, 1957.

Gablick, Suzi. *Has Modernism Failed?* London: Thames and Hudson, 1984.

Gass, William H. "Emerson and the Essay." In *Habitations of the Word: Essays*. New York: Simon and Schuster, 1985.

Genette, Gérard. *Palimpsestes: La littérature au second degré*. Paris: Seuil, 1982.

Hale, J. R. "Machiavelli and the Self-Sufficient State." In *Political Ideas*, edited by D. Thomson. Harmondsworth: Penguin, 1986.

Halsall, Albert. W. *L'Art de convaincre*. Toronto: Paratexte, 1988.

Hamilton, Carol Vanderveer. "Anarchy as Modernist Aesthetic." In *The Turn of the Century: Modernism and Modernity in Literature and the Arts*, edited by C. Berg, F. Durieux, and G. Lermont, 77–87. Berlin: Walter de Gruyter, 1995.

Havel, Vaclav. "Anatomy of the Gag." Translated by M. Schonberg. *Modern Drama* 23, no. 1 (1980): 13–24.

Hemingway, Ernest. *A Moveable Feast*. New York: Jonathan Cape, 1964.

Hilton, Alison. "Zola and the Art of his Time." In *Emile Zola and the Arts*, edited by J.-M. Guieu and A. Hilton, xi–xiv. Washington, DC: Georgetown University Press, 1988.

Hollington, Michael. "Svevo, Joyce and Modernist Time." In *Modernism 1890–1930*, edited by M. Bradbury and J. McFarlane, 430–42. Harmondsworth: Penguin, 1985.

Holloway, John. "Machine and Puppet: A Comparative View." In *Wyndham Lewis: A Revaluation*, edited by Jeffrey Meyers, 3–14. London: Athlone Press, 1980.

———. "Wyndham Lewis: The Massacre of the Innocents." In *The Chartered Mirror*, 118–36. London: Routledge and Kegan Paul, 1960.

Honig, Edwin. *Dark Conceit: The Making of Allegory*. New York: Oxford University Press, 1966.

Howe, Irving. *The Idea of the Modern in Literature and the Arts*. New York: Horizon Press, 1967.

Hulme, T. E. *Speculations*. London: Routledge and Kegan Paul, 1965.

Huyssen, Andreas. *After the Great Divide: Modernism, Mass Culture, Postmodernism*. Bloomington: Indiana University Press, 1986.

Hynes, Samuel. *A War Imagined: The First World War and English Culture*. London: The Bodley Head, 1990.

Ian, Marcia. *Remembering the Phallic Mother: Psychoanalysis, Modernism, and the Fetish*. Ithaca: Cornell University Press, 1993.

Jameson, Fredric. *Fables of Aggression: Wyndham Lewis, the Modernist as Fascist*. Berkeley and Los Angeles: California Press, 1979.

———. "Postmodernism and Consumer Society." In *Anti-Aesthetic: Essays on Postmodern Culture*, edited by Hal Foster, 11–25. Port Townsend, WA: Bay Press, 1983.

Jones, Peter, ed. *Imagist Poetry*. Harmondsworth: Penguin, 1972.

Joyce, James. *A Portrait of the Artist as a Young Man*. St. Albans: Triad/Panther Books, 1977.

Kaufmann, Michael. "T. S. Eliot's New Critical Footnotes to Modernism." In *Rereading the New: A Backward Glance at Modernism*, edited by K.J.H. Dettmar. Ann Arbor: University of Michigan Press, 1992.

Keating, Peter. *The Haunted Study: A Social History of the English Novel 1875–1914*. London: Secker and Warburg, 1989.

Kenner, Hugh. "Mrs. Dukes' Million: The Stunt of an Illusionist." In *Wyndham Lewis: A Revaluation*, edited by J. Meyers, 85–91. London: Athlone Press, 1980.

———. *The Pound Era*. London: Faber and Faber, 1972.

———. "Pursued in Public." Review of *Kenneth Burke in Greenwich Village: Conversing with the Moderns, 1915–1931*, by Jack Selzer. *Times Literary Supplement*, 7 March 1997, 25.

———. *A Sinking Island*. New York: Alfred A. Knopf, 1988.

———. *Wyndham Lewis*. London: Methuen, 1954.

———. "Wyndham Lewis: The Satirist as Barbarian." In *English Satire and the Satiric Tradition*, edited by Claude Rawson and Jenny Mezciems, 264–75. Oxford: Basil Blackwell, 1984.

Kent, Thomas. "The Classification of Genres." *Genre* 16 (1983): 1–20.

Koestenbaum, Wayne. *Double Talk: The Erotics of Male Literary Collaboration*. London: Routledge, 1989.

Kris, Ernst. *Psychoanalytical Explorations in Art*. New York: Schocken Books, 1964.

Kristeva, Julia. *Desire in Language: A Semiotic Approach to Literature and Art*. New York: Columbia University Press, 1980.

———. *Pouvoirs de l'horreur: essai sur l'abjection*. Paris: Seuil, 1980.

Krysinski, Wladimir. "Les avant-gardes d'ostentation et les avant-gardes du faire cognitif: vers une description des langages transgressifs." In *The Turn of the Century: Modernism and Modernity in Literature and the Arts,* edited by C. Berg, F. Durieux, and Geert Lermont, 17–32. Berlin: Walter de Gruyter, 1995.

Lacan, Jacques. *Ecrits*. Paris: Seuil, 1966.

———. *Ecrits*. Translated by Alan Sheridan. London: Tavistock, 1985.

———. "Hamlet." *Ornicar?* 24 (Autumn 1981): 7–31.

Lafourcade, Bernard. Afterword to *The Complete Wild Body* by Wyndham Lewis. Santa Barbara, CA: Black Sparrow Press, 1982.

———. "A Cock-and-Bull Story." Afterword to *Snooty Baronet* by Wyndham Lewis. Santa Barbara, CA: Black Sparrow Press, 1983.

———. "Du purgatoire au panorama." *Etudes Anglaises* 26, no. 2 (1973): 195–211.

———. "Metaphor-Metonymy-Collage." *Enemy News* 25 (1987): 6–11.

———. "Off to Budapest—with Freud." *Enemy News* 15 (1982): 6–10.

———. "Quel mauvais roman que ma vie *Twentieth Century Palette*." In *Wyndham Lewis: Letteratura/Pittura,* edited by G. Cianci, 218–45. Palermo: Sellerio, 1982.

———. "Wyndham Lewis: Post-Moderniste avant la lettre?" *Etudes Anglaises* 35, no. 3 (1982): 280–95.

Langbaum, Robert. *From the Word Below: Essays on Modern Literature and Culture.* Madison: University of Wisconsin Press, 1987.

Lawrence, D. H. *Etruscan Places.* London: Martin Secker, 1932.

———. *Selected Essays.* Harmondsworth: Penguin, 1950.

Lechmere, Kate. "Wyndham Lewis from 1912." *Journal of Modern Literature* 10, no. 1 (1983): 161–66.

Leroy, Claude. "Modernity and Pseudonymity." In *Modernism: Challenges and Perspectives,* edited by M. Chefdor, R. Quinones, and A. Wachtel, 265–73. Urbana: University of Illinois Press, 1986.

Lethen, Helmut. "Modernism Cut in Half: The Exclusion of the Avant-garde and the Debate on Postmodernism." In *Approaching Postmodernism,* edited by Douwe Fokkema and Hans Bertens, 233–38. Philadelphia: John Benjamins Publishing Company, 1986.

Levenson, Michael. "Form's Body: Wyndham Lewis's *Tarr*." *Modern Language Quarterly* 45, no. 3 (1984): 241–62.

———. *A Genealogy of Modernism.* Cambridge: Cambridge University Press, 1984.

———. "The Private Life of a Public Form: Freud, Fantasy and the Novel." In *Critical Reconstructions: The Relation of Fiction and Life,* edited by R. M. Polhemus and R. B. Henkle, 52–70. Stanford, CA: Stanford University Press, 1994.

Lewes, Kenneth. *The Psychonanalytic Theory of Male Homosexuality.* New York: Simon and Schuster, 1988.

Lewis, Wyndham. *America and Cosmic Man.* 1948. Reprint. Port Washington, NY: Kennikat, 1969.

———. *America, I Presume.* New York: Howell, Soskin, 1940.

———. *The Apes of God.* 1930. Reprinted., edited by P. Edwards. Santa Barbara, CA: Black Sparrow Press, 1981.

———. *The Art of Being Ruled.* London: Chatto and Windus, 1926.

———, ed. *Blast.* 1914. Santa Barbara, CA: Black Sparrow Press, 1981.

———, ed. *Blast.* 1915. Santa Barbara, CA: Black Sparrow Press, 1981.

———. *Blasting and Bombardiering.* London: Eyre and Spottiswoode, 1937.

———. "The Caliph's Design." 1919. In *Wyndham Lewis on Art,* edited by W. Michel and C. J. Fox, 216–25. New York: Funk and Wagnalls, 1969.

———. "Cantleman's Spring-Mate." 1917. In *Blasting and Bombardiering,* edited by Anne Lewis, 304–11. London: Calder, 1982.

———. *The Childermass.* London: Chatto and Windus, 1928.

———. *The Code of a Herdsman.* 1917. Reprinted., edited by Alan Munton. Glasgow: The Wyndham Lewis Society, 1977.

———. *The Complete Wild Body.* Edited by B. Lafourcade. Santa Barbara, CA: Black Sparrow Press, 1982.

———. *Count your Dead: They Are Alive!* London: Lovat Dickson, 1937.

———. "Creativity." in *Blast 3,* edited by Seamus Cooney, coedited by B. Morrow, B. Lafourcade, and H. Kenner, 205–30. Santa Barbara, CA: Black Sparrow Press, 1984.

———. *Creatures of Habit and Creatures of Change.* Edited by Paul Edwards. Santa Rosa, CA: Black Sparrow Press, 1989.

———. "The Crowd-Master." 1915. In *Blast 2.* Santa Barbara, CA: Black Sparrow Press, 1981.

———. "Dean Swift with a Brush." 1921. In *The Complete Wild Body,* edited by B. Lafourcade, 359. Santa Barbara, CA: Black Sparrow Press, 1982.

———. *The Diabolical Principle and the Dithyrambic Spectator.* 1931. Haskell House, 1971.

———. "The Do-Nothing Mode: An Autobiographical Fragment." *Agenda* 7, no. 3–8, no. 1 (1969): 216–21.

———. *The Doom of Youth.* New York: Robert M. McBride, 1932.

———. *Enemy of the Stars.* 1932. In *Collected Poems and Plays,* edited by Alan Munton, 143–91. Manchester: Carcanet, 1979.

———. "Essay on the Objective of Plastic Art in Our Time." 1922. In *Wyndham Lewis on Art: Collected Writings 1913–1956,* edited by Walter Michel and C. J. Fox, 200–215. New York: Funk and Wagnalls, 1969.

———. *Hitler.* London: Chatto and Windus, 1931.

———. *The Hitler Cult.* London: Dent, 1939.

———. *The Ideal Giant.* 1917. In *Collected Poems and Plays,* edited by A. Munton, 121–39. Manchester: Carcanet, 1979.

———. "Inferior Religions." 1927. In *The Complete Wild Body,* edited by B. Lafourcade, 149–54. Santa Barbara, CA: Black Sparrow Press, 1982.

———. *The Jews: Are They Human?* London: George Allen and Unwin, 1939.

———. "The Kasbahs of the Atlas." 1933. In *Wyndham Lewis on Art,* edited by W. Michel and C. J. Fox, 260–65. New York: Funk and Wagnalls, 1969.

———. *Left Wings over Europe.* London: Jonathan Cape, 1936.

———. *The Letters of Ezra Pound and Wyndham Lewis.* Edited by Timothy Materer. London: Faber and Faber, 1985.

———. *The Letters of Wyndham Lewis.* Edited by W. K. Rose. London: Methuen, 1963.

———. *The Lion and the Fox.* 1927. London: Methuen, 1951.

———. *Malign Fiesta.* London: Methuen, 1955.

———. "The Meaning of the Wild Body." 1927. In *The Complete Wild Body,* edited by B. Lafourcade, 157–60. Santa Barbara, CA: Black Sparrow Press, 1982.

———. *Men without Art.* 1934. Reprinted., edited by Seamus Cooney. Santa Rosa, CA: Black Sparrow Press, 1987.

———. *Monstre Gai.* London: Methuen, 1955.

———. "Morpeth Olympiad." In *Blasting and Bombardiering.* London: Eyre and Spottiswoode, 1937.

———."Morpeth Olympiad." In *Blasting and Bombardiering,* edited by Anne Lewis, 66–68. London: Calder, 1982.

———. *Mrs. Dukes' Million*. 1908–10. Reprinted., edited by Frank Davey. Toronto: Coach House Press, 1977.

———. *The Mysterious Mr. Bull*. London: Robert Hale, 1938.

———. *The Old Gang and the New Gang*. London: Desmond Harmsworth, 1933.

———. *Paleface*. London: Chatto and Windus, 1929.

———. "Physics of the Not-Self." 1932. In *Collected Poems and Plays,* edited by A. Munton, 195–204. Manchester: Carcanet, 1979.

———. *The Red Priest*. London: Methuen, 1956.

———. *The Revenge for Love*. 1937. Reprint. Harmondsworth: Penguin, 1983.

———. *Rotting Hill*. 1951. Reprinted., edited by Paul Edwards. Santa Barbara, CA: Black Sparrow Press, 1986.

———. *Rude Assignment*. 1950. Reprinted., edited by Toby Foshay. Santa Barbara, CA: Black Sparrow Press, 1984.

———. *Satire and Fiction*. 1930. Folcroft, Pennsylvania: Folcroft Press, 1967.

———. *Self Condemned*. 1954. Reprinted., edited by R. Smith. Manchester: Carcanet, 1983.

———. Snooty Baronet. 1932. Reprinted., edited by B. Lafourcade. Santa Barbara, CA: Black Sparrow Press, 1983.

———. *Tarr*. 1928. Harmondsworth: Penguin, 1982.

———. *Time and Western Man*. London: Chatto and Windus, 1927.

———. *Unlucky for Pringle*. Edited by C. J. Fox and R. T. Chapman. London: Vision Press, 1973.

———. "The Vita of Wyndham Lewis." 1949. Reprint edited by Bernard Lafourcade. *Enemy News* 20 (1984): 10–15.

———. *The Vulgar Streak*. 1941. Reprinted., edited by P. Edwards. Santa Barbara, CA: Black Sparrow Press, 1985.

———. "The War-Baby." 1918. In *Blasting and Bombardiering,* edited by Anne Lewis. London: Calder, 1982.

———. *The Writer and the Absolute*. 1952. Westport, CT: Greenwood Press, 1975.

Lockridge, Lawrence S. "Coleridge and the Perils of 'Self-Realization.'" In *Coleridge's Theory of Imagination Today,* edited by C. Gallant, 257–75. New York: AMS, 1989.

Lodge, David. "The Language of Modernist Fiction." In *Modernism 1890–1930,* edited by M. Bradbury and J. McFarlane. Harmondsworth: Penguin, 1976.

MacCabe, Colin. "The Revenge of the Author." In *Subject to History: Ideology, Class, Gender,* edited by D. Dimpson, 34–46. Ithaca: Cornell University Press, 1991.

Mallalieu, H. B. "Social Force." *Twentieth Century Verse* 1–18, 148. New York: Krauss Reprint, 1966.

Mallarmé, Stéphane. "The Impressionists and Edouard Manet." In *Modern Art and Modernism,* edited by F. Frascina, C. Harrison, and D. Paul, 39–44. London: Harper and Row, 1982.

———. *The Poems*. Translated by Keith Bosley. Harmondsworth: Penguin, 1977.

———. "Prose." In *Oeuvres complètes,* edited by H. Mondor and G. Jean-Aubry, 55–57. Paris: Gallimard, 1945.

Marinetti, Filippo. *Les mots en liberté futuristes*. 1919. Reprint. N.p.: Le Arti, 1986.

Materer, Timothy. "Lewis and the Patriarchs: Augustus John, W. B. Yeats, T. Sturge Moore." In *Wyndham Lewis: A Revaluation,* edited by J. Meyers, 47–63. London: Athlone Press, 1980.

————. *Wyndham Lewis the Novelist*. Detroit: Wayne State University Press, 1976.

McKeon, Michael. *The Origins of the English Novel 1600–1740*. Baltimore: Johns Hopkins University Press, 1987.

McLuhan, Marshall. "The Lewis Vortex: Art and Politics as Masks of Power." In *Letteratura/Pittura,* edited by G. Cianci, 167–70. Palermo: Sellerio, 1982.

Menand, Louis. *Discovering Modernism: T. S. Eliot and His Context*. New York: Oxford University Press, 1987.

Meyers, Jeffrey. *The Enemy: A Biography of Wyndham Lewis*. London: Routledge and Kegan Paul, 1980.

Michel, Walter. *Wyndham Lewis: Paintings and Drawings*. Berkeley: University of California Press, 1971.

Miller, Karl. *Doubles: Studies in Literary History*. Oxford: Oxford University Press, 1985.

Milton, John. *The Complete Poems*. Edited by B. A. Wright and introduced by G. Campbell. Everyman's Library. London and Melbourne: Dent, 1986.

Mitterand, Henri. *Le discours du roman*. Paris: Puf, 1980.

Moore, T. Sturge. *Art and Life*. London: Methuen, 1910.

Morrow, Bradford, and Bernard Lafourcade. *A Bibliography of the Writings of Wyndham Lewis*. Santa Barbara, CA: Black Sparrow Press, 1978.

Nicholls, Peter. *Modernisms: A Literary Guide*. Berkeley and Los Angeles: University of California Press, 1995.

Normand, Tom. *Wyndham Lewis the Artist: Holding the Mirror up to Politics*. Cambridge: Cambridge University Press, 1992.

Norris, Margot. "The Postmodernization of *Finnegans Wake* Reconsidered." In *Rereading the New: A Backward Glance at Modernism,* edited by K.J.H. Dettmar. Ann Arbor: University of Michigan Press, 1992.

O'Keeffe, Paul. Afterword to *Tarr: The 1918 Version*. Santa Rosa, CA: Black Sparrow Press, 1990.

Ortega y Gasset, José. *The Dehumanization of Art*. Princeton: Princeton University Press, 1968.

Orwell, George. *Collected Essays*. London: Secker and Warburg, 1961.

Parker, D. "*Tarr* and Wyndham Lewis's War-Time Stories." *Southern Review* 8 (1975): 166–81.

Pasche, Francis. "Symposium on Homosexuality." *International Journal of Psychoanalysis* 45 (1964): 210–13.

Pearce, Richard. *The Politics of Narration*. New Brunswick, NJ: Rutgers University Press, 1991.

Perl, Jeffrey. *Skepticism and Modern Enmity: Before and After Eliot*. Baltimore: Johns Hopkins University Press, 1989.

————. *The Tradition of Return: The Implicit History of Modern Literature*. Princeton: Princeton University Press, 1984.

Perloff, Marjorie. "Modernist Studies." In *Redrawing the Boundaries: The Transformation of English and American Literary Studies,* edited by S. Greenblatt and G. Gunn, 154–78. New York: Modern Language Association of America, 1992.

Petro, Peter. *Modern Satire: Four Studies*. Amsterdam: Mouton Publishers, 1982.

Pirandello, Luigi. *On Humor*. Translated and edited by A. Illiano and D. P. Testa. Chapel Hill: University of North Carolina Press, 1974.

Plato. *The Republic*. Translated and edited by F. M. Cornford. New York: Oxford University Press, 1956.

Poli, Michèle. "Blast." In *Blast 3,* edited by Seamus Cooney, co-edited by B. Morrow, B. Lafourcade, and H. Kenner, 51–57. Santa Barbara, CA: Black Sparrow Press, 1984.

Pound, Ezra. *ABC of Reading*. Norfolk: New Directions, 1934.

———. *Guide to Kulchur*. New York: New Directions, 1970.

———. *Literary Essays*. Edited and introduced by T. S. Eliot. London: Faber and Faber, 1954.

———. *Selected Prose 1909–1965*. Edited by W. Cookson. London: Faber and Faber, 1973.

Pritchard, William. *Wyndham Lewis*. New York: Twayne, 1968.

Pykett, Lyn. *Engendering Fictions: The English Novel in the Early Twentieth Century*. London: Edward Arnold, 1995.

Quilligan, Maureen. *The Language of Allegory: Defining the Genre*. Ithaca: Cornell University Press, 1979.

Quinones, Richard. *Mapping Literary Modernism: Time and Development*. Princeton: Princeton University Press, 1985.

Raby, Peter. *Samuel Butler: A Biography*. London: The Hogarth Press, 1991.

Randolph, Marie Claire. "The Medical Concept in English Renaissance Satiric Theory." In *Satire: Modern Essays in Criticism,* edited by R. Paulson. Englewood Cliffs, NJ: Prentice-Hall, 1971.

Rank, Otto. *The Don Juan Legend*. Translated by G. G. Winler. Princeton: Princeton University Press, 1975.

Reid, Fred. "The Disintegration of Liberalism 1895–1931." In *The Context of English Literature: 1900–1930,* edited by M. Bell, 94–125. London: Methuen, 1980.

Richards, I. A. *Principles of Literary Criticism*. London: Kegan Paul, Trench, Trubner, 1934.

———. *Science and Poetry*. New York: Norton, 1926.

Russell, John. *Style in Modern British Fiction*. Baltimore: Johns Hopkins University Press, 1978.

Ruthven, K. K. *Ezra Pound as Literary Critic*. London: Routledge, 1990.

Ryan, Judith. *The Vanishing Subject: Early Psychology and Literary Modernism*. Chicago: University of Chicago Press, 1991.

Said, Edward. "The Text, the World, the Critic." In *Textual Strategies: Perspectives in Poststructuralist Criticism,* edited by Josué V. Harari, 161–88. Ithaca: Cornell University Press, 1979.

Sartre, Jean-Paul. *What Is Literature?* Translated by B. Frechtman. Gloucester: Peter Smith, 1978.

Saul, Leon, and Aaron Beck. "Psychodynamics of Male Homosexuality." *International Journal of Psychoanalysis* 42 (1961): 43–48.

Schneidau, Herbert. *Waking Giants: The Presence of the Past in Modernism*. Oxford: Oxford University Press, 1991.

Schwartz, Sanford. *The Matrix of Modernism*. Princeton: Princeton University Press, 1985.

Scott, Bonnie Kime, ed. *The Gender of Modernism: A Critical Anthology*. Bloomington and Indianapolis: Indiana University Press, 1990.

Seaman, L.C.B. *A New History of England 410–1975*. Brighton: Harvester Press, 1981.

Shelley, Percy Bysshe. "A Defence of Poetry." In *English Critical Essays: Nineteenth Century*, edited by Edmund D. Jones. Oxford: Oxford University Press, 1932.

Sherry, Vincent. *Ezra Pound, Wyndham Lewis and Radical Modernism*. New York: Oxford University Press, 1991.

Shklovsky, Victor. "Art as Technique." In *Contemporary Literary Criticism: Literary and Cultural Studies*, edited by R. C. Davies and R. Schleifer, 55–56. New York: Longman, 1989.

Sieburth, Richard. "Pound's *Dial* Letters: Between Modernism and the Avant-Garde." *American Poetry* 6, no. 2 (Winter 1989): 3–10.

Sisson, C. H. "The Politics of Wyndham Lewis." *Agenda* 7, no. 3–8, no. 1 (1969): 109–16.

Socarides, Charles. "A Theory of Aetiology in Male Homosexuality." *International Journal of Psychoanalysis* 49 (1968): 27–37.

Spender, Stephen. *The Struggle of the Modern*. London: Hamish Hamilton, 1963.

———. "Writers and Politics." *The Partisan Review* 34, no. 3 (1967): 360–81.

Stevens, Wallace. *The Necessary Angel*. New York: Vintage Books, 1951.

Stevenson, Randall. *Modernist Fiction: An Introduction*. London: Harvester-Wheatsheaf, 1992.

Suleiman, Susan. *Authoritarian Fictions*. New York: Columbia University Press, 1983.

Symons, Julian. *Makers of the New*. London: André Deutsch, 1987.

———. "Wyndham Lewis's First Novel." *Critical Observations*. London: Faber and Faber, 1981.

Todorov, Tzvetan. *Les genres du discours*. Paris: Seuil, 1978.

Trotter, David. *The English Novel in History, 1895–1920*. London and New York: Routledge, 1993.

———. *The Making of the Reader*. London: Macmillan, 1984.

Tuma, Keith. "Wyndham Lewis, *Blast*, and Popular Culture." *EHL* 54, no. 1 (1987): 403–19.

Wagner, Geoffrey. *Wyndham Lewis: A Portrait of the Artist as the Enemy*. London: Routledge and Kegan Paul, 1957.

Watson, George. *Politics and Literature in Modern Britain*. London: Macmillan, 1977.

Wees, W. C. *Vorticism and the English Avant-Garde*. Manchester: Manchester University Press, 1972.

Whitman, Jon. *Allegory: The Dynamics of an Ancient and Medieval Technique*. Oxford: Clarendon Press, 1987.

Whitman, Walt. *Leaves of Grass*. Edited by S. Bradley, H. W. Blodgett, A. Golden, and W. White. New York: New York University Press, 1980.

Wiedeman, G. H. "Some Remarks on the Aetiology of Homosexuality." *International Journal of Psychoanalysis* 45, no. 1 (1964): 214–16.

———. "Survey of Psychoanalytic Literature on Overt Male Homosexuality." *Journal of the American Psychoanalytic Association* 10, no. 2 (1962): 386–409.

Williams, Raymond. *The Politics of Modernism: Against the New Conformists*. Edited by T. Pinkney. London: Verso, 1989.

Wordsworth, William. *Selected Poems and Prefaces*. Edited by Jack Stillinger. Boston: Houghton Mifflin, 1965.

Worringer, Wilhelm. "Abstraction and Empathy." In *Modern Art and Modernism*, edited by F. Frascina, C. Harrison, and D. Paul, 159–64. London: Harper and Row, 1982.

Young, Alan. *Dada and After: Extremist Modernism and English Literature*. Manchester: Manchester University Press, 1981.

Zamyatin, Eugeni. "On Literature, Revolution and Entropy." In *The Idea of the Modern in Literature and the Arts*, edited by I. Howe, 173–79. New York: Horizon Press, 1967.

Zola, Emile. *Ecrits sur l'art*. Edited by Jean-Pierre Leduc-Adine. Paris: Gallimard, 1991.

Index

233

178, 180, 183, 185, 189–91, 198; and father figure, 169, 193–95, 200–201; and freedom, 164–65, 168, 184, 185–88; and identification/delusion, 190–92, 195–201; of the intellect, 180–82, 188, 189, 190–91, 192, 195, 196–98, 199, 201–02; and Labour, 164; and Liberalism, 164, 165; and lost generation, 163; and mass media, 164–65, 168; Marxism/Marxist, 15, 69, 158, 159, 165, 169, 186, 187; and mind-body dualism, 169–70, 172, 174, 181–86, 190–92; as pathos, 176–78, 191–92; and patriarchy/masculine principle, 16, 167, 192–95, 199, 200, 201-2; and personality, 180, 185, 189, 192, 194; and power, 173–76, 177–78, 185, 198; and propaganda, 190–91; and racism, 183–84; and radicalism, 15–17, 168, 170, 171, 182–83; and revolution, 164, 170–71; and ruled/ ruler/ruling, 164, 177, 180–82, 185, 192, 195–97, 198–202; and socialism, 165; and Stalinism, 170; totalitarian, 178–79, 185; and youth/Peter-Panism, 16, 165, 166, 168–69, 189, 200–201; and Unionists, 164; and utopia, 44, 51, 165, 170–71, 175, 178–79, 180, 184,185, 187–88; and the Wild Body, 169–70, 172, 178, 185–86, 187, 190, 191; and WWI, 163–63, 173, 189, 193, 199. *See* allegory; avant-garde; feminism; genre; great divide; homosexuality; narration; prosopopoiea; tradition

Pope, Alexander, 23
Postmodernism, 14, 21, 125, 128–32, 148, 158–59
Poststructuralism, 13, 25, 148, 153
Pound, Ezra: and aesthetic of the present, 136; art as science, 127; and dandyism, 132; and the doctrine of the Original Sin, 172; and imagism, 137; Lewis on, 166; Lewis to, 50; in connection with mask, 135; as modernist, 17; and modernist style, 79; on the object, 126
Pritchard, William, 178
Prosopopoeia: and allegory, 67, 69–70, 73–75; and dandyism, 135; definition

of, 67; and the essay, 59; and gender, 93, 97, 101; and genre, 28; and hallucination, 72–73; in relation to the mask, 67, 69, 101, 120, 135; and narration, 67–71; and personification, 67, 69–70, 74, 180; and political discourse, 175–76, 180; and satire, 72–73. *See* Wild Body
Pykett, Lyn, 14, 88
Pynchon, Thomas, 132

Queneau, Raymond, 130
Quilligan, Maureen, 65, 76, 201
Quinones, Ricardo, 26
Quintillian, 66

Rabinow, Paul, 130
Raby, Peter, 48
Randolph, Marie Claire, 142
Rank, Otto, 114
Read, Herbert, 163
Realism: and abstraction, 139–40; and allegorical style, 80–81; and deixis, 80; and the role of detail, 79–80, 137, 143; and language, 79–80, 136, 149, 151; and modernism, 19–29, 68–69, 79, 136–39, 140, 141–44, 145, 147; and modernity, 136–37; and naturalism, 137, 142, 144, 145; scientific ethos of, 137, 140, 142–43, 144. *See* allegory; dualism; empiricism; mimesis; perspectivism; satire; time
Reality, 38, 41, 143; and hallucination, 72–73; and illusionism, 57, 64, 120, 135, 176; and the object, 123, 126–27; and perspectivism, 137–38
Reid, Fred, 164
Republic, The, 181
Richards, I. A., 127–28, 129
Riopelle, Jean-Paul, 79
Robbe-Grillet, Alain, 130
Romanticism: parody of, 18–19, 68, 69, 109, 117; and perception, 38; and realism, 138
Roosevelt, Franklin, 192
Ruskin, John, 191
Russell, Bertrand, 123
Russell, John, 77, 81
Ruthven, K. K., 62
Ryan, Judith, 24, 37, 38, 41–42